®rr-some

Research into the Orr Family

Brian J. Orr

HERITAGE BOOKS
2007

HERITAGE BOOKS

AN IMPRINT OF HERITAGE BOOKS, INC.

Books, CDs, and more—Worldwide

For our listing of thousands of titles see our website
at
www.HeritageBooks.com

Published 2007 by
HERITAGE BOOKS, INC.
Publishing Division
65 East Main Street
Westminster, Maryland 21157-5026

International Standard Book Number: 978-0-7884-4266-7

iii
CONTENTS

iv

Photographs, Maps, Illustrations

PREFACE AND ACKNOWLEDGMENTS

Like so many family history researchers I had the intention of one day writing the definitive history of my family. As time went by I occasionally reminded myself to get on with the work, but was interrupted for thirty or more years making a living, buying a home and raising a family. I eventually returned to my genealogical brick wall—the ancestor who cannot be traced no matter what I do. The situation had not changed so I decided to look further afield at the wider family of Orr, and to start upon a study of our origins and our bid to populate the world. The one trait that is apparent is that our ancestors were prolific. Families with ten, twelve, or sixteen children are quite common in the eighteenth and nineteenth centuries; the record stands at three wives and twenty two children. But, of course, infant mortality was also very high with about half the children born dying by their tenth birthday. Second and sometimes third marriages, were also more common then as there was no social security—widows with young children needed a man about the house and an income to keep them. A secondary feature is our wanderlust as we dispersed to seek our fortunes around the world. All the more ancestors to find no doubt, but also more to disappear into the mists of time in some far flung corner of the former British Empire.

I have had to accept that there is no prospect that all the Orr families will one day be linked together. This work is therefore about the origin of the Orrs, the places from whence we came and where we have migrated to. It is made up of Orr information gathered over a period of some forty years; from ongoing research by myself; research for articles I have written; my own web site pages; magazine articles, and three books about the Scottish Reformation; the Presbyterian Kirk, the Covenanters and the Ulster Scots (the Scotch Irish). I have also taken the opportunity to add historical and social aspects to illustrate the wider picture and explain how our ancestors lived. Not least among the records are the contributions by Orr descendants from around the world, some of whose information has been included. I hope this work goes some way towards repaying that generosity. Please note, however, all information is offered `as is`. Although every care has been taken by me to provide reliable data, it is not in any way guaranteed to be correct. As is also custom and practice where a date of death is not known, the birth and marriage dates after 31 December 1899 are omitted on the assumption that the person may still be alive.

Finally, my thanks to Sandy Pittendreigh of the Dumfries and Galloway FHS; Debora Spano in Berkshire, New York; Vinson Tate in Ohio; Barbara Holt and Merrilee Palmer in New Zealand; Margaret Gower; Terry Orr for the image of Loch Orr Castle; Sandy Orr in Scone; and Ken Guest for information as well as all for the use of their photographs.

B. J. Orr

INTRODUCTION

It is not my intention to produce a `how to` guide for researching in the UK or elsewhere, there are many such books already as well as free tutorials available on www.rootsweb.com and www.genuki.org.uk to help you. However, a few general words to set the scene about researching your Orr ancestors may be appropriate in the light of my own experience

There are great expectations when first we start researching our ancestors, often without first making a serious efforts to glean all and any information possible from living family members. It is essential to make the effort and sit down with elderly grandparents, great aunts and uncles and gently pick their memories. Also obtain access to any old records, photographs, postcards, insurance policies, wills, family bibles, diaries, land records, deeds, birth, christening, confirmation, marriage and death certificates, diaries, letters, scrapbooks, etc. before they are cast out as rubbish, especially when there is a house clearance following the demise of a relative. Your relatives may think you are a pest but in years to come you will be glad you braved their wrath.

The past ten years or so has seen a quantum leap in the amount of information that is becoming available via the Internet. Both national organisations and local family history societies are generating more and more data in digitised form for on line interrogation, for sale on CD, or on microfiche. The Rootsweb organisation hosts a variety of groups that are engaged in collecting and making available a wide range of data, including the transcription of ships' passenger lists—a vital source for immigrants. Most local societies have projects that are transcribing data from local archives, such as early census data, church registers, and gravestone memorials. This wealth of information is a stark contrast to earlier days when research meant a special trip, perhaps overnight stays, and hours in archives plodding through large tomes of closely written records. Don't be fooled into thinking that all the answers are there on the Internet—perhaps much of the last hundred and fifty years will be, but once beyond the inception of mandatory registration of births, marriages and deaths, there is still a reliance on material that may only be available in archives in a distant town state, or even country.

Be warned, however, that there is an increasing amount of rubbish filtering on to web sites which is uncorroborated and without the source specified. This is in turn being replicated in all innocence by web surfers accepting the data at face value, then sometimes exacerbating matters by uninformed guesswork and fanciful `leaps of faith`. If you have good grounds to make assumptions then make a note of the reasons in your file so that you and other researchers can help validate them.

At the end of the day there is absolutely no substitute for seeing, copying, or making a note of, the original or certified source documents. Always record your sources.

Scotland, the home land of the Orrs, is especially fortunate to have had most of the Old Parish Registers (OPR) of the Church of Scotland filmed and digitised. With subsequent mandatory civil registration of births, marriages and deaths from 1855, it means there is a very substantial on line facility that goes back as far as 1580 in some parishes. This is a pay site at www.scotlandspeople.gov.uk. I should mention that this is not a total record for Scotland, so don't be disappointed if an ancestor is not found straight away. The population moved around quite a bit following the available work, and the sought after birth, marriage, or death may be in a different parish or shire. Maybe the ancestor was not a kirk goer, or was a dissenter, or not of the Presbyterian faith, or perhaps Catholic. These will not appear in the OPR. Before 1855, there were occasions when children were not christened, sometimes for years, because of taxation and religious discrimination. Also, under Scottish law, a man and woman can live together as man and wife without the formality of a church or civil wedding; all that is required is a declaration that they are man and wife. Similarly, a child born out of wedlock (a natural birth as it is sometimes called) is automatically legitimised by the subsequent marriage of the couple.

Compulsory registration was implemented in England and Wales in 1837. In Ireland it was mandatory for Protestants from 1 April 1845 and Catholics from 1 January 1864. There is a subsequent division of responsibility for records in Ireland between Dublin and Belfast from 1922 when Eire or the Irish Republic was formed. Regrettably many records, including most of the early Census records were destroyed in a fire in 1922 or used as waste paper in WW II, so dependence falls on supplementary records and, critically, knowledge of the ancestors` religion along with as exact a definition of where they lived that you can obtain. It is particularly useful if you can determine the `townland` (a specific area within a parish) as these are used in many old rental and tax records to identify a family.

If you are confining your research to a particular country or region it is well worth joining the appropriate local Family History Society who will have lists of members` interests; probably have a resource centre with a members library; and local publications and microfiche for sale. Whether or not you join them, I would encourage you to visit these societies and benefit from the members experience and local knowledge. Visitors are always welcome and for a small charge for temporary membership, access can normally be had to their local record holdings. Anyone visiting Edinburgh should place a visit to the Scottish Genealogy Society at the top of their list of things to do. It is within yards of the General Record Office and National Archives, the National Library of Scotland, the Museum of Scotland and the Edinburgh City Library—a veritable paradise for the researcher.

Web Sites

The major reference sites remain www.rootsweb.com, www.familysearch.org and www.ancestry.com for data, and www.cyndislist.com for links to interesting sites. Importantly, these organisations endeavour to maintain the links they give. The data sites are being continuously updated and expanded so return trips can be fruitful. In each country there are national organisations as well as archive sites at national, county and local level, such a the Public Record Office (PRO) at Kew, London; the Public Record Office in Northern Ireland (PRONI) and the General Record Office in Dublin, and Edinburgh. The national libraries and their on line book catalogues can be very useful, both in ascertaining what published works there might be and in obtaining information (for which a charge may be made). The Linenhall Library in Belfast is one (www.linenhall.com) and the National Library of Scotland (www.nls.uk) is another. Bodies such as the USA Genweb and the UK`s Genuki organisations provide information about a location— not only the county, but also the parish, the registration district, or in Ireland the Barony, the Poor Law Union and the townland; as well as post and zip codes. A favourite search engine is www.google.com which seems to be able to find just about anything. Give it a try, type Orr in the search panel and see what is produced.

The Church of Jesus Christ of Latter Day Saints (the Mormons)

The records of the Church of the Latter Day Saints (LDS) are well known and a very useful starting point for the beginner at www.familysearch.org. If there is a LDS Family Research Centre near you, then a visit is well worth the effort. The International Genealogical Index (IGI), is a major resource if used intelligently. Just remember that the data has been collected for Church purposes and cannot be taken as absolutely correct—errors in transcriptions and copying of old records do occur. Use the information to guide you to the source documents so that you can verify the facts. The

IGI contains information as it appeared on the original record or in a submission and cannot be changed. If you find an error, an alternative to correcting the information is to submit the accurate data to the Pedigree Resource File by clicking on the Share tab on the web site's home page and following the instructions. The Pedigree Resource File is a collection of pedigrees that have been lodged with the Church—there were over 160 Orr related files the last time I looked, so check in case others have already done work in your area of interest.

A useful resource is the Library Catalogue available on CD and on line. The Catalogue lists in country order, within counties/parishes by subject a wide range of documents, histories, records of every type that have been filmed—not just births, christenings and marriages. If you are going to attempt some serious research it will be worth the while to look and see what is available from Salt Lake City and delivered to your local Family History Centre—mostly for only a very modest handling charge.

Interest Lists on Rootsweb.

There are thousands of interest lists covering a multitude of subjects including the Orr-List, and the Scotch-Irish List. Other lists are by geographical district, county or state, and there are special interest lists such as Army units and ethnic groups. These are a valuable resource and have many knowledgeable researchers subscribing to them, as well as other potential cousins searching for the elusive ancestor in that locality. A word of caution—do not be greedy and subscribe to too many lists at one time—some lists are very busy and you could be swamped by e-mail. Sit in for a few days and get a taste for the topics under discussion, and post your queries. You can always come back to a list, and it is possible to search the list's archives—another good way to find out if your special interests have been mentioned. For an index to more than 24,000 RootsWeb-hosted genealogy mailing lists and easy (free) subscribing options, visit http://lists.rootsweb.com/

E-mails

The e-mail facility has changed for ever how we communicate and a trendy shorthand language all its own has developed. Expedient though that may be, please do not let it be at the expense of common courtesy. There is an increasing use of nicknames or pseudonyms in e-mails and e-mail addresses. Many serious researchers consider it singularly rude to receive e-mails that are unsigned and, worse, sometimes in a demanding tone wanting all the available information. Some researchers will not even answer such mail. It is also less than helpful for follow up correspondence if all you have is a terse and cryptic e-mail address only to find later that your contact has changed their Internet Service Provider and not told anybody. By all means protect your privacy if you so wish, but remember that you are seeking and hopefully exchanging detailed information about your relatives with a possible family member. In these circumstances keeping your name a secret is both pointless and mistrustful. There has to be some give and take and exchange of information if you want to obtain maximum cooperation. Remember, too, that people may have spent many years, and probably a considerable amount of money, on their research. If there is likely to be ongoing communication the offer of a postal (snail mail) address would probably be welcomed, and it adds to the feeling that you are `one of the family`.

DNA

The latest development has been DNA tests by Orrs in California, Illinois, Iowa, Liverpool, Ohio, Ontario, and Ulster, which has revealed a common ancestor with Donegal Orrs through a Joseph and Andrew Orr in Muff Parish, and to James, John and Thomas Orr from the Newtownards–Donaghadee area of County Down. Interestingly this reflects the migration pattern of the descendants of Patrick Orr, younger son of James Orr of Ballyblack (1607) some of whom went to Donegal and Armagh. The elder son, James stayed in

County Down. The numbers that have taken DNA tests are relatively few and more would be very welcome.

Part I

THE ORR ROOTS

The Orr Name

Edward MacLysaght, an authority on Celtic names, states that the name derives from the parish of Orr (Urr) in Kirkcudbrightshire. It is also the name of an old Renfrewshire family and is most common in the west of Renfrewshire and in particular in the parish of Lochwinnoch. The Gaelic scholar, Mac Giolla Domhnaigh, says that the name was also used as an anglicisation of Scots Gaelic Mac Iomhair, 'son of Ivar', a name also made MacIver, MacIvor, MacUre and Ure. Some others derive the name from the Gaelic odbar donn, odbar, meaning 'sallow` (of complexion) and donn, meaning 'brown'. I am not too sure about sallow, the vast majority of Orrs I have ever met, or seen in photographs and paintings have generally been of a healthy, ruddy, complexion, or weather beaten and tanned.

Robert Bell in his *Ulster Surnames* says that in Ireland the name is common only in the Province of Ulster, where it is chiefly found in counties Antrim, Down, Londonderry and Tyrone. Although in Ulster for four hundred years, and probably longer because of the closeness of the West coast of Scotland, the roots of the family lie squarely in Scotland. The Orrs and Ures are an acknowledged sept (a family giving allegiance to another more powerful family) of Clan Campbell.

George Black in his *Surnames of Scotland* tells us of Hugh de Hur who was a member of an assize court in the Marches of Grange of Kircwynni and the land of Culven in 1289. Hugo of Hurr, probaby the same family, was witness to a charter by the Kirkconnel family in Kirkgunzeon. And Hugh de Ur was a juror on an enquiry as to the priveleges claimed by Robert de Brus, Earl of Carrick, in 1304. What these references indicate is that an area of land called Urr had already been defined and made a barony by the mid 1200s; and was being adopted as part of a person's name.

Some Myths Rejected

I have seen several claims that the Orr name is derived from McGregor which is inconsistent with the facts. It is <u>not</u> a diminutive form of McGregor, the Orr name had been been in existence in its own right for over 300 years *before* the McGregor name was banned in 1603. It is, however, possible that a MacGregor might have taken the Orr name when that clan was forced to give up his own - in the same way that Rob Roy MacGregor took the name of his arch enemy Campbell as his new surname - but that is an entirely different thing. The chances of an adoption having happened is probably very small indeed, not least because Orr is essentially a Lowland name. But on the other hand, if you are certain to be transported or lawfully killed on sight for just having the name MacGregor, it might not be such a bad idea to take a name of a southern Scottish family.

Neither is there any evidence that the Orr name is a derivative from the French d'Or (meaning gold) from the Huguenots, or from the name of Spanish sailors washed ashore from wrecked ships of the Spanish Armada. Again, the name existed for several hundred years *before* the Huguenot's were forced to migrate in the late sixteenth century and at the invitation of William III ca 1690. The Spanish Armada was sunk in 1588. In America some interest has been generated concerning a dark skinned (not necessarily black) people labelled the Melungeons to whom the Orr name has been linked. Again it may be that Orrs have intermarried with native peoples but they do not derive the name Orr from them.

Existence of the Orr Name in Scotland Since at Least 1296

A reference book from Inveraray Castle (*Your Clan Heritage*, A McNie, 1988), the home of the Duke of Argyll and Chief of Clan Campbell, lists the names associated with the clan and includes Orr:

> ORR. Old Renfrewshire name, originally either from extinct placename or from Gaelic odhar, of sallow complexion. The numerous occurence of Orrs in Campbelltown, Kintyre since c. 1640 likely due to movement from Renfrewshire. John Or in Moy listed as Campbell of Cawdor family, 1578.

Andro Craefurd (Andrew Crawford) author of *The Cairn of Lochwinnoch* ca 1836 deeply researched the history of the Lochwinnoch area and in his notes observes that

> the Orrs, the Montgomeries, the Brydines, the Kirkwoods, the Glens, the Sempiles have charters from five hundred years. [from the Abbott at Paisley].

This indicates that the Orrs had been leasing land since the early 1300s and is consistent with the record that a Hew Orr or Urr swore allegiance to King Edward I (the Ragman Rolls) in 1296.

There are many variations in spelling as a result of officials in the past writing the name as it sounded and it was not until the mid nineteenth century that a consistent form appeared. You might try to imagine a stereotype Scotsman with a broad accent pronouncing Orr as Urr, Ure, Oorr, Oare, Owr, Owar, Ower, Oar, Or, Oarr, Oayre, Oure, Our, - maybe he was just .. err ... clearing his throat or reluctant to admit he was a MacGregor !

The Orr connection to Clan Campbell is rooted in the feudal system where small families gave allegiance to a larger, more powerful, family. Clan or family membership comes about through three means: birth, as generally understood by having one of the surnames of a clan or family; marriage; a woman may choose to wear her own family tartan e.g. her father's; and thirdly by adoption. The Orrs would appear to have become a sept through adoption thus we have John Or in Moy listed as a Campbell of Cawdor family in 1578.

Clan Campbell itself is believed to stem from the race of O`Duibhne who owned the shores of Loch Awe and were the original Oire Gaidheal, or Argyll, the "Land of the Gael ". That race is said to have ended with the heiress Eva, daughter of Paul of The Sporran (named so as he was the carrier of the Kings money bag) who married Archibald or Gillespie Campbell. A charter of David II in 1368 gave to Archibald Campbell all the lands of Loch Awe. Colin Mor Campbell of Lochow was knighted by Alexander III in 1288 and it is from him that chiefs take their title "Mac Cailean Mor" The Duke of Argyll is the Chief of Clan Campbell and he resides at Inveraray Castle which is a must visit if you get to the vicinity of Loch Fyne - about 45 miles north west of Glasgow.

Inveraray
Castle
Photo by the
author

The road past Inveraray (the A 83) south will take you to
Lochgilphead from where you can go to the Mull of Kintyre and on
a good day see the coast of Ireland. Campbeltown harbour was one
of the points of departure across the Irish Sea for migrants to Ulster
- just 21 miles from the Mull of Kintyre. The earliest Orrs resident
in Campbeltown seem to be in 1641. There are several family
groups from 1659 until about 1860 when they all disappeared.

Campbeltown Harbour   Photo by the author

The early families possibly migrated to Ulster and the Colonies,
although increasing industrialisation in the eighteenth and
nineteenth century would have encouraged more and more people to
move to Clydeside where there was work and better pay for the
former fishermen. A single family group existed on the island of
Gigha where they appear to have been the `hereditary` ferryman.

The Irish Connection

The earliest Orr recorded (to date) in Ireland is a Richard Orr of
Clontarf., near Dublin who appears in an index of wills where his
testament is recorded in 1563. Clontarf in the Diocese of Dublin, is
the site of a famous victory by King Brian Boru over the Vikings in

1014. Richard is not a very common name in Scotland and poses the possibility that he may have come from elsewhere. The locality around Dublin was known as `the Pale` in Elizabethan times, and was the area settled by mainly English migrants and adventurers.

The presence of Scottish Orrs in the Province of Ulster came about primarily through the acquisition of land in Co Antrim and Co Down by two Scottish landlords, Hugh Montgomery and Sir James Hamilton, both from Ayrshire. They purchased a great deal of land between 1603 and 1607 and took with them tenants from Scotland to settle on their new estates. Later there was the Plantation of Ulster (1610-1630) which saw thousands of Scots settling on escheated land in the other counties of Ulster.

As far as is known a James Orr and his wife Janet McClement, were the first of the name to settle in the parish of Ballyblack, County Down, on the estates of Hugh Montgomery in 1607. We know of their descendents through the work of Gawin Orr of Castlereagh, who researched and documented some 2,900 relatives in his epic `Ulster Pedigree`. This has been added to and published by Ray A Jones in 1977 under the title of *Ulster Pedigrees Descendants, in Many Lines, of James ORR and Janet McClement who Emigrated from Scotland to Northern Ireland ca 1607*   This book is in the Latter Day Saints Library in Salt Lake City, Call no 929.2415 Or7j; and on fiche #6036613. A long title but it is the most comprehensive public record of Orrs in Ulster there is. A list of names of people who married Orrs, and are mentioned in the Ulster Pedigree is in Appendix 8.

The Norse, English or Norman Connection Since 1202

It is another possibility that the Orr name has a Norse origin from their word `Orri ` meaning `blackcock` (a game bird) The possible Nordic origins is supported by the existence of several Swedish, Norwegian and Finnish families of Orre some of whom emigrated to America. The Norsemen were very active along the western shores of Scotland and the Isles; and had a major presence on the Isle of Man. The Angles gave way to the Norsemen in the ninth century and for the next two hundred years they held sway until the land passed to the Scottish throne under Malcolm Canmore (1057-93).

An interesting link appears in the Lincolnshire Assize Roll of 1298 with reference to a Roger Orre b ca 1202. That the name Orre should turn up so early on the east coast of England where Norman knights from William the Conqueror's time had lands, raises all sorts of possibilities. As indicated earlier, Hew Orr or Urr swore allegiance in 1296. His name is also variously given as Hew or Hugh del Urre, meaning Hew *of* Urr. It was custom and practice for the Norman knights who did not have surnames as we know them, to take the name of their fiefdom or barony, as part of their name. This soon became a necessary practice and a requirement at Court so that the king might know from whence they came. Another tenuous link is that to Richard Orr of Clontarf who may have settled in Ireland during the reign of Elizabeth I. It is within the realms of possibility that the two knights were of the same family and Richard might even be a descendent, but that is conjecture.

A Viking Connection

Recently DNA comparisons have been made that show the possibility of some Viking markers which gels with a source of the name `orre`. There are a number of Orre families in Sweden that supports this argument; they are mainly in the 1800s but there was a Sven Orre son of Lars Orre in Sweden in 1660. The Orre spelling was common in Western Scotland - Ayrshire, Lochwinnoch and Glasgow around 1650-1720. The Vikings or Norsemen (of which there are three strands of origin - Denmark, Sweden and Norway) were very active indeed down the western seaboard of Europe with the Danes mainly engaged in England, France, Belgium, Holland, and Germany. The Swedish Vikings were mainly in central Europe through Finland, they founded Russia and were active down into the Caspian Sea and the Mediterranean. The Norwegian Vikings sallied forth initially against England then focussed on Scotland and Ireland. Other Norwegian Vikings led by Eric the Red ventured to Iceland and Greenland where they created a republic in 930 AD. His son Leif is credited by some as having discovered America - 500 years before Columbus.

In England the Vikings of Danish origin were very active and fought many bloody battles in the 8th -10th century. Importantly, after the blood letting was over they turned to settling the land and brought with them sophisticated manufacturing processes, poetry, literature and a democracy that gave women equal rights with men. They ruled the Dane Law - the land north and east of a line roughly between London and Liverpool which included the Midlands, East Anglia, Yorkshire, and the ancient kingdom of Northumbria, which had been agreed with King Alfred the Great in 886 AD. A unique genetic marker for the Danish Vikings has not been isolated because they and the earlier raiders cum settlers - the Angles and the Saxons, originate in much the same region of Northern Germany and Denmark.

The Norwegian Vikings do have a unigue genetic marker. They mounted raids on monasteries and the like in England (Lindisfarne in 793) but were mainly in evidence in Scotland (Iona in 795 AD, the first of three raids in the next ten years) and Ireland. In 870 AD they stormed the fortress of Dumbarton after a four month siege, and attacked the Pictish fortress at Dunnottar on the east coast in 890 AD. There was effectively a Viking Age in the west of Scotland that lasted from ca 800 AD to 1050 AD during which the Vikings ruled a small empire from their base in the Orkneys and Shetlands. One of their Saga`s is the thirteenth century story of `The Saga of the Earls of Orkney`, otherwise known as the *Orkneyinga Saga*.

The Vikings were also dominant on the Isle of Man for a long time and exercised their influence down the west coast of Scotland and the Western Isles. They were prominent in Cumbria, the northernmost part of England on the south side of the Solway Firth, where they appear to have settled for many years around Penrith. A quite high incidence of DNA compatibility has been found by researchers. It is therefore quite possible that a Norwegian Viking gene should turn up in the Orr line that hitherto has been traced only as far as the mid thirteenth century in west and south west Scotland. The rich pasture lands of the valley of the River Urr in Dumfriesshire emerges into the Solway Firth south of Dalbeattie (which was once an ancient port for the area) and would have been accessible to Vikings both as raiders by sea and as traders from across the Firth in Cumbria, just a few mile away.

The Place

Of the various options it is most likely that the Orrs took their name from a parish in the south west of Scotland where there is the Parish of Urr (Pre 1975 Parish ref. 884 in Dumfries and Galloway Region) to the north west of the town of Dalbeattie. Locally the area is known and the name pronounced, as Orr. One of the explanations for the name of the Parish of Urr is that it is derived from the Norse ur, a word for the wild ox (the auroch), that in ancient times abounded in the river valley of the Urr. There is also the earthwork called the Motte of Urr nearby and several other Urr features - Urr Water or river which flows to the sea from Loch Urr, through the Haugh of Urr and beneath the Old Bridge of Urr into the Urr Estuary and the Solway Firth.

Edward MacLysaght is quite firm in his opinion that the name is derived from the parish of Orr or Urr in the Stewartry of Kirkcudbrightshire. The parish is quite long being some fourteen miles in the North - South direction and between one and six miles wide. Overall the area is about thirty five square miles. Through the Parish runs the Waters of Urr or River Urr that has its origins in Loch Urr. The Loch is in fairly wild moorlands and is approached by service roads that run through modern pine plantations. The landscape looks rather bleak with a small headland that juts out into the loch, with a copse of trees on the far shore.

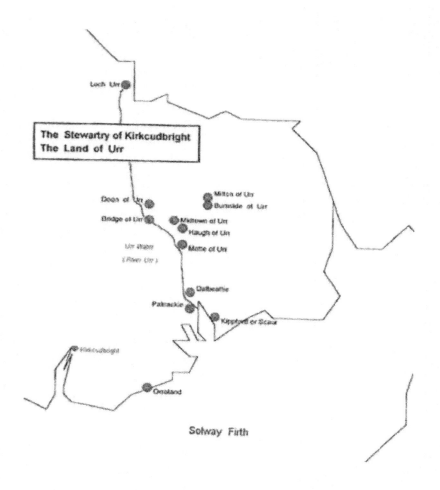

The Parish of Urr

Map drawn by the author

Certainly the district and parish was referred to as Orr [*sic*] as long ago as 1684 in *A Large description of Galloway* by Rev Andrew Symson. This was a response to the request for information for a new map by Sir Robert Sibbald, following his securing a patent from King Charles II as His Majesty`s Geographer for Scotland. Symson wrote:

> The Bishop of Edinburgh is patron hereof, as depending on New Abbey. The kirk of Orr is twelve miles distant from the town of Kirkcudburgh, and twelve miles distant from the town of Dumfreise. The parish of Orr is bounded eastwardly with the parish of Kirkgunnion; on the southeast with the parish of Cowend; and on the south and south west with the parishes of Bootle and Corsemichael, from both which parishes it is separated by the river of Orr; on the north west it is bounded with the parish of Kirkpatrick Durham; on the north by the parish of Irongray; and on the north east, it is bounded with the parish of Lochruiton.

He says of the river Orr:

> Orr hath its rise from Loch Urr or Loch Orr, which loch is situated betwixt the parish of Balmaclellan, on the west side, and the parishes of Glencairn and Dunscore, on the east side. In this loch, there is an old ruinous castle, with planting of sauch or willow trees for the most part about it. where many wild geese and other water fowles breed; to this place there is an entrie, from Dunscore side, by a causey which is covered with water knee deep. This loch is replenished with pikes; many salmon are also found there at spawning time.......... This river is foordable in many places; being foordable also at Kipp Ford when the tide obstructs not, although, at spring tides the sea water flows up as far a Dub O`Hass. However, if the water be at any time great, there is a stone bridge over it, call`d the Bridge of Orr, which joynes the parishes of Kirkpatrick Durham and Corsemichael together.

The Statistical Account for Scotland 1799 has an interesting footnote about the Parish of Urr. This refers to Loch Urr/Orr and a castle in the vicinity during the time of Sir William Wallace (1300) belonging to the Seaton family. Sir Christopher Seaton was a companion of Wallace who was allegedly caught in Fife, where there is another Loch Orr (modern spelling Lochore). But the explanation that Bruce was expected in Dumfries (and anyone on the run who knew the hills and moors of Galloway is unlikely to have been hiding in Fife), is quite convincing. Innes MacLeod in *Discovering Galloway* tells that there was a crannog on the south west side of the loch and an underwater stone causeway to the shore with remains of three or four enclosures and possibly a 13th century hall. A six acre premonitory at the south west end has a ditch and bank across the landward end and may have been as a bailey to an island castle. A correspondent, Terry Orr, has an eighteenth century drawing of a Loch Orr that shows a castle in the background which is remarkably similar to this description. I believe they are one and the same.

The river Urr flows twenty six miles from its source in rather desolate moorland through some beautiful wooded valleys and farmland to the sea and the Solway Firth. For about ten miles the river is the western boundary of the parish. The river at one time had very good fishing from which large salmon have been taken. The estuary of the Urr is fairly shallow with mud banks exposed at low tide and is home to much bird life.

13

Loch Urr   Photo by the author

Loch Orr   Image courtesy Terry Orr

Urr Parish Church   Photo by the author

The village hall, Haugh of Urr   Photo by the author

Views up and down river at the Bridge of Urr. Photos by the author

The Urr Estuary at Kippford
Photos by the author

The

Water of Urr

Photos by the author

The Motte of Urr

This is a 12th century `motte and bailey ` construction - a fortified area, built on rising ground with earthworks creating a deep and wide ditch around it, is on the outskirts of Dalbeattie. The buildings on the mound and the fence round it would have been constructed from wood. Remnants of burnt wood have been found dating back to the 12th century and signs were found that the fortifications were subsequently rebuilt.

The Motte of Urr is said to be the most extensive motte and bailey castle in Scotland. Its position in the valley of Urr Water does not look especially commanding from a military standpoint now, but in its day was probably a more dominant feature and may well have been built on the site of an earlier Anglo Saxon fort.

The Motte of Urr. Reproduced from *The Parish of Urr*, D. Frew (1909)

Also known as ` The King`s Mount` the motte stands on the west bank of the River Urr, about a mile from the parish church and about 2.1/2 miles from Dalbeattie. It is thought that there was a town adjacent to the motte on the east side. Standing in a broad meadow the river appears at one time to have divided, perhaps by human hand, and surrounded the motte, thus giving it the appearance of an island. Its shape is of an oval hill which rises sharply from the river bank, the south side being a reasonable slope but the other sides rather steep. The whole is surrounded by a ditch that is about 15m wide. On the base platform rises the central plateau on which sits the conical mount - about 85 feet above the river bank. The two diameters of the conical mount are 100 feet and 92 feet. It is also surrounded by a ditch that is 537 feet round and between 10 and 12 feet wide and about 14 feet deep.

It is easy to imagine that with wooden palisades in place and steep slopes and ditches to climb, that it was a substantial fortress in its day. Excavation at the top showed that the topmost 2 metres had been added after a disastrous fire ca 1170-1180 had destroyed timber fences and houses. There was a rectangular wooden tower or blockhouse in the middle of the motte and a timber palisade with foxholes or pits around the edge for archers to fire down through the slits or embrasures. Coincidentally this feature is also found in similar constructions in Ireland. There is evidence of rebuilding and new foxholes added after the fire, and coins and pottery indicate that there had been occupants until the 14th century.

Actual references to the occupation of the Motte are few and not until ca 1456 does it appear in the Exchequer Rolls as a farmstead that pays rent. In the Registrum Magni Scilli or Register of the Great Seal - an early register of royal grants and licences in Scotland, there are two references to grants by King James V - 1535 ` Moite de Wr` and ` 1541 Moit de Ur.`

The Tradition of `The King`s Mount`

The tradition is that Robert the Bruce came to the area in the course of his wanderings and one morning found himself near the Motte. There he encountered an English knight, Sir Walter Selby, and was forced to fight him. As they gave battle they were observed by the wife of Mark Sprotte, who lived on the Motte, while she was preparing her husband's breakfast of brose or porridge. She saw that Robert the Bruce was in danger and rushed out and tackled the Englishman, bringing him ignominiously to his knees. The Bruce chose not to take advantage of his fallen opponent and sheathed his sword and allowed Sir Walter to get up. Having washed themselves in the river they went to the Sprotte home for rest and refreshment. Here the good lady produced but one bowl with one spoon which she gave to the Bruce saying she would not feed an Englishman in her house. Partly to defeat her vigilance and partly to reward her for her care of him, the Bruce told her to go out and run as best she could and he promised to give her all the land which she covered while he took of the bowl of porridge. The good lady did as she was bidden and while she was gone the two men shared the bowl and the one spoon.

In due course some twenty Scotch acres of land was granted the Sprottes who became the Sprottes of the Mount and the land remained in the family for some five hundred years. The condition the Bruce made was that on any occasion a king of Scotland passed through the valley of the Urr a bowl of brose or porridge was to be presented to him in ` King Robert's Bowl`.

Urr Features

There are several other Urr features - Urr Water which flows to the sea from Loch Urr and in the 11th and 12th century passed through the port of Hur which was between Dalbeattie and the old port of Dub O` Hass. The Milton of Urr was a village on the 17th century old military road though there are suggestions of medieval and Roman occupations as far back as the 2nd and 3rd centuries. Recent archaeological digs at Drumlanrig has revealed a substantial Roman fort. After about 1800 it was a busy thoroughfare with a sawmill, corn mill, school and a smithy. The Haugh of Urr was another busy crossroads with several inns for the tired and thirsty traveller, with the Old Bridge of Urr a crossing point on the river between parishes.

The terrain is of rolling hills, none of which are exceptionally high, but enough to give splendid views. Any hill walker is well advised to dress properly as mists can descend very quickly and the open moors are shelterless and windswept. In winter months blizzards and `white-outs` from driven snow are common The river valley has good soil and rich pastures while sheep and cattle, including the famed long haired black Galloway, are reared on the higher pasture. The most common colour is black, although a small number of animals are dun in colour or red. These cattle are known for their double coat, which combats the cold and wet. They are medium sized, compact and well-fleshed animals bred for generations to live off the poorest of land. Their hardiness is second to none and they are famed for their outstanding mothering qualities. This is the main reason Galloway are in great demand as a "hill cow", her calf is an easily fleshed beef animal, which in turn, are much sought after, due to the succulent taste of their meat. Another local breed of cattle to be seen is the `Beltie ` named from the broad white cummerbund around its girth. This breed, a probable Dutch cross with the Galloway, is thought to have been imported from Holland as long ago as the eleventh century. The Beltie as a beef animal produces exceptionally lean and flavorful meat, and their heritage has conditioned them to survive in very

A Galloway `Beltie`
Photos courtesy A. Pittendreigh

harsh climates, including parts of the U.S.A. The region suffered terribly from foot and mouth disease in 2000/2001 and is gradually rebuilding its livestock.

A modern shepherd's `bothy`
Photos courtesy
A. Pittendreigh

A common feature is the use of stone walls rather than wire fences around the smaller fields; and stone pens are still in use for holding sheep and cattle.

Stone sheep pens
Photo courtesy
A. Pittendreigh

It is easy to see that this land of forests and mosses was once home to now extinct species of wild boar, wolf, bear, deer and the urus or auroch. The latter was a large black ox like, animal standing six feet at the shoulders and with fearsome forward pointing horns. The auroch became extinct ca 1627 when last seen in Poland. It is possible that the Urr/Orr name stemmed from the Latin name, similarly the Norse word urus also means wild ox and boar. The spelling of the place has varied from Vr, Ure, Hurr, Whur and Wur but the sound of it remains reasonably constant. The Basques from northern Spain are said to be the forebears of the Celts and date from about 500 BC, In their primitive language Urr signifies water, or close to water. So it is reasonable to believe that Urr means from `from the river` or similar phrase and applied to the Celts who lived on its banks.

The early populace

The earliest peoples of whom there is definite information were Celts, although there is conjecture that there may have been a small dark haired peoples who have disappeared. The Celts were hunters and had the name Selgovae (derived from the Gaelic for hunter) and also known as Picts or painted people from the tattoos with which they adorned themselves. Their original dwellings would have been the caves and, in time, shelters constructed with stakes in the ground and covered by leafy branches. These progressed to wattle and daub - sticks and mud, and eventually more substantial buildings of hewn timbers, with gaps filled by clay and roofed with straw, ferns and turf. The Rev David Frew wrote a definitive work *The Parish of Urr, A History, (1909)* and has this to say about the early people of Urr.

" The ancient barony of Urr probably determined the bounds of the parish, when it came to be formed, some time in the twelfth, or early part of the thirteenth century. To that period of religious revival in Scotland, under the influence of Margaret, wife of Malcolm Canmore, and her son David I, is ascribed the general division of the country into bishoprics and parishes. The latter, as a rule, were associated with the existing baronies, and made conterminous with them: the parish of Urr would be delimited accordingly, on the lines already fixed by the barony. The subsequent partition of the barony in the time of Bruce may be related in some way to the appearance of two parish churches in Urr simultaneously, which will be noticed later. The condition of things in Galloway, and consequently in Urr, about the time of its erection into a parish, shows some improvement upon the rudeness of existence in former days. The religious revival instituted by Queen Margaret, and other influences at work in the province since its incorporation into the Scottish kingdom, had not been without a salutary effect upon the social life of the people.

The land was still, to a great extent, covered with wood and swamp; but agriculture had risen to the level of a recognised industry, and was as far advanced in its methods as it was for three or four centuries afterwards. Besides black oats, rye, and long-bearded barley, such quantities of wheat were grown, that Edward I was able to draw upon them for the support of his army during his campaign in Galloway. The rise of monastic institutions in the province, and the distribution of parish clergy among the people, helped to spread the knowledge of agriculture, as well as other refining influences. Of course the cultivation of the soil still proceeded upon somewhat elementary lines. The possibility of reclaiming wet lands by drainage, and enriching poor ones with fertilising substances, was not yet understood, hence tillage was confined to the higher-lying regions, even practised upon the summits of considerable hills; and, when the portion of land utilised became worn - out and unfruitful, it was left to recover itself by the healing virtue of time. This explains the traces of past cultivation still visible on heights where no modern agriculturist would dream of attempting to grow a crop.

The plough was of primitive structure, and was drawn by quite a herd of oxen, ten being no infrequent number. Where it could not be worked, or failed to take effect, the spade was brought into requisition. The harrows were simply bunches of whins or thorns tied to the tails of the oxen. When the grain had been gathered and dried, it was ground in a small stone handmill called a quern. This usually consisted of two round flat stones, the upper one having a narrow hole or funnel driven through its centre, and the lower one a wooden or metal pin inserted in it, on which the other revolved, and crushed the grain. Some of these stones have been- found in and around the parish of Urr, after having been used for other purposes, and are now carefully preserved. Much of the grain was not put through the quern, but made into malt, and brewed into ale. The mountains, forests, and uncultivated parts generally were no longer given over to wild animals, but stocked with black cattle, sheep, goats, and swine; which, in the absence of fences, had to be assiduously herded off the cultivated lands.

The clothing of the natives was still largely composed of animal skins; though wool had begun to be used, and, either in its natural state or spun into yarn, was woven into a coarse kind of cloth, which was utilised for raiment. Flax was grown in very few places, and linen consequently almost unknown. Shoes were hardly ever worn by the lower classes, though pieces of hide were sometimes tied upon the feet to cover and protect them. As usual in an undeveloped stage of society, the drudgery, and indeed most of the work, was left to the women, the time of the men being divided between idling and fighting.

The houses of the poorer inhabitants remained very much as they had been for centuries: small huts of wooden beams and branches, plastered over with clay or mud, and roofed with heather, sod, or turf, which the cattle shared with the owner and his family. Large castles, however, after the Norman style, with thick stone walls and numerous apartments, moats and draw-bridges and other fortifications, began to be built by the nobles; and it was at this period the abbeys and monasteries arose, and grew into the splendid proportions which may still be traced and admired in such magnificent ruins as those of New Abbey and Dundrennan. "

A novel feature, although surprisingly quite common in the region, are the houses built on islands, usually man made by driving timbers into the bottom of a lake and backfilling with branches and stones to give a foundation on which to build a house. These `crannogs`, as previously mentioned in Loch Orr, have an Irish origin and are found mainly in Ireland and Scotland with a recent discovery in Wales. They had hidden, secret, paths to them which would zig zag beneath the water so only those in the know could safely access them. Excavations in the Milton Loch in 1953 exposed a large farmhouse on a circular timber platform and a wooden gangway. Elsewhere the land dwellers have left many traces of their passing with hill forts, hut circles and burial cairns.

A Roman geographer, Claudius Ptolemaeus of the second century placed a large settlement of Caer-bantorigum, one of the four main towns of the Selgovae, in the vicinity of the Motte of Urr. The Roman legions were active in the area in 79 AD and it appears that for three hundred years they occupied the valley of the Urr and probably used the site of the Motte as an encampment. Little is known of the inhabitants after the Romans left Britain in 407 AD and we must assume that there continued to be trade, movement and inter marriage with the Irish Picts just twelve miles across the sea from the Mull of Kintyre.

The Norsemen and the Normans

St Columba went to Iona in A. D. 563 and his followers enjoyed over 200 years of relative tranquillity. However, the Norsemen were especially active along the western isles and through the Irish Sea to the region of Dublin where they had a large trading settlement. Iona was attacked by raiding Norsemen in 795, 801, 806, 825 and 986. Rebuilt in 1074 it became a cathedral in 1500. All the religious buildings on Iona were later broken up during the Reformation, although the Celtic Cross of St John was saved. It wasn't until 1910 that the abbey was restored. The Norsemen held sway in most of the western Lowlands until the land passed to the Scottish throne under Malcolm Canmore. He in turn granted it as an Earldom to his youngest son, David, in 1107. David I `s reign was one of relative peace and consolidation of the emerging Scotland into one kingdom and the introduction of the feudal system of land tenure. As Prince of Cumbria, David (King David I r1124-1153) had caused an inquisition to be made of the lands and buildings that had belonged to the ancient church. Acting on that information David created the bishopric of Glasgow in 1121. This new diocese stretched from the river Clyde to the Solway and from the Lothians to the river Urr in Kirkcudbrightshire. The consequence was a rapid growth of feudalism with land becoming the basis of power. The feudal system itself made for a closer control by the King who gave land to many foreign Lords and Sheriffs, including Crusaders, Knights of St John, Knights Templar and other Norman knights. At the end of the chain of tenancies was the common man with winners and losers over the tenancies of the smallest acreages. In this respect a growing source of land was the church which received great support from David. In his reign the Culdee churches of the Celts at

St Andrews and Lochleven disappeared and new monasteries arose and existing ones were strengthened.

There was a problem when Donald MacHeth claimed the throne on David's death in 1153, and for three years had the assistance of Somerled, King of the Isles. However, Somerled withdrew his support and continued to make a nuisance of himself elsewhere until slain at Renfrew in 1164. In the meantime Fergus, Lord of Galloway seized his chance to try and break away but was tamed in 1160. Subsequent attempts were made by a succession of Lords of Galloway, Uchtred, Gilbert, Roland and Alan to get rid of the Scottish allegiance but they also lost their struggle. Although subjugated militarily there was a stubborn resistance to change in the south west where the Picts and their descendants maintained a sturdy independence, and continued to speak Gaelic until after the Union of the Crowns in 1603.

In the late thirteenth century the lordship of Galloway was divided up between four members of the ruling famiy, including John Baliol and Alexander Comyn. Under these leaders the men of Galloway were the opponents of King Robert the Bruce whose brother Edward finally subdued the area in 1308. In 1369 the eastern part of the area was given to Archibald Douglas, the Grim, who built the stronghold of Threave Castle.

The earliest records of Urr occur in the charters of Holm Cultran, an abbey in Cumberland, which owned lands in the parish of Kirkgunzeon adjacent to Urr. A Hugo of Hurr and his son Thomas appear as witnesses to several charters. Records also show the lordship of Urr in the possession of Walter de Berkeley (died ca 1194) who was Chamberlain to King William I. From him it passed by marriage to the Balliol family who occupied Buittle Castle. Two witnesses to a Balliol of Urr Charter of 1262 - Adam Clerk and Hugo Sprot, were described as burgesses of Urr. Hugh de Urre del Counte de Dumfres appears In the Ragmans Rolls, declaring allegiance to Edward I in 1296. His lands were later given to Henry de Percy who had been appointed Keeper of Galloway.

A map by Chatelain & Guerdeville dated 1720, in the Museum of Scotland, shows a village of Orr just south of Dumfries. A search of the 1841, 1851 and 1881 Censuses, however, shows few Orrs in the area; in 1881 there was only one family of Urr/Orr then in Kirkcudbright, being a dwelling at Auldon Bank, Troqueer. It is interesting that the two sons of the house, both born in Maxwelltown, are listed with different surnames - James M. Orr aged 5 yrs and his brother Thomas Alexander Urr aged 3 years, demonstrating how easily names were varied in their spelling.

A Time of Turmoil

The evidence is of turmoil in the area which was subject to an ongoing demand by the local lords for feudal service by the men in their respective armies. Towns began to emerge in the reign of William I (1185-1200) such as Dumfries in 1186 and Ayr in 1197. These were intended as secure bases from which the sheriffs helped to pacify the region; and as defences against the lawless bands. They also became the centres from which trade developed in surplus agricultural produce. This was influenced by the success of the Cistercian monks who had developed sheep farming and manufacture of associated goods.

It is sometimes forgotten that feudal military service took the men from the land and it is more than coincidence that famine was common and often followed by pestilence and plague. Thus the turmoil, famine, plague, and constant demands for military service would have been cause enough for the migration of people who had been held in thrall by the local lords for so long. It has to be conjecture that the ancient peoples of Urr migrated northwards to Ayrshire and Renfrewshire. But it is relevant that the main river valleys – Annandale and Nithsdale, run from the south east to the north west and this would have influenced trading routes and migration to areas where Orrs are to be found in number in later centuries. Dalry is about 20 miles and Dalmellington about 35 miles north west of Dalbeattie; and the nearby Nithsdale route runs from Dumfries to Kilmarnock, Lanarkshire, and to the River Clyde and Glasgow.

Conclusion

The available evidence is that the Orrs came from the Parish of Urr, although few are to be found there today. Something cataclysmic happened in Urr, to destroy a substantial settlement like the Motte of Urr. It may have been war or plague, or possibly during a revolt by one of the Lords of Galloway- we may never know. We do know that the coming of the Norman knights to the south west of Scotland saw the replacement of wooden forts and motte and bailey castles, with fine stone castle such as at nearby Buittle, built on a hillock on the western edge of the River Urr. This was the favourite home of John Baliol, erstwhile King of Scotland, and his mother Dervorgilla. The death of the young Maid of Norway, grandchild of Alexander III, meant that the succession to the Scottish throne was in disarray. It was this uncertainty that led to Edward I of England imposing himself as "Lord Paramount" and on 11 June 1291 the four regents of Scotland handed the throne and the kingdom of Scotland into Edward`s hands. There followed the proceedings to determine who should be King of Scotland, which Edward finally decided on 17 November 1292, should go to John Baliol

A feature of affairs at this time was the transfer of the castles or fortresses of Dumfries and Galloway first to Walter de Curry in 1291; then to Robert Siward in 1292. In April 1296 John Baliol resiled from his vassalage and declared for a free kingdom which led to an immediate military subjugation by Edward`s army. About this time Edward, perhaps in a fit of pique, is said to have restored all the lands of Galloway to Thomas, illegitimate son of Alan, the last Lord of Galloway. In September 1296 the castles of Ayr, Wigton, Cruggleton and Botol (Buittle) were committed to the keeping of Henry de Percy when he was appointed Keeper of Galloway. He also received a portion of land in Galloway as, in the later reign of Robert I land consisting of half of the barony of Urr, was granted to Thomas Randolph, Earl of Morray, when it was forfeited by Percy. It was also in this period that William Wallace began his fight for freedom and Edward`s army retaliated with great force burning and looting all places of resistance.

This constant unrest and changing ownership of land would have changed the status for the motte and its occupants. As the people in a feudal society were part and parcel of the land on which they lived, they would have had several changes of loyalties forced upon them each time a new new master came along. It is little wonder that there was a drift of the population away from the area, leaving the motte for lesser nobles or gentry before adoption by farmers. Mottes with earthen slopes and wooden palisades did not serve any real defensive purpose from about the fifteenth century.

Another factor in this period was the emergence of the church as a major land holder. At the end of King David I`s reign (1153) there were nine dioceses, not including Galloway (which remained under the Archbishop of York`s jurisdiction). This expansion meant that the vast wealth and lands of the mediaeval church became a factor in the transformation of a backward country. Perhaps this was a factor in the migration of the Urrs/Orrs to the church lands of Lochwinnoch where they were tenants of the Abbey of Paisley ca 1300. Hughe de Urre, who lost his lands to Henry de Percy, would have known of the bishopric of Glasgow, which king David had created. With contacts at Court and probably the money to be able to make a move, there is the possibility that lands were obtained in the Paisley area. Indeed, he may have been compensated with church land in Lochwinnoch when the barony of Urr was given to others. Conjecture I know, but for now, this is my favorite hypothesis.

Part II

DISTRIBUTION OF ORR

Around the World in 1998

No doubt professional statisticians can suggest more complex methods than those I used, but based on simple counts of entries in phone books, estimates of households on the basis of 2 adults and 2.7 children per family, available Census statistics and lists of registered voters, there were in 1998 about 132,000 Orrs in the world or in round numbers about 28,000 family groups. We already know that the Orrs found the young America in the 1650s and today there are probably over 100,000 scattered across that country. They also went to other former British colonies - to Canada where there are about 7,000 Orrs and Australia about 7000. New Zealand was a later destination and has about 2,000 Orrs There are also families in South Africa, the island of Malta, the West Indies, South America (Argentina) and scattered in enclaves round the world. In the homeland of Scotland there are about 10,000; England has about 11,000 and Ireland (Ulster) about 5,000. *These numbers are of course, just estimates to give a feel for the spread of our name.*

The 1997 Electoral Rolls for England and Wales give a figure of 9710 Orr's entitled to vote. A database for England, Wales and Isle of Man, (from the National Statistics Office as at 9 Sep 2002) had a total population of 54,412,638 and gives the following hits and ranking for variant spellings of Orr. The database is an approximation only and appears to be of voters, ie persons over 18 years old.

ORE 206 ranking 20895
URR 634 ranking 9439
OAR Nil
ORRE Nil.

In summary the world population of Orrs alive in 1998 was *very*
approximately:

Country	Primary count	Est. Households	Calc. Popn.
Australia	1703	1552	7294
Canada	1639	1476	6937
England	3915	2516	11826 *
IOM & CI	16	12	57
New Zealand	521	411	1932
Scotland	3640	2204	10339
Ulster	2029	1132	5322
USA	18708	18708	87928 **
Wales	110	67	315
Totals	32281	28078	131950.

* Electoral Roll (over 18 yrs) 9710. ** US Census (1990) 88799.

New Zealand

The settlement of New Zealand by the British post dates that of
Australia by a generation or two and really commences in the
1850s. The majority of early settlers went under the auspices of the
New Zealand Company but by the 1840 a a significant proportion of
organized settlement was church based, such as that at Otago by
members of the Free Church of Scotland (the followers of Reverend
Norman McLeod who arrived via Nova Scotia.). By the close of the
nineteenth century about a quarter of the population of New
Zealand were Scots or of Scottish origin.

Analysis of New Zealand White Pages (1998) shows there were 521
listings for Orr which after making allowance for `couples` results
in an estimated 411 family groups giving an estimated population
including children, of 1932.

Australia

The calculated figures that follow are made from count and analysis
of the Australia White Pages Directory (1998 version). Because

spouses/partners are frequently listed together and separately eg A B Orr & C D Orr, the `couple is treated as a single family unit. The family count is therefore a count of listed entries as amended.

The population per state has been calculated as family groups x 4.7 (2 adults + 2.7 children) being the factor previously used and validated as reasonable with the USA; and the known large families which the Orrs tended to have until very recent times.

State	District	Count	Adjmt	H/holds	Calc. Popn.
S. Australia	Adelaide	81	14	67	315
	Borossa Vly.	18	2	16	75
	Port Augusta	8	2	6	28
	S. East	2	1	1	5
	York Pen.	2	1	1	5
	Totals	111	20	91	428
Queensland	Brisbane	143	30	113	531
	Beaudesert	7	1	6	28
	Cairns	12	4	8	38
	Dalby Roma	3	1	2	9
	Gold Coast	42	11	31	146
	Maryboro	20	4	16	75
	Rockhampton	54	16	38	178
	Sunshine Coast	46	16	30	141
	Toowoomba	10	2	8	38
	Townsville	12	2	10	47
	Totals	349	87	262	1231
ACT	Canberra	134	4	30	141
N. Territory		16	6	10	47
Tasmania	Hobart	14	3	11	52
	Burnie	5	1	4	19
	Launceston	15	2	13	61
	Totals	34	6	28	132
Victoria	Melbourne	203	27	176	827
	Bairnsdale	20	3	17	80
	Ballarat	58	13	45	212

Bendigo	44	11	33	155
Geelong	17	2	15	70
Mildura	8	2	6	28
Mornington	42	11	31	146
Shepparton	20	4	16	75
Warrnambool	10	3	7	33
Wangarratta	14	2	12	56
Warragul	2	1	1	5
Totals	438	79	359	1687

State	District	Count	Adjmt	Households	Calc. Popn.
N.S.W.	Sydney	200	9	191	898
	Albury	15	5	11	52
	Bega	6	1	5	23
	Bathurst	16	3	13	61
	Broken Hill	3	1	2	9
	Campbelltown	7	2	5	23
	Central coast	27	6	21	99
	Cooma	3	1	2	9
	Dubbo	30	8	22	103
	Goulburn	3	-	3	14
	Kempsey	17	5	12	56
	Lismore	31	6	25	118
	Muswellbrook	7	3	4	19
	Newcastle	61	16	45	212
	Nowra	6	2	4	19
	Penrith	11	4	7	33
	Tamworth	17	2	15	71
	Wagga Wagga	12	2	10	47
	Windsor	4	1	3	14
	Wollongong	22	4	18	85
	Totals	499	81	418	1965

State Popn.	District	Count	Adjmt	Households	Calc.
W. Australia	Perth	160	41	119	560
	Central Country	10	2	8	38
	Great Northern	9	3	6	28
	South Western	43	11	32	150
	Totals	22257	165	776	

Total calculated Orr population @ 1998   6407.

Canada

State	District	Count	Adjmt	Households	Calc. Popn.
Alberta		Nil			Nil
British Columbia		320	10	310	1457
Manitoba		108	6	102	479
New Brunswick		34	2	32	150
Newfoundland		3	-	3	14
Nova Scotia		56	3	53	249
N W Territory		4	-	4	19
Ontario		1013	61	952	474
Pr Edwd Island		6	1	5	24.
Quebec		94	4	90	423
Saskatchewan		Nil			Nil
Yukon		1	-	1	5
Totals		1639	87	1552	7294.

Distribution in the United Kingdom

It is not surprising that the Orrs are well distributed throughout the United Kingdom despite having their roots in Scotland and Ulster. Like so many other families in the 18th and 19th centuries they were driven to find work wherever it was available. It is significant that the education and work ethic of the Presbyterians guided them towards the professional classes and the `white collar` trades as these emerged through the Industrial Revolution. Thus we see them in especially in the law, teaching, medicine, engineering, manufactures, wholesale and retail distribution, and the army; as well as keeping a foot in the farming community. This expansion of interests drove them to the relevant centres of activity and the larger towns and cities. A further group were engaged in various types of mining, being involved in lead, coal and iron ore mines in Scotland (Ayrshire and Fife) and subsequently in the vast coal fields of Northumberland and Durham. This association with mining is correlated by the number of Orr`s that ended up in the mining area of Pennsylcvania. A note about some Orr fatalities in the UK coal fields is at Appendix 16.

The distribution below is taken from a computer analysis of the Electoral Rolls for 1997 and is therefore as accurate a count as can be obtained of the adult (18 and over) Orrs in the UK. For the purposes of calculating the population including children the family base has been taken as 2 adults + 2.7 children. Adjustments were made to reduce the count to households listed and then the family factor applied. This is necessarily arbitrary but also based on information gathered and consequent `feel` for the average family size. In the very small populations in some of the Islands the factor has not been applied. *I would reiterate that these figures are approximate and only serve to show where we were residing at the time.*

England by County

County/shire Popn.	Voters	Adjustment	Households	Calc.
Avon	67	28	39	183
Bedford	55	26	29	136
Berkshire	77	30	47	221
Bucks.	61	27	34	160
Cambs.	43	14	29	136
Cheshire	94	39	55	259
Cleveland	54	20	34	160
Cornwall	10	1	9	42
Co Durham	92	33	59	277
Cumbria	121	39	82	385
Derbyshire	41	15	26	122
Devonshire	99	42	57	268
Dorset	58	24	34	160
East Sussex	74	28	47	221
Essex	126	50	76	357
Gloucester	52	22	30	141
Hampshire	92	32	60	282
Hereford	8	2	6	28
Hertford	70	24	46	216
Is of Wight	17	4	13	61

Kent	113	36	77	362
Lancashire	364	118	246	1156
Leicester	69	21	48	226
Lincolnshire	23	10	13	61
London	321	68	253	1189
Merseyside	216	81	135	635
Middlesex	80	25	55	259
Norfolk	43	16	27	127
N. Humber	83	38	45	212
N. Yorks	68	24	44	207
Northampton	71	27	44	207
N`thumberland	92	32	60	282
Nottinghamshire	53	24	29	136
Oxfordshire	57	22	35	165
Shropshire	6	2	4	19
Somerset	24	7	17	80
S. Humber	32	13	19	89
S. Yorkshire	58	24	34	160
Staffordshire	40	12	28	132
Suffolk	36	14	22	103
Surrey	144	57	87	409
Tyne & Wear	249	102	147	691
Warwickshire	28	9	19	89
W. Midlands	109	36	73	343
W. Sussex	60	22	38	179
W. Yorkshire	90	28	62	291
Wiltshire	42	15	27	127
Worcestershire	32	16	16	76
Totals	3915	1399	2516	11826.

Isle of Man and the Channel Islands

I of M	8	4	4	19
Ch Isles	8	-	8	38
Total	16	4	12	57

Scotland

Aberseen	54	18	36	169
Angus	80	35	45	212
Argyll	16	4	12	56
Ayr	449	184	265	1246
Berwick	14	4	10	47
Caithness	2	-	2	9

Clackmannan	35	13	22	103
Dumfries	38	16	22	103
Dunbartonshire	84	35	49	230
East Lothian	50	21	29	136
Fife	175	71	104	489
Inverness	28	11	17	80
Isle of Bute	2	1	1	2
Isle of Islay	4	2	2	9
Isle of Lewis	4	3	1	3
Isle of Mull	1	-	1	1
Isle of Skye	1	-	1	1
Kincardineshire	9	6	3	14
Kirkcudbright	22	9	13	61
Lanarkshire	1328	518	810	3807
Midlothian	306	107	199	935
Moray	17	6	11	52
Nairn	2	1	1	2
Orkney	1	-	1	1
Peebleshire	4	2	2	9
Perthshire	72	31	41	193
Renfrewshire	458	172	286	1344
Ross	13	6	7	33
Roxburghshire	12	5	7	33
Selkirkshire	13	4	9	42
Stirlingshire	132	54	78	367
W. Lothian	206	93	113	531
Wigtownshire	8	4	4	19
Total	3640	1436	2204	10339.

Ulster				
Antrim	954	399	555	2609
Armagh	125	60	65	306
Down	591	264	327	1537
Fermanagh	27	10	17	80
Londonderry	171	81	90	423
Tyrone	161	83	78	367
Totals	2029	897	1132	5322

Wales				
Clwyd	29	13	16	75
Dyfed	19	8	11	52
Gwent	6	4	2	9
Gwynned	9	1	8	38

Mid Glamorgan	13	7	6	28
Powys	5	1	4	19
S Glamorgan	14	4	10	47
W Glamorgan	15	5	10	47
Totals	110	43	67	315

Distribution of Orr Families in the USA.

Estimate based on analysis of the 1997 US Phone Book.

State	Count	State	Count	State	Count
Alabama	423	Kentucky	237	N Dakota	23
Alaska	51	Louisiana	179	Ohio	836
Arizona	305	Maine	89	Oklahoma	407
Arkansa	300	Maryland	267	Oregon	275
California	1581	Massachusetts	289	Pennsylvania	275
Colorado	336	Michigan	655	Rhode Island	30
Connecticut	176	Minnesota	273	S Carolina	431
Delaware	57	Mississippi	218	S. Dakota	62
Dist Columbia	36	Missouri	471	Tennessee	609
Florida	12078	Montana	123	Texas	1321
Georgia	765	Nebraska	126	Utah	154
Hawaii	35	Nevada	109	Vermont	59
Idaho	153	New Hampshire	58	Virginia	481
Illinois	827	New Jersey	362	Washington	439
Indiana	514	New Mexico	107	West Virginia	96
Iowa	277	New York	705	Wisconsin	165
Kansas	248	N Carolina	724	Wyoming	54

Total of 18708 family units.

Interrogation of the US Census Bureau facility at: http://www.census.gov/genealogy/www/freqnames.html gave 88799 Orrs in the 1990 Census, representing 0.019% of the population and the 636th most common name.

The base numbers above are, of course, only the homes with telephone connections that are listed. Experience suggests that to find the approximate total of Orrs in a state that are alive, including children, you need to multiply by a factor of 5.

Where the Orrs Were in the 1881 Census of England, Scotland & Wales

NOTE: *The figures are per Census place and include therefore persons born outside the area'*

Scotland: Location – Shire, and Number

Aberdeen 3	Angus 156	Argyll 74	Ayr 803
Banff 2	Berwick 49	Clackmannan 2	Dumfries 4
Dunbarton 136	East Lothian 34	Elgin 10	Fife 60
Forfar 56	Haddington 34	Inverness 4	
Kirkcudbright 15	Kincardine 1	Lanark 1442	
Linlithgow 16	Midlothian 365	Moray 10	Nairn 2
Peebles 13	Perth 33	Renfrew 586	Ross &
Cromarty 2	Roxburgh 38	Selkirk 125	Stirling 170
West Lothian 47	Wigtown 50		

Totals	Scottish Lowlands	3417
	Scottish Highlands	464
Total		3881

England & Wales

Bedford 8	Berkshire 14	Cheshire 45	Cumberland 79
Derby 8	Devon 25	Dorset 1	Durham 79
Essex 15	Gloucester 15	Hampshire 20	Hertfordshire 2
Is of Man 10	Is of Wight 20	Kent 60	Lancashire 428
Leicester 9	Lincolnshire 2	Middlesex 116	Norfolk 5
Northampton 6	N`thumberland 60	Nottingham 1	Oxford 1
Shropshire 1	Somerset 6	Staffordshire 6	Suffolk 14
Surrey 61	Sussex 10	Warwickshire 3	Westmoreland 9
Wiltshire 1	Worcestershire 24	Yorkshire 84	Royal Navy 4
Channel Isles 6	Anglesey 1	Glamorgan 5	

Total England and Wales: 1266

The General Record Office for Scotland

There is a free search facility at www.scotlandspeople.gov.uk which gives global details of the location of the name in the GRO. There is also helpful guidance on how to start researching in Scotland, as well as comprehensive notes on how to use the pay system for detailed searches and how to obtain official certificates.

The name search facility shows the number of names in a data set. The number of records for ORR between 1553 and 1899 in each set are:

Old Parish Record Births/Christenings (1553-1854)	6261
Statutory Index Births (1855-1899)	5811
	12072
Old Parish Record Marriages (1553-1854)	4210
Statutory Index Marriages (1855-1899)	2455
	6665
Statutory Index Deaths (1855-1924)	4284
Old Parish Record Unknown (1553-1854)	2
1891 Census	4133
Total	27154

A later record count of ORR between 1553 and 1951 is:

OPRI & SRI Birth & Christenings (1553-1901)	12357
OPRI & SRI Marriages (1553-1926)	4643
SRI Deaths (1855-1951)	4284
1891 Census	4133
1901 Census	4429
Total	34896

A look at more recent figures in 10 year steps revealed:

1900/1910	+137 births, + 770 marriages; +990 deaths.
1910/1920	+805 marriages; +1128 deaths.
1920/1930	+437 marriages to 1926 only; +903 deaths.
1930/1940	+ 886 deaths.
1940/1950	+ 936 deaths.

Birth figures are only available up to 1901 and marriages up to 1926 which rather distorts the picture, but the death rate is fairly constant at about 90-100 per year in Scotland. Given that there are much smaller family groups in the 20th century and the void created by the two World Wars, it is reasonable to assume that the Orr population is gradually reducing in the homeland but increasing elsewhere.

As family history researchers we are concerned primarily with the dead and an attempt was made to evaluate how many ancestors there might be. The only place with anywhere near reliable figures is Scotland where the death rate is about 100 pa. This would produce a about 28,000 records since 1600. This figure is very likely underestimated since families were much larger, and child mortality greater, in earlier times. As a *very rough* rule of thumb measure, it would appear that for every living Orr there are 3 deceased records which gives a total world base of possibly 400-500,000 records. Discovering and relating such a huge volume is an impossible task - even if the relevant records existed and were available.

Scottish Naming Conventions in the 18th - 19th Century

In the 18th and 19th centuries families tended to name their children in a specific pattern, which occasionally can give some guidance to family names. It was also common for the wife's maiden surname (the maternal grandfather) to be used as a second christian name of some if not all children. This can be a valuable guide when the wife's name is otherwise unknown. It is sometimes confusing to find perhaps three or even four children of the same name. This usually indicats that the earlier named child/children has died.

Males

First-born Son Father's father
Second-born Son Mother's father
Third-born Son Father
Fourth-born Son Father's eldest brother
Fifth-born Son Father's 2nd oldest brother or
Mother's oldest brother

Females

First-born Daughter Mother's mother
Second-born Daughter Father's mother
Third-born Daughter Mother
Fourth-born Daughter Mother's eldest sister
Fifth-born Daughter Mother's 2nd oldest sister or Father's oldest
sister

In some cases you will find that the order is reversed with the first and second children, i.e. the First-born son being named after the Mothers father and the Second-born son after the Father's father. If this is the case then the daughters are also usually reversed.

It sometimes happens for some special reason such as repaying a kindness, that a close friends` surname might be given to a child as a second christian name. In some instances the name of a person might have been the witnesses at marriage, or god parents at a christenings. Remember, too, that witnesses are likely to be relatives, often sisters and aunts, signing under their married name.

Top ten Christian names

This analysis is derived from my Scottish Orr database holding 15212 names at the date of sampling. The count of names includes variant spellings eg Isbel, Isabel, Isabella, Isobel etc. are all under Isabel. These are mainly names occurring between ca 1600 – 1900.

Name	%	Name	%
John	10.73%	Margaret	7.82%
James	10.05	Janet	6.35
William	8.40	Agnes	4.83
Robert	5.46	Mary	4.78
Thomas	3.57	Elizabeth	3.56
Alexander	2.11	Jean	3.34
David	1.63	Ann	2.49
Andrew	1.10	Isabel	2.22
Hugh	0.91	Jane	1.95
George	0.91	Marian	1.30

Part III

MIGRATION AND IMMIGRATION

Scottish Migration to Ulster

There had long been movement of Scots across the Irish Sea to the shores of Ireland by way of trade and as galloglass (mercenary soldiers). But there were also small settlements on the Antrim coast which increased in number when the authority of the Lords of the Isles was broken in the fifteenth century. The intrusion of the Scots was very unwelcome to the English government at that time and many attacks were made on them. However, it seems that by the late sixteenth century the presence there of the McDonnells in particular, led by Sorley Boy, was inevitable. In 1586 Queen Elizabeth I granted him a large portion of Antrim in return for submission and acknowledgement of the Crown's superiority.

As a Scot Sir Randal MacDonnell was a favourite of James VI/I and received the area called the Glynnes and the Route in 1603. For his achievements as a planter he was made Viscount Dunluce, and then Earl of Antrim in December 1620. What this marked was the beginning of colonisation of Ulster. It meant also a greater English direction in Irish affairs which until then had been more of a feudal dependency. The indebtedness of Earl of Antrim to the Crown was later reflected in the provision of troops to join with the Marquis of Montrose in his campaign against the Presbyterian Covenanters in 1644-5.

The principle of Planting peoples on sequestered land evolved from Henry VIII 's accession to the throne of Ireland in 1541 and it was under his policy of `Surrender and Regrant` of lands that the Irish princes received English titles. Con O`Neill became Earl of Tyrone; Murrough O`Brien the Earl of Thomond; and Macwilliam Burke of Galway, Earl of Clanrickard. The significance of the policy is that having the land regranted to them meant that in any subsequent default of misbehaviour the lands were liable to seizure by the Crown. Under Edward VI a more aggressive policy led to seizure of lands in reprisal for insurrection and in 1556 under Queen Mary I a plantation scheme for most of Leix and Offaly was declared with the counties being renamed Queens County and Kings County. The policy of seizure and grant to English landlords continued under Elizabeth I. This policy underlies the later resentment of the indigenous population whose ancient tribal land was settled by `foreigners`.

It should be remembered that until 1707 and the Act of Union, Scotland was a foreign country to England and throughout the 17th and 18th centuries England herself was in constant turmoil. The accession of James VI to the English throne in 1603 brought new problems for the Scottish people who had already suffered for generations through the power vacuum over succession to James IV following his death at Flodden Field in 1513. There had been a string of young kings and a queen with Regents running the country, which interacted with the religious ferment of the Scottish Reformation; and the rejection of Catholicism and French influence in Scotland. This was followed by the turbulent times of Mary Queen of Scots who was forced into abdicating in favour of her infant son, James VI. Scotland was thus seen as a threat to English interests, especially trade, even though they soon had a common king.

It was some years before James VI reached his majority and took hold the reins of power but when he did he set about dealing with the kingdom`s problems, especially lawlessness. The Band Act of 1602 addressed the growing lawlessness on the Scottish - English Border and required compliance from the lords and their control of the Border Reivers. In the Highlands the MacGregors were hounded with fire and sword and their name expunged as an example to others. At the same time a survey was made of `surplus` men which led to their transportation. The Act was renewed in 1617 with further transportations taking place.

The Hamilton and Montgomery Settlements

The Scottish migration to Ireland was initiated by the acquisition of land by two Ayrshire familes - Sir James Hamilton from Dunlop, and. Hugh Montgomery Sixth Laird of Braidstone. Both men were private adventurers before the formal Plantation scheme commenced in 1610. There was much wheeling and dealing with the last of the Irish Earls, O`Neill, before he fled in 1607. His lands began to change hands in 1603; By 1606 the settlement by the Scotsmen began in earnest with both landowners taking Scottish families with them to their lands in Counties Antrim and Down. These two counties were excluded from the Plantation scheme of 1610 having already accomplished the substantial Scottish - Protestant settlement that the king desired.

Sir James Hamilton, later Viscount Clandeboye came from the Dunlop area of Ayrshire, where his father was the Rev Hans Hamilton. The family had owned lands in Raploch, Lanarksshire for some 400 years which they seemed to have lost at some stage hence James` enthusiasm for taking up as much he could in Antrim and Down. He was the eldest of six sons James, Archibald, Gawin, John, William and Patrick; and was largely tutored by James Ussher, later Bishop of Meath, Archbishop of Armagh and Primate of Ireland.

Hugh Montgomery was the eldest son of Adam, fifth Earl of Braidstane b ca 1560 made Viscount Montgomery of the Great Ards in 1622. The Montgomery lands and the lordship of Braidstane was in the bailliary of Kyle, county of Ayr. Until the middle of the 17th century the lands were within the Parish of Beith consisting of two divisions - Braidstane and Giffen. There were changes to boundaries after 1649.

The Montgomery Manuscripts, written ca 1680-1700 as memoirs by William Montgomery, son of Hugh, quotes some details of the earliest tenants who are mainly family. The manuscript goes on to record that in June 1606 settlers began to arrive including the brothers of Hamilton - Gawin and John. Other families included Maxwell, Rose, Barclay, More, Baylie

On the Montgomery lands settlers included John (or James) Shaw of Greenock, brother of Sir Hugh's wife (Elizabeth Shaw); Patrick Montgomery of Black House or Craigbowie (husband of Christian Shaw, sister of Elizabeth, and thus Hugh Montgomery's brother in law) and Cunningham of Glengarnock - related to the Shaws. George Montgomery, brother of Hugh, was appointed to the bishoprics of Derry, Raphoe and Clogher in 1605.

The Montgomery`s tenants began to arrive in 1607 as Proclamations in Glasgow, Ayr, Irvine, Greenock and other south western parts of Scotland, especially around Braidstone, declared leased land on easy terms. This drew large numbers of Scots to Ulster and later, many went to Donegal and what is now Londonderry. Co. Antrim was the main centre for the Scottish settlers during the early 17th century with settlement of the MacDonnell land in Antrim and the Baronies of Dunluce and Glenarm. In Co. Down the Hamilton and Montgomery estates were the main Scottish areas up to about 1614. Hamilton recruited tenants for his estates in County Cavan from Clandeboye, while some lands were leased to tenants who themselves recruited Scots. Thereafter further land disputes inhibited growth. This period also saw the Incorporation of Bangor, Newtown and Killyleagh to ensure there was a Protestant majority. Most of the burgesses came from the Lowlands with about 200-300 males in Co Down by 1614. In all it is estimated that some 10,000 Scotsmen were brought to Ulster by the Montgomery and Hamilton plantations.

Mainly early Presbyterian settlers, those on the Hamilton Estates in the 1600's, included: Anderson, Lemon, Getts (Geddis), Moore,

Lowry, Herron, Kerr, Bole, Shaw, McBratney, McKee, Clark, Wilson, Scott, Burns, Brown, Megra (Megraw), Gibson, Grant, Dempster, Bowman, Love, Guelston (Gelston), Gillespie, Burgess, Walker, McVey (McVeigh), Dixon (Dickson), Milliken (Milligan), Piper, Martin, Huddleston, Davidson, Hamilton, Maskelly (Miskelly), Kennedy, Frame, Petticrew, Thompson, Paterson (Patterson), Fraizer (Frazer), McKibben, Curry, Maxwell, Boyd, Gamble, Bennett, Porter, Carr (Kerr), Douglas.

Under the patronage of George Montgomery, more influence in the Church was exercised by the appointment of Scottish Bishops such as Andrew Knox, Bishop of Raphoe, 1610. There were 7 ministers from Scotland in 1612 and 15 ministers of which 12 were from Scotland in 1622. An interesting side issue was the volume of denizations granted to Scots - denization was necessary in order to have the rights and privileges of an Englishman and therefore eligible to have title to land. There were some 300 denizations approved in 1619. thus a further 300 families planted in Ulster.

The Plantation Scheme, 1610–1630

On 4 September 1607 The Earls of Tyrone and Tyrconnel with 30 relatives and 60 friends and followers fled from Ireland into exile. These included Maquire, owner of half Fermanagh, It was decided that all the lands of Shane O'Neill were forfeit, as a result large portions of counties Tyrone, Donegal, Coleraine, Armagh, Cavan and Fermanagh reverted to the Crown and thus available for redistribution.. On 29 September 1607 the Privy Council approved a Plantation scheme. There was a short lived rebellion by Sir Cahir O'Dogherty which led to the sacking of Londonderry on 19 April 1608; and the use of Scottish levies from Ayr to take Carrickfergus - the first use of Scottish troops by the English for conquest abroad. The troops remained in Ulster and became a further source of tenants.

In January 1609 proposals had been made for the plantation of Tyrone which became the plan for the division of the escheated lands in the six Counties. The Proclamation of the Plantation in Scotland on 8 March 1609 opened the doors for the settlement of thousands of Scots in Ulster. The original applicants for land tended to come from within 25 miles of Edinburgh. They were generally persons of substance and position and the applications were by way of family ventures with mutual action as cautioners' (guarantors). It was the urban middle class and petty gentry who were most enthusiastic. In all the Scottish undertakers received some 81,000 acres.

The nine baronies set aside for the Scots were mainly around the periphery of the escheated lands. The Scottish Baronies were Boylagh, Banagh and Portlough in Donegal; Strabane and Mountjoy in Tyrone; Knockninny, Magheraboy in Fermanagh; Clankee and Tullyhunco in Cavan; and, the northern half of The Fews in Armagh.

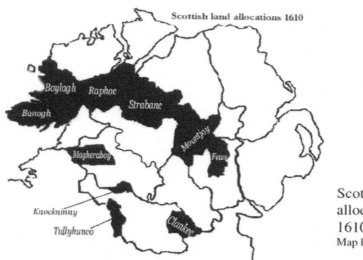

Scottish land allocations 1610

Scottish land
allocations
1610
Map by the author

The Scottish origin of the undertakers influenced migration and to a large degree the family location of many Scots. As a very broad indication only, the families were dispersed at this time:-

Donegal - Cunningham, Campbell.

Fermanagh - Home, Johnston, Armstrong, Elliot, Little, Irving, Beaty - all Border names.

Tyrone - Stewart, Hamilton, Elliott, Armstrong, Johnson, Graham, Scot, and Irving.

Antrim - Stewart, Boyd, Hamilton.

Down - In the 1630 muster: 53 Montgomery's, 44 Hamiltons then Campbells (Ayrshire - Hamilton estates) Johnston, Kennedy, Scot, Bell, Maxwell, Gibson, Dixon, McKee - mainly from the vicinity of Ayr, Renfrew, Wigtown and Lanark. When Derry was granted to the City of London in 1610 among the South Western Scots who were compensated were the families of Boyd, Patterson and Wray.

The Muster Rolls of 1630 provide a basis for analysing the extent of Scottish migration. The extant Rolls provide a total of 13,147 adult males which suggests a total population in excess of 30,000, of which about 60% were Scottish.

Orr in the Plantation and after.

The earliest Orr found in Ireland is that of Richard Orr of Clontarf who died ca 1563. Whether he was of Scots origin or otherwise can only be conjecture, however there are no doubts about James Orr and Margaret McClement, from Ayrshire, who settled in Co Down in 1607 as part of the Montgomery settlement before the Plantation proper.

It is highly probable that there were a number of Scottish Orrs in the early influx of new settlers under the Plantation Scheme of 1610 although documentation is quite another thing. There is one Orr listed in the early denizens this being James Orr, of Raphoe in County Donegal who was granted denization 20 November 1617. It is probable that this Orr originated from either Ayrshire or

Galloway. It was from these regions that the Scots settlers in the County Donegal baronies of Boylagh and Banagh, and Portlough, originated. There was a Thomas Orr in East Inishowen and a Donnell Orr in Raphoe in the 1630 Muster. By the time of the Hearth Tax Rolls in 1665 there were quite a few Orr families - William Orr in Conleigh; John and William Orr in Letterkenny; John Orr in Castlefin; Alexander Orr in Raphoe (Beltany); Joseph Orr in Drumay; John Orr in Donoughmore; Joseph Orr in Taughboyne (Gortree) and Thomas Orr in Taughboyne (Taughboyne).

Robert Bell in his *Book of Ulster Surnames* says that there were settler families in Co Tyrone in 1655. *The Hearth Money Rolls and Poll Tax Returns for Co Antrim, 1660-1669* show a reasonably well off William Orr in Antrim Town with 2 hearth taxes (ie he had a house with two fire places, or perhaps two houses) in 1666 and 1669. In the Parish of Raloo in 1669 there was a Robert Orr (townland of Ballyrickard More) and a Widow Orr (townland of Ballywillin). In the Parish of Ballymoney there was a Pat Ore (townland of Ballymoney) in both 1666 and 1669 Hearth Money Rolls. In the Parish of Dunluce a John Orr (townland of Ballybogy) in 1669. In the Parish of Larne John Oure (townland of Larne Parish & Town) in 1669. In the Parish of Ballinderry John Orr (townland of The New Park) in 1669.

The Estate Records of the large landowners are held at PRONI and are a source for some tenancies, but not necessarily all of them since tenancies were often sublet. The records of the Earl of Antrim and the Earl of Abercorn indicate some early Orr tenants. A Patrick Orre with two other men, was granted the tenancy of Drumlee in Finvoy Parish 24 July 1637. It is a possibility and no more, that he may have been the second son of James Orr of Ballyblack. The Estate Records of the Earl of Abercorn for 1794 gives the following: Robert Orr - Burntha; Joseph Orr- Castletown; Robert Orr- Castletown; James Orr- Fiddyglass; John Orr – Legnathraw;

Matthew Orr – Legnathraw; Samuel Orr- Lismaghery; David Orr – Moness; Matthew Orr – Moness.

Tracing James Orr and Janet McClement

The Old Parish Registers of the Church of Scotland, most of which have been filmed by Latter Day Saints (the Mormons) and included in the International Genealogical Index (IGI), only takes us back to 1682 or so in Beith which is adjacent to Lochwinnoch Parish in Renfrewshire. The earliest dates for births, marriages and deaths in the Parish Registers for Beith are - 1661, 1659 and 1783 respectively. The earliest records for Lochwinnoch are 1718. This means that we have to turn to the Kirk Session records and the Commissariot Registers, the original church court testaments, in the hope of an entry. Both of these localities were in the Glasgow Commissariot. That far back in time one might expect to find something in the minutae of the Montgomery family papers - such as a list of tenants, rents, and workers, who went to Ireland. But William Montgomery could find no list of tenants in the family papers when he was writing the *Montgomery Manuscripts* in 1698-1704; so the chance of finding anything three hundred years later is frankly nil.

The *Manuscripts* says:

> ... it is evident that a large number of settlers had come with sir Hugh Montgomery to the Ards during the first four years of his colonisation. It is to be regretted that no list of these original settlers can now be found. Among them, were several named Orr who appear to have originally settled in the townlands of Ballblack and Ballykeel, and were the progenitors of a very numerous connexion of this surname throughout the Ards. The earliest recorded deaths in this connexion, after their settlement in the Ards, were those of James Orr of Ballyblack, who died in 1627, and Janet McClement his wife, who died in 1636. The descendents, male and female, of this worthy couple were very numerous, and as their intermarriages have been carefully recorded, we have thus, fortunately a sort of index to the

names of many other families of Scottish settlers in the Ards and
Castlereagh.

But we can go forward from James Orr and Janet McClement
thanks to the work of Gawain Orr of Castlereagh who spent a great
deal of his life researching his family history and creating his *Ulster
Pedigree*. This work provides information on about 2,800
individuals although the dates of births, marriage and deaths
information is rather lacking. A list of surnames of persons who
married an Orr has been compiled from the Pedigree. and is at
Appendix 8.

The Movement to and from Ireland and Subsequent Migration to the Colonies

A small but important point to remember is that until the
Revolutionary War and the creation of the United States of America
in 1776, the whole of north America - the US and Canada, was
one English colony, although in dispute with French. Elsewhere
there were the colonies in the West Indies and later Australia and
New Zealand. There were no passport requirements under British
law to move from Scotland to Ireland and thence to the Colonies.
This meant that there were no central records required to be kept of
who went where, and people passed largely unhindered across
county and state lines. Research in this period has to depend on
whatever commercial shipping lists, manifests and passenger lists
that were kept by the ship`s captain or the owners of the vessel.
Some families kept in touch by letter, and these can be a most
interesting source of information; occasionally the church registers
might say that a family had left the parish for America etc. I prefer
to refer to these people as migrants in this period - they became
emigrants and immigrants when the respective colonies became
independent countries.

The rationale behind the movement of people to and from Scotland
and Ireland and migration to the Colonies is a complicated mixture

of economic, religious and political pressures. From the earliest times there was a flow of people between the Western Isles and what we now know as Northern Ireland - at its narrowest point the sea crossing is a mere 21 miles. The employment of Scotsmen as `galloglass` (mercenaries) was common from about the 13 century onwards. Intermarriages of the leading families in Scotland and Ireland was common as long ago as 320 AD when Aileach daughter of Ubdaire, King of Alba married Eochaidh Doimhlein, brother of the King of Ireland.

Much has been written about the accession of James VI to the English throne of England in 1603; the struggles of the Presbyterian Covenanters - with its own consequences of religious persecution; the 1715 and 1745 Jacobite Rebellions, and the later Highland Clearances. In Ireland there was a complex weave of religious and social discrimination set against the seizure and redistribution of native Irish owned land for political reasons since Tudor times. Importantly, this history effected the English Parliament`s attitudes to Irish and Scots issues. Within Ireland bigotry and distrust ran rife not only because of religious differences but also exploitation of power; absentee landlords and a government whose mind was elsewhere having little regard for the `local` problems in Ireland. Not least was the ongoing differences with France and Spain that threatened war again and again.

The 17th century was possibly the busiest time in the history of Britain with the autocratic rule of Kings who believed absolutely in their Divine Right. Non Conformists of all kinds, Presbyterian, Puritans, Independents, Quakers, Congregationalist as well as Roman Catholics were on the receiving end of discriminatory laws in the entire Kingdom of Britain. The despotic leanings of Charles I, Charles II and James VII/II brought civil strife, with wars between Scots and English and Irish. Oliver Cromwell ruthlessly brought peace and sanity to the three kingdoms for a few brief years. In Scotland throughout most of the century, until 1690, there was the ongoing struggle of the Presbyterians and the hard line dissenters or Covenanters, large numbers of whom migrated first to Ulster then to the New World.

Later there was the agrarian revolution in Scotland whereby crofting began to be replaced by hill farming, particularly sheep, and enclosures of land in the lowlands changed farming patterns and tenancies. The consequence was the movement of displaced peoples from the glens and farms to the coastal and industrial towns. This helped create the slums of Glasgow in the industrial crucible of the Clyde valley; and filled the emigrant ships which departed from Fort William, Greenock and Glasgow heading to the USA.

Economic and Social Reasons for Migration

The motivation to migrate from Scotland and Ulster because of religious persecution was certainly a serious cause between about 1630 and 1720. After this period the factors became much more economic and social as both agrarian and industrial revolutions began to exert influence.

The early days of the Plantation saw land being let to settlers at a shilling per acre and less.. A hundred years later the poorest land was renting out at six or seven times as much – mountain land at 5 s.8d an acre and `strand` land at 7s.0d an acre. By the early 1700s landlords were beginning to question the need to retain their tenants. Leases were still offered for 21 and 31 years or for three lifetimes, these were reasonably generous and usually made direct with the tenant. But there gradually arrived on the scene the middlemen, often groups of individuals joining in a partnership who rented large tracts of land and sublet. Inevitably prices rose. By the 1750s the landowners were beginning to revert to direct leases and there was the popular observance of the `tenants rights`. By this the custom and practice was that the tenant had first choice at renewing the lease when it became due with no one else making an offer until that had been rejected. This gave a value of perhaps two or three times the rent to purchase the `interest` and was a useful additional source of funds for the intending migrant. But the landlords, having had secure ownership while their tenants had cleared the land and improved it, saw the opportunity to vastly increase rents for this land. The `Ulster Tenants Rights Custom` allowed the sale of goodwill, but increased rents also meant less income for sons and sons of sons who wished to retain the `family` lands. Many of the poorer sort in County Down lived in constant fear of arrest of crops for non payment of rents. *Two Centuries of Life in Down* by John Stevenson, gives a colourful picture of the life of our ancestors and illustrates the significant increase in land rentals during the eighteenth century that caused very many to migrate to America. In the parish of Dundonald for example, 4000 acres leased in 1705 for three lives and 31 years was £297.16s.5d had increased in 1802 to £1850 p.a. Woodside, a single farm of 45 acres, rose from 2s.6d an acre in 1741 to £2.10.0d an acre in 1809. In Portaferry the rental of an estate of 3,225 acres rose from £738 (4s.6d per acre) in 1641 to £1,440 (9s.0d per acre) a hundred years later

Agriculture and industrial growth was fastest in the east of Ulster during the 1700s and reflected the distribution of the population. Following the accession of William III and Mary in 1690 there was encouragement to Hugenots to bring their skills to Ulster, In consequence there was much investment in the domestic linen industry with spinning and weaving on home looms. Alongside this the agriculture was of small flax crops and sufficient produce for the home. The majority of these small farms cum weavers did not grow produce for the commercial market. As a result they suffered when poor harvests and famine struck and they were forced to purchase supplementary foods, seed and stock. In better times increased incomes gave the excuse for an increase of rents which contributed to smaller lettings of land, and more small tenants. Expansion also meant more subsidiary industry with bleach greens, textile finishing, more commerce, transport facilities and so forth.

In the west of Ulster the expansion was more leisurely with a focus on yarn spinning and supply of yarn to the North of England mills. Agriculture was perhaps more market orientated as farmers made good use of rich pastures for fattening cattle for sale. But they too had to endure the rising rents and the relative boom and bust cycles from recession, bad harvests and famine.

In the eighteenth century therefore the various pressures saw surges of migration from time to time. 1710-1720 was a busy time for migration from Ulster, as was 1730-1740 and 1750-1775. The numbers who migrated vary considerably such as an average of 4000 a year in the 1760s. Other estimates suggest 6000 a year between 1725 and 1770, and 12,000 a year between 1729 and 1750. Whatever the true number the reality was that thousands of people, many small farmer and weavers among them, set out for a new life in America during the eighteenth century.

Migration to the colonies took place from ports all round Ireland but in later years many younger people went via England where they worked to get their passage money, or signed up as `indentured servants` (fancy words for slaves in many cases). So there were regular movements of people from Ireland, through the ports of Londonderry, Portrush, Larne, Belfast, Portpatrick, Warrenpoint, Dundalk, and Drogheda to Glasgow, Liverpool, Fleetwood, Ardrossan, Greenock and. London. From Dublin, Cork, Wexford, Waterford, the main interim destinations were Bristol, Liverpool, Glasgow, Plymouth. This movement of would be migrants is another reason why it is very difficult to track down where an ancestor departed from the home land.

The main ports of departure for direct sailings during the 1700s were Londonderry, Larne, Belfast, Newry and Portpatrick usually to Pennsylvania, New York, South Carolina, Massachusetts, Maryland; and occasional voyages to Georgia, Delaware, Nova Scotia and Prince Edward Island. The prime driver in this migration was commerce and migrants had to travel on cargo ships until purpose built passenger ships came along in the 19th century. Emigration was aided by a series of enactment's in the US after 1783 when Ulster enjoyed a virtual free trade status; so good trade gave opportunities to travel.

Another significant change that is often overlooked was in the type of person emigrating. Very broadly, before 1770 many emigrants were single persons and became indentured servants who were employed as laborers. They also took on the hard and dangerous jobs in the new frontiers. After 1783 the emigrants became more fare paying and were skilled workers and tradesmen. Whole families migrated, and importantly they had some money in their pockets to invest in their trade and their new country. In the 18th century there were positive moves to encourage settlement in lands as far apart as South Carolina where land was given to immigrants; and recruitment for Prince Edward Island in Canada. Even as late as 1888 there were Emigration agents in most towns in Ulster..

Emigration from Ireland - After the Rebellion of 1798

Those of them who had been caught up in the rebellion, continued to pay a heavy price. Most found their way back to their homes-or what was left of them. In some parts of the country, the cycle of violence continued sporadically There were disturbances in Galway, with widespread houghing (rustling) of cattle, and a rising in Clare. On the Wexford-Wicklow border there were shootings and chapel burnings.

Dr. Troy, the Catholic Archbishop of Dublin, wrote confidentially to the Castle, as the Parliament in Dublin was called, to complain that no "priest can appear in the North Eastern parts of that distracted county nor in the neighbourhood of Arklow " The root of the trouble seems to have been some unemployed Protestant yeomen who calling themselves the "Black Mob". had taken to robbery. As no one dared prosecute them. they put up threatening notices-demanding leases only for "true sons of Moll Doyle" - and for a time it looked as though a new round of persecution was beginning. In the country as a whole the boom in rents and the slump in employment continued; snow fell in April, and the summer was as wet as the summer before had been fine. In many areas the harvest failed and people were on the verge of famine. Predictably, the result was a wave of emigration to England and Scotland soon rising to an average of 50,000 a year. Compared with the tidal wave during and after the Great Famine, this was only a ripple.

The British industrial cities, where the Irish took refuge, had problems enough without them. Like all emigrants who lack capital and education, the Irish had to take the worst jobs and live in the worst ghettos. Many migrants to Glasgow fell victims to the typhus epidemics of 1818, 1835-37, and 1847. Their children went out to work as child labourers in the mills and the mines of the new Britain. The political prisoners sent abroad generally fared worse than the voluntary emigrants.

Pressed Men

About five hundred revolutionaries were pressed into the navy, or sent overseas in the British army. To serve for any length of time in the West Indies was, for the rank and file, virtually a death sentence. In fact, owing to overcrowding on the tenders, some of these new recruits died even before the ship "Hillsborough" arrived to take them to barracks in England for training. A further group of 318 Irish convicts were sent to Emden in September 1799 on board the "Alexandria" and two other ships- their fate was to serve in the army of the King of Prussia. According to one account, they ended their days in the salt mines.

Transportation to Australia

Other political prisoners were transported, according to practice, to Botany Bay. In 1799 the "Minerva" and the "Friendship" sailed with two consignments of this sort, totalling about 230 prisoners. A Matthew Sutton was among them. In a letter to his father he described the scene before the "Friendship" sailed: The prisoners were stripped, scrubbed, dressed in canvas shirts, and ironed (chained) together, 120 in one long room; already a malignant fever was sweeping the ship and several men had succumbed. A further consignment from Ireland followed in the "Atlas" and "Hercules", mainly consisting of political prisoners. Conditions on board were bad even by contemporary standards. The Governor of the penal colony protested to Whitehall: "these ships have lost 127 convicts out of 320 put on board, and the survivors are in a dreadfully emaciated and dying state". At the official enquiry it turned out that to carry more cargo for his own profit, the captain of the "Atlas" had grossly overloaded the ship, and it was so low in the water that the ventilators could not be opened. In addition, according to the ship's surgeon, the captain had loaded the convicts "with heavy irons on their legs and one round the neck with a large padlock as an appendage".

By 1802 Irishmen made up a quarter of the population of Botany Bay. Political prisoners included three Catholic priests: Father James Dixon, brother of the celebrated Captain Dixon of Wexford, Father James Harrold from Kildare and Father Peter O'Neill from Cork. But the majority of them, like the hard core of the movement in the field, seem to have been artisans:- weavers, carpenters, blacksmiths, masons and so on. The authorities were, however, in constant fear of a rising, and in 1804 some sort of conspiracy was discovered, which led to the hanging of eight men. The new prison governor sent out in 1805 was hardly the man to calm things down- he was Captain Bligh, late of the Bounty. (In fact Bligh was later deposed by the local military commander for ill-treating the prisoners, and himself imprisoned.). In due course, some of the prisoners were released and found their way back to Ireland, including Father O'Neill in 1802, and Joseph Holt, the Wicklow partisan, in 1814. Others were assimilated into Australian life, like James Meehan who became Deputy Surveyor-General of New

South Wales. To-day there is a war memorial in Sydney to the men of '98.

In Ireland in January, 1799, the third group of political prisoners-the seventy-six United Irish leaders who had signed the "Treaty of Newgate" with the Government, were still in custody, and still complaining bitterly about their treatment. In fact the Government's plan to ship them off to America had miscarried because President Adams regarded them as too dangerous to admit. Most of them were packed off to a Scottish fortress-Fort George in the Highlands-for the duration. At the Peace of Amiens in 1802 they were allowed to banish themselves to France. Next year renewed hostilities gave them renewed hopes of French help to liberate Ireland. Leader of this second revolutionary movement was Thomas Addis Emmet's twenty-four year old brother, Robert, who had been an undergraduate at Trinity in 1798, and escaped to France. The older United Irish leaders were unenthusiastic and so were the people; thus Robert Emmet's rising ended in a scuffle in a Dublin street. Years later his speech before execution was to echo round the world - much as William Orr's dying declaration had moved the Irish peoples in 1797.

The Famine in Ireland and Scotland

The Famine didn't happen in Ulster' has been one of the most unchallenged myths in recent Irish History. *The Famine in Ulster* by Christine Kinealy and Trevor Parkhill corrects that distortion by giving an account of how each of the nine counties and the city of Belfast, fared during this great calamity. Ulster was indeed spared what a local newspaper called 'the horrors of Skibbereen'. Nonetheless, the severity of the famine for much of the population, particularly in the winter of 1846-7 is all too apparent in each of the counties. Ninety-five inmates of Lurgan workhouse died in one week in 1847; 351 people queued to get into the Enniskillen workhouse in one day and emigration continued at an ever increasing pace while hospitals overflowed with fever cases.

In Scotland following the 1745 Jacobite rebellion there was positive action to remove power from the clan chieftains with widespread seizure and redistribution of lands. Alongside this was the forced change to an agrarian society with the development of hill sheep farming to replace the traditional crofting. A product of this was smaller farms and higher rent charges from landowners. Sheep rearing led to greedy landlords and a policy of moving people out of the glens to the coasts and disillusioned Highlanders to the ports of Fort William, Greenock and Glasgow and thence emigration. The situation was compounded in the 19th century when a policy of Highland Improvements continued the creation of larger sheep farms with forced removal of tenants. But this lasted only until the middle of the century when the plan faltered because of competition from Australia - where many of the exiles had fled.

This period saw frequent famines, the worst of which followed the potato blight of 1846 which affected much of rural Scotland as well as Ireland. Here were epidemics of cholera, and whole families were found dead in the rotting straw of their huts. In the food riots which followed both blight and pestilence was rife. Emigration to the colonies was now regarded by the Government as a noble purpose and supported by government funds and private subscription. Similar activities took place, albeit on a smaller and less emotive scale, in Kent and Sussex in England, whose salt-marshes and rolling Downs were ripe for sheep farming. But it was Scotland and Ireland that suffered the most and whose populace for one reason or another sought foreign climes.

Orr Down Under - Australasia

Scottish migration to Australasia should be seen as part of a movement which has its roots in the early modern period. The tradition of emigration from Scotland is long established - in the seventeenth century the Scots were settling throughout northwest Europe, especially in the Netherlands, Poland as well as Ulster, as a consequence of religious persecution. Emigration (post 1776) to contemporary USA direct from Scotland was small scale and only became significant after the middle of the eighteenth century; and migration to Australia started ca 1830. The reasons for such migration were complex but included religious and political persecution, economic and social opportunities, plus military service abroad when there was little else available at home. Both the trans-Atlantic emigration and that to the Antipodes had one general feature that, with some exceptions, movement from the Highlands of Scotland tended to be in family groups, whereas that from the Lowlands was of individuals.

As an emigrant destination Australia came relatively late on the scene. Early in the 17th century Dutch sailors discovered the West and North coasts and exploration led to the discovery of Van Diemens Land (Tasmania) In 1688 and 1697 Dampier investigated the North and North West coasts but no settlements were made. It was left to Capt. Cook to land on the more inviting Eastern coast at Botany Bay on 29 April 1770. He reported the land as suitable for colonisation. Loss of the American colonies in the War of Independence led the British government to turn to Australia for alternative overseas settlement.

Captain Arthur Phillip commanded the First Fleet of 11 ships which brought out from England 1,500 people including 800 convicts to found the fist colony at Sydney, in January 1788. The first settlements at Sydney Cove and Paramatta were laid out by a German Baron Augustus Theodore Henry Alt, Governor Phillip`s surveyor. In 1797 a Capt. MacArthur introduced the merino sheep and by the 1830s a substantial trade in high quality wool was in place. The first settlers in Van Diemens Land arrived about 1803 and Tasmania as it was renamed, became an independent state in 1851. About the same time the Great Dividing Range was crossed and opened up the Bathurst Plain which was suitable for sheep grazing and allowing expansion of the New South Wales colony in Sydney.

In *An Atlas of Irish History* Ruth Dudley Edwards explains that many of the convicts transported from 1791 were Irish and by 1803 there were 2,086 of them. Despite the popular belief that they were largely political prisoners, in fact over 60% of them had been sentenced for criminal offences. An Irish priest sentenced for political offences held the first mass in 1803 and by 1836 there 21,898 Catholics in the country, mostly Irish and half were convicts. The Catholic community and convicts suffered from severe discrimination. With the appointment of the first Bishop in 1835 serious organisation of the Australian Catholic Church began. With the appointment of a large number of Irish bishops during the 1860s the ultra Irish nature of the church was exaggerated and it is only in recent years that the church has become more Australian than Irish.

An analysis of the British Colonies in 1861 showed the proportion of Irish in the relevant populations:

	Irish as percentage of the population
Western Australia	21.3%
Queensland	18.4%
Victoria	16.1%
New South Wales	15.6%
South Australia	10.0%

Between 1788 and 1868 about 150,000 convicts were shipped to Australia, however, because of the different legal systems in Scotland and the rest of the British Isles, relatively few Scots arrived as felons - probably the most prominent Scots shipped in chains were the Scottish Martyrs of 1794-1795.

There were no Orrs in the First, Second and Third Fleets, but four Orrs were sentenced to deportation from Ireland. They were:

Edward Orr, a tailor, b ca 1794, sentenced in Co Tyrone 1814 to 7 years. Arrived aboard the "Canada"

John Orr, sentenced to Life. Arrived on board the "Friendship" (1800)

Margaret Orr, b ca 1748, tried at Carlow 1792, deported for 7 years. Arrived aboard the "Boddington".

William Orr, of Co Antrim was sentenced to transportation for life. He arrived aboard the "Friendship" (1800) and was the only one noted as having been a "rebel". He escaped and after an adventurous time in the East Indies he actually returned to Ulster. His story is told in *Remember All the Orrs* by R H Foy.

Australia is my parental home and that of my seven siblings. In consequence there is a growing community of my direct bloodline. Interestingly a sister in law is of the Penrose family from Tasmania and is a relative of several famous persons (see Claims to Fame) including Dr Arnold of Rugby School fame, and the Huxley family. A brother in law is a descendant of a long line of Wheatons from Devon and his mother was from the Tilbee line in Kent.

Some of the earliest colonial administrators of Australia were Scots such as Captain Richard Hunter, Lachlan MacQuarie and Sir Thomas Brisbane. By the 1830s Australia was receiving a small but steady flow of migrants from Scotland which was increasingly encouraged by groups such as the Highlands and Islands Emigration Society. The discovery of gold generated an increase of settlement in Australia in the 1850`s, and by the end of the century Australia and New Zealand rivalled the United States and Canada as destinations for Scottish migrants

New Zealand was first discovered in 1642 by Tasman, and the islands were visited by Captain Cook and the coasts explored in 1769, 1773, 1774 and 1777. Seal hunters from Australia were probably the first Europeans to settle and a timber trade was started. However, lawlessness was rife and eventually, in 1840, the sovereignty of Queen Victoria was announced. In that year the first permanent settlement of Wellington was founded. Despite trouble with the native Maoris further settlement took place with the Free Church of Scotland sponsoring a settlement at Dunedin (S Island) in 1848 and the Church of England the settlement at Canterbury in 1850. The Dominion of New Zealand was created in 1907. After the Maori Wars of 1845-48 and 1860-70 the native population eventually settled into peaceful coexistence. It is relevant that the early settlers were very isolated and relied on communications by sea, both one with the other and the outside world.

Canada

There are strong historical links through fishing with Nova Scotia ("New Scotland") and Newfoundland which was recognised by King James VI in 1625 when the Scottish colony was first established. From much the same time there was a special relationship with Irish fisherman who regularly fished off the Newfoundland Banks and often brought additional shore side labour with them for salting and packing the catch. But the majority of Scottish migration to North America was in the 18th century to the thirteen colonies along the Atlantic seaboard. Canada was generally an afterthought and for sufficient reason, it was easier to farm in the southern (American) colonies where cheap land was being made available to migrants on the new frontiers. Apart from climate, there were the continuing differences with France over ownership of the colony so that migration to Canada in any numbers did not begin until ca 1815.

A large number of migrants went from Islay to New York State and from the Highlands and Ireland to Nova Scotia. This latter movement is particularly well documented. From Perthshire, settlement was in Prince Edward Island, predominantly on small farms. Migration from South Uist and Benbecula was the result of religious discrimination there; and that from the Highlands was due to loss of land tenancies and from rising taxes. Greater security was to be had in PEI with opportunity to buy and be your own master although the physical hardships were great. The early Orrs in Canada appear mainly from the late 1790s in Chatham Township, Kent County, Ontario. They also were prominent in York West Township, while a Jane Orr married in 1754 in Halifax Nova Scotia, and Ann Orr married there in 1759. In the 1800`s there was an increasing emigration and several hundred Orrs spread across the country.

The migration of Empire Loyalists from the USA (who mere mainly Scottish) in 1783 paved the way for Scottish migration to Canada which peaked in the period after the War of 1812, and 1865 when formal record keeping came along. By the late 19th century Scots were well established in Canada, occupying key positions in government, they owned the largest banks and insurance companies, were patrons of educational institutions and as entrepreneurs engaged in major operations. Although outnumbered they had an affinity for Canada.

The Talbot and Selkirk Settlements

The personal initiatives of two individuals stand out in the movement and settlement of emigrants from Britain to Canada in the early 1800s, those of Thomas Talbot and Thomas Douglas, 5th Earl of Selkirk. Talbot's work helped settle a critical part of southern Ontario between Amherstburg and Niagara on what was then and is now known as the "Talbot Road", a route which proved crucial in the defence of Canada following the American invasion of 1812-1814. In return for grants of land and tools, migrants swore allegiance to the Crown, paid taxes, and agreed to maintain their part of the Talbot Road which ran across the front of their property, while in return, Talbot gained huge land holdings for his personal estate.

The Selkirk Settlements were principally in the Red River area of Manitoba in an area which also would prove critical to the future history and economy of Canada. Selkirk's efforts were pivotal in opening the west of Canada to large-scale settlement. The work of both men took place in the early 1800s, both were involved in inducing migrants to come to Canada then settling them once they arrived. It was a novel scheme at the time given the haphazard approaches to migration which there previously had been.

Buchanan and Robinson Settlements

There were other agents engaged in the settlement of emigrants especially from Ireland. These organisers were Buchanan, and Robinson. Buchanan was active between 1817 and 1818 and placed his protestant settlers in the area north of Port Hope. In ` *Irish Emigration and Canadian Settlement* " by Cecil Houston & William Smyth the Peter Robinson migration is mentioned and there is a sketch map of the settlements in Canada, 1817-25. A note says that in 1823 Robinson took 571 Cork people to settle on military reserves in the Rideau country and two years later he repeated the project with 2050 people to the Emily and Douro districts. It is interesting that in the book Robinson`s parties are referred to as Catholic. The reference source is given in the appendices as Wendy Cameron`s "*Selecting Peter Robinsons Irish Emigrants* " Histoire sociale/social history, 1978 (p) 29-46.

Emigration to the USA

For nearly 400 years there has been a stream of emigrants leaving Glasgow and other ports in the west of Scotland for destinations overseas. In the early seventeenth century the majority were headed for the Plantation of Ulster, while a few were sailing to the continent and a handful to Nova Scotia. As transatlantic trade developed, the economic links led to settlement overseas, particularly along the American East coast and in the West Indies.

The Union of England and Scotland in 1707 removed most restrictions on Scottish trade with the English colonies. Soon Glasgow virtually monopolised the tobacco trade with the Chesapeake, which led to further settlement in America. Within a generation Glasgow and Greenock became two of the most prominent ports in British intercontinental trade and the main exit ports for Scots migrants. There are three significant areas of settlement where Highland communities were established: Jamaica, North Carolina and Prince Edward Island (PEI). The first distinct migration from Scotland, mainly Presbyterian, was to South Carolina in 1682 where the settlement of the Stuartstown and Ashley River area survived for twenty years. Such early experiences as this - and later in New Jersey - were used as a basis for future ventures including the disastrous Darien (Panama) settlement. Notable personages from Argyll and Ayrshire were involved in these early days - leaders included Lord Neil Campbell and Ewan Cameron of Locheil.

Other establishments, of the 1720s and 1730s, were in the Savannah area of Georgia and around Cape Fear in North Carolina. The rate of migration was to increase rapidly in the mid eighteenth century due to changes in land tenure in Western Scotland and the Highlands. Families moving to small plantations and farms was a significant feature of migration to North Carolina;

The pioneering spirit is clearly seen in the fact that so many Scots went to areas where land was available either free or very cheap. The land itself tended to be in the remoter parts, in need of clearance and often required defence against the native Indians. Thus they took land 40-50 miles inland from Philadelphia, and similarly in Maryland. An Ulster settlement was established at Donegal, Pennsylvania and spread from there into the Cumberland Valley and then to Virginia and Carolina.; the Shenandoah Valley and Appalachian Mountains.. The ancestors of these settlers moved on to Arkansas and Missouri, and with fresh immigrants via New Orleans moved into Mississippi to join those immigrants coming down the Ohio Valley. Even then, still seeking space, they migrated to Texas and the Mid west - Indiana, Illinois and Nebraska. Today there are about 100,000 descendants of these early American Orr`s scattered across all states of the USA.

The Ulster Scots

The term Scotch Irish is a particularly American expression to describe the Ulster families of Scottish origin who migrated to America (the USA). It is often confused as meaning Roman Catholic and native Irish rather than Protestant/Presbyterian of Scots origin. In the UK they are properly referred to as the Ulster Scots (Scotch refers to the drink). The main ports for the migrants from Ulster were Belfast, Londonderry, Larne, Newry and Portpatrick. The definitive work *Ulster Emigration to Colonial America, 1718-1775* by R J Dickson gives a wide range of factors and figures pointing out that peaks in migration reflected periods of shortages and recession in Ulster. Thus peaks were in 1718-9; 1727-9; 1735-6; 1740-1; and 1745-6. He also gives the approximate number of sailings from the main ports during 1750-1775 as: Belfast 143, Londonderry 128, Newry 84, Larne 57, Portpatrick 30. The destination of these vessels were mainly to Philadelphia, New York, South Carolina, Maryland and Massachusetts with odd sailings to Georgia, Virginia, the West Indies, Nova Scotia and Prince Edward Island. It also happened that many people transhipped at these ports for other destinations, which makes tracing them more difficult two or three hundred years later.

Sholto Cooke in his *The Maiden City and the Western Ocean* gives an absorbing story of the special relationship that existed between the American ports, and the ships of City of Londonderry. For about a hundred years – through the nineteenth century, Londonderry was a focus for migrants as the ships that brought flax seed and timber into Ulster took human cargo on the return trip. The trade with the American ports was of course interrupted by the War of Independence and again by the War of 1812-14, while in Europe there was the ongoing wrangles with France and Spain and the risk of being taken by privateers. After the Peace of Ghent in 1815 the Londonderry ships – all sailing ships, were busily engaged in taking between 4 – 5,000 migrants annually to Philadelphia and New York, then proceeding to Canada to collect return cargoes of grain from Quebec and softwood timber from St John. The growth of trade with Canada after the ending of the French wars subsequently saw St John develop as a passenger port and many migrants would tranship there for onward travel to the USA. Grain was also shipped between Baltimore and Londonderry, while in the winter season voyages were to Charleston, Savannah and New Orleans. The importance of the trade was reflected in the growth of the City itself with the population doubling to about 40,000 between 1851-1900. In time, however, the wooden sailing ships were overtaken by the building of iron ships and the development of steam. This in turn led to migrants going to the larger ports of Liverpool or Glasgow to take passage on the larger, faster and more comfortable steam ships.

Many a lurid tale is told of the privations suffered by migrants, and there is no doubt that in the early days – the 18th century and earlier, they were indeed tough, sometimes lasting for 60 or more days and very much at the mercy of the seasonal winds and weather. By 1832 a Liverpool ship`s captain was saying that the average trip was forty days westward (Liverpool to New York) and twenty three days eastward on the return journey. The Londonderry sailing ships were averaging about 27-28 days westward, and 19 days eastward and largely reflected the improved designs that had been made in the ships. On the down side were the disasters brought about by nature and occasionally by unscrupulous masters. In 1832 the brig Hebe took 83 days from Belfast to St John with 17 passengers dying of want (starvation) and one of smallpox. Another ship, the Brutus from Liverpool to Quebec, had 81 deaths on board from cholera.

In summary there was an increasing flow of Dissenters from Ulster to America in the 18th century which was the consequence of restrictions on the Irish woollen trade (1698), and the imposition of the Test Act (1704-1781) which denied public office to the Presbyterians and other nonconformists. There was also the levy imposed on renewal of leases thus preventing farmers from taking advantage of any improvements they made. In the nineteenth century the position was reversed as the main migrants became Catholic, the Presbyterian grievances having been largely remedied by repeal of the Test Act and given security of tenure on farms. In the poorer districts of Ireland the increasing population was creating congestion, there was no industry to speak of and the already small farms were increasingly subdivided until they were incapable of supporting a family. An increasing feature of migration became the passenger bookings for America and Canada facilitated by earlier migrants putting up the money to bring out their friends and family. The average fare to the United States was between £4-5 and to Canada between £3.10s and £4.

Early Settlers in America

Below is a summary of settlements [No.]extracted from *A Genealogical and Historical Atlas of the United States of America.* by E. Kay Kirkham, 1976. It serves to give an indication where to look for the earliest Scots Irish ancestors. It should be remembered that the Lowland Scots were by and large Protestant (Presbyterians), and the Highland Scots were initially Gaelic speaking Catholics. Also, Irish Catholics and Protestant Irish and Scots were all unable to practice their faiths as they saw fit in the early days of settlement because they were still subject to repressive English laws. A sore point to them all was that they were required to pay tithes (taxes) to the Anglican Church. These factors would have influenced their decisions to move inland to the frontier regions where they were less likely to be overseen and prosecuted for their religion.

The main Scots-Irish emigration to the US began around 1714 with the earliest known migration shown in 1652. Many went to the

western counties of Pennsylvania, between the Susquehanna River
and the Allegheny Mountains. A large group went down the
Shenandoah Valley in 1732. By 1745, the Scots-Irish were a quarter
of the population of Pennsylvania. That increased to about one third
of the population by 1770. It is said that Protestant Irish formed four
fifths of the Pennsylvania Continental line units of the
Revolutionary War. It should be noted that these were
overwhelmingly Presbyterians from Ulster. The native Irish
emigrants were a feature of the post Famine period in Ireland, in the
1850s.

Delaware
Dutch (1651) [1]; Scots (1692-1750) [14] (Census says most were
Presbyterians); Swedish (1627) [1]

Georgia
English (1751) [1]; German (1732-1757) [2]
Scots (1732-1798) [20] (Most were not Highland Scots)

Kentucky
Scots Catholics (1785) [1] Presbyterian Scots (1775-1793) [42]

Massachusetts
English (1630-1660) [3]; French (1662-1721) [5]
Irish (1675-1714) [2]; Scots (1652) [1]
Scotch-Irish (1718-1783) [18]

Maine
Irish (1735) [1]
Scots (1736-1785) [13]
Acadians (1755) [1]

Maryland
English (1634) [1]; Swedish (1638) [1]; German (1757) [1]
Quakers (1660) [1]; Huguenots (1666) [1]; Scots-Irish (1720-1788)
[20]; Scots (Presbyterian) (1649-1715) [8]

New Hampshire
Scots-Irish (1719-1776) [16]

New Jersey
Dutch (1617) [1]
Quakers (1676) [2]
Scots (1700-1775) [60]

New York
Dutch (1614) [5]Scotch-Irish (1640-1768) [70]
Italian (1656) [1]; Quakers (1657) [3]
Huguenots (1688) [1]; Scots (1741-1796) [9]
Irish (1764) [1] (300 persons)

North Carolina
Barbadians (1665) [1]; Quakers (1680) [22]; Scots (1683) [5]
Huguenots (1700) [1]; German (1710) [6]
Scotch-Irish (1719-1800) [67]; Moravians (1753) [1]

Pennsylvania
Quakers (1680) [7]; Irish (1683) [1]; Scots-Irish (1698-1800) [150]
Amish (1700) [1]; Huguenots (1700) [1]; German (1810) [9]

Rhode Island
French (1686) [1]

South Carolina
Huguenots (1562) [3]; Barbadians (1670) [3]
Scotch-Irish (1684-1799) [76]; Quakers (1680) [4]
English (1695) [1]; German (1732) [5]; Irish (1732) [1]

Vermont
Scots-Irish (1763-1778) [13]

Virginia
English (1607) [1]; Quakers (1660) [19]; Scots-Irish (1603-1798)
[80]; Huguenots (1685) [2]

West Virginia
Scotch-Irish (1737-1798) [19]

As well as these settlements there are numerous places designated
Orr something or other: e.g., Orr-Acres, Airport, Bay, Branch,
Canyon, Chapel, Church, City (Minnesota), Creek, Coulee, Dam,
Ditch, Ferry, Gulch, Hill, Island, Lake, Mill, Mount, Park, Point,
Pond, Ridge, School, Springs, Stream, Swamp, Well. The range of
places where they are found points to both the wanderlust of the
Orrs; their willingness to take on the former frontier wilderness; and
the creation of homes just about anywhere in the USA. Thus there
have been towns called Orr in Oklahoma, Pennsylvania, Minnesota,
Colorado, Kentucky, Michigan, Maryland, Arizona and West
Virginia; there have been Orrvilles in Ohio, Alabama, Indiana,
Missouri, Pennsylvania, South Carolina. Ranches in Colorado,
Montana, Nebraska, Utah, New York; and cemeteries in Alabama,
Indiana, Kentucky, North Carolina, Tennessee, Georgia, South
Carolina, Oklahoma, Ohio to name but a few.

The West Indies

Scotland has had direct social and economic links with the West Indies for nearly 300 years. This only became possible once Spanish power began to wane in the early seventeenth century. The first vessel known to have sailed to the West Indies was the ` Janet of Leith ` which left Leith in 1611 Settlement there began as early as 1626 when James Hay, Earl of Carlisle, a Scot, was appointed as Proprietor of Barbados by Charles I, which led to a number of Scots settlements.

From Barbados the English spread their settlement to nearby islands and by the 1650s had taken Jamaica from the Spaniards. There vas a constant demand for settlers and servants which was partially supplied by Scots indentured servants through English ports, transportees such as Cromwellian prisoners of war, Covenanters, or criminals shipped directly from the Clyde or from Leith; and, by a small flow of migrants from Scotland. Some of the survivors from the Darien Scheme in the Isthmus of Panama settled in Jamacia and the smaller islands. Scots could also be found among the Dutch islands in the Caribbean. After 1707 all restrictions on trade between Scotland and the English colonies were abolished which led to a significant expansion of what had been an illicit trade, and in turn the settlement there by Scots.

The West Indies became a destination for many individuals and some families who were seeking to re establish their fortunes rather than a permanent home. Some Orrs are shown in *The `Ulster Pedigree`* as having gone to the West Indies. A strong Presbyterian or Methodist background did not stop them from indulging in the slave trade. It should be borne in mind that the Scottish were very prominent in the tobacco trade and the sugar/molasses/rum trade and had connections with the West Indies where slaves were common, including some `indentured` white people. Scotland routinely sentenced felons to slavery, and the term transportation in those days meant exactly the same. Slavery as a trade increased dramatically in the 18th century with floating slave `factories` housing 4-500 souls moored off the coast off the Guinea Coast, West Africa. In the UK the industrial revolution was undoubtedly funded by slavery with cities such as Bristol and Liverpool benefiting. Elsewhere the newly rich sought to build impressive country homes such as Harewood House in Yorkshire, and the town of Leamington Spa was built by slave owning plantation owners and merchants. So the Scottish/Irish/Ulster traders were well situated to expand their interests, including the use of slave labour, when they migrated to Alabama and Georgia.

An Account of White People come to Jamacia by Virtue of Several Acts for Introducing and Encouragement of White Settlers passed the 15th May 1736, the 21st May 1743, the 2nd July 1747 and October 1750. With the Quantity of land granted them - lists a Samuel Orr granted 110 acres of land in Portland District, patent granted 29 August 1745. In Antigua a baptism is recorded of Louisa Augusta Orr (a free coloured person) on 12 February 1823 (born 17 October 1822), daughter of Robert Orr and Elizabeth Mevozies.

Settlement there was more likely to be temporary than settlement in the mainland American colonies. Settlement in Jamaica was more of the entrepreneurial type - of single young men, who established trade in sugar and rum, became overseers of plantations making money to develop their social position often with the intention of returning to Scotland. Society on the plantations was based on slavery. Slaves were taught Gaelic and ordered to use it since escape was nigh impossible to areas where Gaelic was not spoken. Slavery was exploited fully for profit. In 1763 the French ceded most of their Caribbean islands to the British, which led to settlement in Grenada, Tobago, St Vincent and Dominica. After the American War of Independence many Loyalists, including a number of Scots, settled in the West Indies. Planters produced sugar, cotton, tobacco, rum, and mahogany which was shipped back to Britain for processing and subsequent export to European markets. The main Scots ports involved were on the Clyde but

Aberdeen and Leith were also concerned. Companies based in these ports would recruit managers and servants to work in the West Indies through advertisements in papers such as the Aberdeen Journal. The part played by Scots. in the settlement and economic development of the Caribbean was significant, where their organisational skills and enterprise were positive contributions - whatever the apologists of Empire might opine. Orr`s were among them as indicated in their wills recorded in the National Archives, Kew. These include Joseph Orr of Saint Thomas in East Surrey County, Jamacia who died there ca 1798 (Probate 11 September 1798); a John Orr merchant in Kingston, Jamacia   probate granted 21 October 1814; and Thomas Orr, described as a Planter of the Island of Tobago, had his will probated 12 February 1817. Thomas certainly had slaves as he mentions them in his will.

Part IV

ORR IN SCOTLAND

As previously noted, our name is of Scottish origin and possibly comes from the Parish of Urr in the Stewartry of Kirkcudbright. Since about 1290, however, we have been mainly in the counties of Renfrew and Ayrshire. The Orr name is now quite common throughout Lowland Scotland having spread through Lanarkshire, across to Edinburgh, Haddingtonshire into Fife and even the Highlands. By the time of the 1881 Census Orrs were dispersed throughout the whole of England, Scotland and Wales. Orrs from Ayrshire were probably the first of the name to migrate to Ulster ca 1607 in what became the Plantation of Ulster.

The evidence is that a Hugh del Urre rendered homage in 1296 to Edward I (The Ragmans Rolls – a document acknowledging loyalty to Edward I), and a John Or was a follower of Campbell of Cawdor in 1578. The rental of Paisley Abbey which owned quite a bit of the land in the vicinity had Orrs as tenants in the 14th century and probably earlier. Orrs were also in Campbelltown in Kintyre from ca 1640 probably having migrated from Renfrewshire. It is likely that from here they migrated across the Irish Sea to County Down. In the Charter records of Paisley Abbey there is a summons at the instance of Robert, Abbott of Paisley, dated January 1504 against John, Lord Rope of Hawshed; Alan Or; Ninian Or; Johnne Or; Johnne Or; William Glenne; Johnne Dunlop and Johnne Whytefuird. The charge is in coarse Latin " pro injustis intro mifsione, occupatione, laboratione, et manoratione terrasum " which translates roughly that they had occupied land and put the populace in fear ie had been bad landlords (assuming they rented the land from the Abbey).

A General Description of the Shire of Renfrew by George Crawfurd (1710) was updated by George Robertson in 1818.

Extracts from this book give details of the population of Renfrewshire by parish ca 1818 and a record of the land valuations for the Parish of Lochwinnoch. Among the proprietors are several Orrs. Much of the land in the area is owned by some of the ancient families, especially Semple who were the hereditary Stewarts (Stewards) of the Barony of Renfrewshire since the 1300s. Beltrees had a charter in 1477 given to a William Stewart and his spouse Alison Kennedy, passing to Lord Semple in 1559. Achinames belonged to the Crawfords as long ago as 1100 when two brothers Sir John and Sir Gregan were rewarded for services by King David I. Gavan and Risk belonged to the Boyds ca 1205 and the Glens were in Barr from ca 1450 and passed to the Hamiltons in 1710.

There were Orr`s also in the neighbouring Kilbarchan Parish where Jok and John Orr are mentioned in Sir John Craufurd`s Protocol Book. This tells us that in 1541 Gabriell Sympyll of the forty shillings land of Toris, commissioned his sergeant officer [bailiff] Jok Orr to evict Jok Andro, Pate Blackburne, Hobe Luif, George Park and William Lang. An entry on 1 April 1550 records that Lord Sempill sent his sergeant John Layng to the Weitlands and seized all John Orr`s goods and gear. In both instances the actions were probably taken for non payment of rents.

Lochwinnoch

Lochwinnoch is a small town in Renfrewshire on the side of a Barr Loch and Castle Semple Loch. Just 4 miles south of Lochwinnoch over the shire border, in Ayrshire, is Kilbirnie which faces the town of Beith across Kilbirnie Loch. Dalry is about 3 miles further south. These are the parishes in which the Orr name appears time and time again. Andro Crafurd [Andrew Crawford] wrote (ca 1836) in his notes for *The Cairn of Lochwinnoch*: "Lochwinnoch was the headquarters of the Orrs for above 500 years", and that Orrs were tenants of Paisley Monastery since the 1300s. Although the period from then to ca 1700 is vague there is a rich vein of Orr ancestry to mine in the locality as shown by the Orr residents listed in Fowlers Directory 1831/1832.

The main occupation was farming and it is there we find some significant family records of the Orrs of Risk, Kaim and Midhouse farms, In all the Orrs occupied at different times, some 30 farms in the vicinity, almost all being tenants of a superior land owner. It is only in later years ca 1600 onwards, that they appear as freeholders and selling or renting their lands to others.

The Orrs were mainly Presbyterian and there is record in the *Cairn of Lochwinnoch* that at least three of them were committed to jail at Stirling on 1 November 1684. They were Robert Orr of Millbank; John Orr of Jamphraystock; and John Orr of Hills. Imprisonment at that time would probably have been for refusing to take an oath or suspicion of conventicling activities, although the Cairn account refers to refusal to take the Test or to give a Bond. In those circumstances they were hazarding their lives. From 1681 heritors had been required to take action against conventicles (outdoor prayer meetings and church services) and to report them to the authorities (even if they did not know they were taking place !). Land owners were in an invidious position being held responsible for the actions of their tenants and many were fined for alleged compliance when they were not even aware that tenants were engaged in an alleged illegal activity. In 1684 the Justiciary Courts were set up and conventicling declared treason. In July 1684 a Committee of Public Affairs pursued the magistrates to clear the backlog of prisoners held locally with instruction to imprison or discharge from custody; only to be followed by an Order in Council of 1 August 1684 to clear the prisons and the guilty to be executed within six hours of sentencing.

Such was the panic about loyalty to the King that four further Circuit Courts were set up on 6 September 1684 to take `justice` out to the people. The Lords given power included the Earl of Mar, Queensberry, Balcarres and the infamous John Graham of

Claverhouse, with any two to act as judges. They were actually given a list of some 28 offences that they were to enforce with the objective of 'extinguishing disaffection'. How on earth it was expected that enforcing Draconian laws, with possible execution a high possibility, was going to remove disaffection I have yet to fathom out. Such was the confused state of affairs and overcrowding of the prisons that it is likely the three Orrs would have been arraigned and possibly fined, required to take an oath and give a bond for good behaviour. At least they do not appear in the lists of the executed. Two later Orrs, James Orr and William Orr, also believed to be from Lochwinnoch, were among the prisoners brought to Burntisland, Fife, on 20 May 1685 and marched to imprisonment in Dunnottar Castle. It is known that William Orr took the Test and was released on 26 July 1685. No Orrs appeared in the lists of those from Dunnottar that were transported in August 1685, and it is likely that James Orr was also released on taking an oath and giving bond.

In the 19th century Fowlers Directory (1826/1827 and 1831/1832) of Lochwinnoch, Newton of Beltrees, How Wood, and neighbourhood listed some 22 Orr families in the immediate area. Extracts from *The Cairn of Lochwinnoch* lists farmers since at least 1654.

Orr, Alexander, surgeon Harvey Square (1826, 1831)
Orr, James, Auctioneer, Calder Street (1826, 1831); beer and porter dealer (1836)
Orr, James, bookseller and stationer, High Street (1831)
Orr, James, flesher, and vintner, High Street (1831)
Orr, James, of Langyard, farmer, (1826, 1831)
Orr, James, farmer East Johnshill (1826, 1831)
Orr, James, of Newton of Beltrees, farmer Glenhead (1826, 1831)
Orr, John, farmer, East Barnaich (1826, 1831)
Orr, Mrs. of Fairhills (1831)
Orr, Robert, farmer, Westhills (1826, 1831)
Orr, Robert of Auchinhane, farmer (1826, 1831)

Orr, Robert, of Cruiks, farmer (1826, 1831)

Orr, Mrs. Thos. stationer, hardware, and toyshop, Cross (1826, 1831)

Orr, Thomas, grocer and tea-merchant, High street (1826, 1831)

Orr, Thomas, Lochwinnoch Inn (1826)

Orr, Thomas, of Risk, farmer (1826, 1831)

Orr, Thomas, (Orrian Academy,) behind the Cross well (1826,1831)

Orr, William, carding master, Calderpark mill (1826, 1831)

Orr, William, farmer and grazier, Auchinhane (1826, 1831)

Orr, William, merchant, High street (1826, 1831); stationer (1836)

Orr, William, of East Johnshill, cattle dealer (1826, 1831)

Orr, William, of Kaim and Greenbrae, farmer (1826, 1831)

Orr, William, of Linthills, farmer,:(1826, 1831)

There was also involvement of many Orrs in the community apart from their trade shown above.

A William Orr was precentor at the Parish church

Alexander Orr was president of the Sabbath Schools Committee

Thomas Orr was treasurer of the Sabbath Schools Committee

Thomas Orr was a teacher at the Orrian Academy, with 70 pupils.

Hugh Orr was a clerk in the Lochwinnoch Friendly Society, High St (1812)

Alexander Orr was treasurer of the Lochwinnoch Library, Chaple St (1823)

A Mrs Orr was secretary of the Lochwinnoch Benevolent Society (1836)

James Orr of Cross was secretary of the Lochwinnoch Farmers Society (1827)

Alexander Orr was vice president of the Home Mission (1831)

The Orrs also feature in the Fowlers 1836 Directory for Paisley:

Orr, Andrew, spirit dealer, 23 High St (1836)

Orr, Francis, Accountant, 9 Gauze St (1836)

Orr, James grocer, 6 Walneuk St (1836)

Orr, John Jnr & Co, cotton spinners, Underwoode (1836)

Orr, John cotton spinner, house Underwood St. (1836)

Orr, John Shawl manufacturer, 39 Causeyside (1836)

Orr, John Mrs, house 57 Causeyside (1836)

Orr, Robert of Ralston (1836) this family was a major contributor to printing on linen in Paisley. Also in Pigot 1825.

Orr Robert, of Lylesland (1826) also in Pigot 1825.

Orr Robert, builder, 31 George St. (1836)

Orr Robert, stocking maker, 8 Wardrop St. (1836)

Orr Thomas, Caledonian Inn, Caledonia St. (1836)

Orr Thomas, plumber 97 New Sneddon. (1836)

Orr Thomas, spirit dealer and boatman, Moss St. (1836)

Orr William, joiner and cabinet maker & glazier 9 Gauze St. (1836)

Orr William & Robert, manufacturers 163 Causeyside (1836)

Orr William, Jr. Merchant, house 94 Gauze St (1836)

Orr William, mason

Orr William Mrs, house, 14 Causeyside. (1836).

ORR farmers in the Lochwinnoch area over the centuries

Farm Name	Orr	Year
Aikeins	William	1654
Auchinhane	William	1614
Auchinhane	Thomas	1692
Auchinhane	Daniel	1703
Auchinhane	William	1709
Auchinhane	Thomas, sasine.	1772
Auchinhane	William	1830
Auichinhane	Robert	1830
Auldyards	Robert, sasine	19.11.1662
Auldyards	William	1772

Barfod	William	1654
Banfod	William	1753
Barmaflock	John	1694
Barmaflock	John	1726
Barmochloch	William feued 10/- land	1653
Barmochloch	William, inherits	1736
Barmochloch	William, sasine	1833
Barnaiche	Thomas, Portioner	1646
Barnbrock	Robert	1654
Barnbrock	William	1654
Barnbrock	Robert	1675
Beltreemuir	William, Portioner.	1666
Beltreemuir	Robert	
Beltrees	John	1760
Beltrees	Thomas, Heritour	1695
Beltrees	Thomas	1920
Brigend	John	1694
Brigend	John	1720
Borofield	James	1726
Burnfoot of Calder	Robert	1712
Cruiks/Crooks	Robert	1654
Crooks	Robert	1830
Crooks	Jane	1881
Crooks	Robert	1906 sold
East Johnshill	James	1830
East Johnshill	William	1830
Easter Hills	Janet	1726

East Hills	John	1694
East Barnaich	Thomas	1684
Fairhills	Robert	1675
Fairhills	James	1730
Fairhills	James	1814
Gavilmoss	Thomas	1772
Geilsyard	Robert, Portioner	1663
Glenhead	Robert	1855
Greenbrae	John	1753
Greenbrae	William	1830
High Linthills	John	1881
Hills of Barnaigh	John	1675
Jeffreystock	John	1692
Kame	William, Portioner	1560
Kame	William, Portioner	1645
Kame	Robert, Portioner	1645
Kame	Robert, Valuation Roll	1650
Kame	William, feued 20/- land	1653
Kaim	William	1654
Kaim	Robert	1654
Kame	Robert, Valuation	1654
Kaim	John	1666
Kaim	William, Portioner	1666
Kame	William, Portioner	1680
Kame	William, Poll Tax	1695
Kame	Robert	1730
Kame	William	1732

Kame	William inherits	1736
Kaim	William	1770
Kaim	William	1814
Kaim	William	1830
Kame	William, sasine	1833
Kame	William, Portioner	1840
Kaim Hills	Robert	1814
Langyard	Robert	1654
Langyard	James, Portioner.	1666
Langyard	James	1692
Langyard		1715
Langyard	Robert	1753
Langyard	Robert, Portioner	1772
Langyard	James	1791
Langyard	James	1830
Langstillie	James	1632
Langstillie	James	1656
Little Gavan	James	1726
Linthills	John	1814
Linthills	William	1830
Lorabank	Robert	1818
Lorabank	William	
Market Hill	Robert	1830
Midhouse	John	1654
Midhouse	William	1726
Midhouse	Thomas	1735
Milnbank	Robert	1526
Milnbank	Robert	1630

Milnbank	Robert	1654
Milnbank	Robert	1662
Milnbank	Robert	1675
Milnbank	Robert	1710
Milnbank	Hugh	1713
Milnbank	Robert	1744
Milnbank	Robert	1752
Milnbank	Thomas, sasine	27.3.1772
Milnbank	Robert	1818
Milnbank	Robert	1881
Moneyabrock	John valuation	1654
Newton of Beltrees	James	1830
Plantilly	William	1653
Risk	William	1643 bought
Risk	William, clare constate	22.8.1656
Risk	James	1752
Risk	William	1814
Risk	William	1820
Risk	Thomas	1830
Risk	James	1830
Risk	Robert	1881
Saltcoats	William	1791
Strandhead	James	1709
Stripe	William	1833
South Gavane	William	1834
Strandheads	James	1726
Thornbraehead	William	1834

Westhills	James	1691
Westhills	William	1818
Westhills	Robert	1830
Westerhills	James	1703
Westerhills	John	1753
West Knockbartnoch	Robert	1881

ORR Farmers in the Lochwinnoch Area (Index to Map)

Item	Farm Name	Orr	Year	
1	Aikeins	William	1654	
2	Auchinhane	Thomas	1692	
	Auchinhane	William	1726	
	Auchinhane	Thomas	1772	
3	Barfod	William	1654	
4	Barnbrock	Robert	1654	
	Barnbrock	William	1654	
	Barnbrock	Robert	1675	
5	Bridgend	John	1694	
6	Cruiks/Crooks	Robert	1654	
	Crooks	Robert	1906	sold
7	East Johnshill	James	1830	
	East Johnshill	William	1830	
8	Easter Hills			
	East Hills	John	1694	
9	East Barnaich	Thomas	1684	
10	Fairhills	James	1814	
11	Hills of Barnaigh	John	1675	
12	Gavilmoss	Thomas	1772	
13	Greenbrae	John	1753	
14	Jeffreystock	John	1692	
15	Kaim	William	1654	
	Kaim	Robert	1654	
	Kaim	William	1814	
	Kaim Hills	Robert	1814	
16	Langstille	James	1656	
17	Langyard	Robert	1654	
18	Linthills	John	1814	
19	Lorabank	William		
20	Market Hill	Robert	1830	
21	Midhouse	John	1654	
22	Milnbank	Robert	1654	
	Milnbank	Robert	1675	
23	Moneyabrock	John	1654	
24	Newton of Beltrees	James	1830	

25	Risk	William	1643 bought
26	Saltcoats	William	1791
27	Stripe	William	
28	South Gavane	William	1834
29	Strandheads	James	1726
30	Thornbraehead	William	1834
31	Westhills	James	1691
	Westerhills	James	1703
	Westerhills	John	1753

Orr Farms in the Lochwinnoch area over the years.

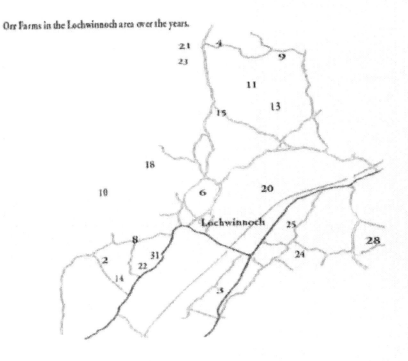

A Local Historian`s View

The following extract from Lochwinnoch historian Elizabeth Anderson`s *History of Lochwinnoch* adds further to our knowledge of the Orrs.

> You would perhaps note that Blair is still in the Kerse, and Millar was about Lochhead until very recently. What about Orr ? The Orrs were everywhere, but Andrew Crawford (Cairn) complained bitterly, in 1853, that that ancient family had not taken sufficient care of title deeds and other documents. Orr of the Langyard had lost all documents prior to 1703; the Kaim lost theirs in a fire of 1711; Jaffraystock, then called Jamphraystock, sent theirs to Edinburgh when they sold out to Macdowall, and had not had them returned, when Andrew Crawford was frantically recording Lochwinnoch history before it was lost. He did, however, unearth a great deal of Orr history. One important wedding was that of Robert Orr at Markethill, (a Midhouse Orr), to Janet Orr, daughter of William Orr of Lorabank and Auchinane. Documentation of that wedding is in the possession of Janet Orr Ferguson, a direct descendant. Lorabank was part of the Estate of Langyards, which was in the possession of Orrs for several generations.

Many Orrs emigrated to America of whom John Orr, born in 1724, settled in Richmond, Virginia. His son was the captain of a ship which was caught by the British in the Revolutionary War, and eventually he landed at Largs with no money. He refused help from his Lochwinnoch relatives when they gave advice about the spending of the money. He got home without their help. His brother, William, born 1731, was a surgeon in the American service. Both were loyal to the new country. The infant Congress was allegedly held in the Orr household.

Hugh Orr, born in Lochwinnoch in 1717, and trained to be a gunsmith and door-lock filer, went to America in 1737, and settled in Bridgewater, Massachusetts, His story is told later.

An interesting comment on the prolific Orrs is contained in a history of Lochwinnoch prepared by the Scottish Women`s Rural Institute c1960, kindly copied for me by the Community Museums Officer, Paisley Council. They were so many Orrs that nick names were often used to distinguish one from another.

Without a doubt, the most common Lochwinnoch name was 'Orr'. Search through the Register of Marriages, and you will find the name 'Orr' again and again. Mr. William Glen has in his possession his family tree', back to 1802, and there the name keeps recurring. Andrew Crawfurd, in his notes on Alexander Wilson, mentions this fact. "Lochwinnoch was the headquarters of the Orre for above 500 years" To distinguish the different Orr`s secondary names or even nick-names were resorted to. Wilson's pirn winder was Pirn Peggy (Orr), to distinguish her from Lochside Peggy, Gentle Peggy and Gospel Peggy.

A more recent Orr, related to William Glen, was Robert Orr of Cruicks Farm. He and his cronies William Stevenson of Gateside and Robert Speir of Balgreen, delivered milk to Lochside Station, but instead of going on Sunday, they delivered twice on Saturday. Every Saturday night they raced home with their ponies and traps, very often risking disaster as their wheels came perilously close. Mr Speir of Balgreen ("The Pamphlet" named after one of his ponies) was extremely reckless. Another caper was to leave the pub after the milk delivery, go like the wind up Calder Street, along Braehead, and down the Craw Road - all with a pony and trap. It makes one's hair rise to think of it. In Johnshill can be found a relic of the days of horses. No 5 Johnshill, the house with the crowstepped gables, has a tethering ring in the wall.

A Short Statistical Note about Lochwinnoch

The Statistical Accounts of Scotland cover, 1791-1799 (the first), and the period to 1845 (the second). These were prepared by the ministers in the 938 parishes in Scotland, and provide a wealth of information about each district, its geology, farming, history, industry and peoples.

The First Account of Renfrew by the Rev James Steven runs to ten pages; the Second Account by the Rev Robert Smith runs to no less than 39 pages. They are well worth a read but for the casual visitor here are some statistics to help explain both the growth of Lochwinnoch and its eventual decline. The figures particularly reflect the growth of cotton working in the district.

Population:

1695	Families 290	
1755		1589 Persons
1791	557	2613
1801		2955
1811		3514
1821		4130
1830		4500
1851		4515

Average annual births, marriages and deaths

1791   28 male   26 female   Total births 54   marriages 22
1845   94   31   deaths 77

Numbers of farmers in the district

1695	186
1791	148
1845	130

Occupations in the district in 1791 reflect a self dependent, still largely agrarian society which has expanded (from ca 1750s) to light industries along its waterways. The first mills and bleach greens were set up in 1740 and 1752.

Farmers   148
Cotton mill workers 380. wages ca 2/6d a day
Weavers   135. In 1791 15 working for local farms; 203 were outworkers for Glasgow and Paisley factories.
Tailors   19
Shoemakers   14
Grocers   2
Bakers 2
Butchers 2
Wrights (artificers, wood/metal workers) 39 1/8d - 2/2d a day
Masons   27   2/-s to 2/2d a day
Smiths 31
Surgeons 2
Ministers 1
Writer (lawyer)   1
School masters   2
Ale sellers 14.

Men servants £10-£12 a year
Maid servants £4 pa.
Day labourer 1/4d - 1/8d a day

Land rents depending on quality of land, were between 12/- to £2 an acre. But poor lands were as low as 5/-s an acre. Farms were let for usually 19 years from £15 to £110 a year. Not more than a third of the land was allowed to be tilled at one time and had to be manured. Crop rotation was a requirement of most leases with ploughing for 2 years and resting for four. There is very good pasture land in the district which was used to good effect for fattening cattle and producing great quantities of milk and butter. In the early 1800s there was a move towards leases for 10-12 years, and for them to be granted perhaps two years before the current lease ran out. This encouraged farmers to keep the tenancies and reap the benefit of their labours. The farms themselves were not large averaging around 50 acres, with some much smaller. Few exceeded 100 acres and there was a move for the larger estates to be broken up into smaller farms thereby creating more rentals and income for the proprietors. Rents were normally due at Martinmas (11 November) and Whitsunday, Martinmas for arable lands and Whitsunday for houses, yards and pasture land.

The Second Account does not give a similar breakdown of employment, but output from the 9 mills in the area had grown until about 1820 when there was a change in trade and weaving practices to fine silks and cambrics. A major influence was the onset of the industrial revolution that saw steam power take over from water wheels and a consequent shift of the cotton industry. The observation is made that the mill workers were drawn and pale from their labours in the mills but nevertheless enjoyed a reasonable diet, including meat daily, and lived well for their times. Their working hours would frighten the modern employee - 12 hours a day Monday to Friday and 9 hours on Saturday for about 2/6d - 3/6d a day (12.1/2p - 17.1/2p today`s currency). The minister comments on the number of ale houses, which in 1791 was 14 and in 1845 risen to 24,

> There are 24 inns in this parish, which are too many, and do an incalculable amount of mischief without being balance by almost any good. The institution of temperance societies led to an inquiry into the amount of ardent spirits and other liquors used here, and the melancholy and astounding fact was forced upon us, that in this, as in neighbouring parishes, three or four times more money is expended in this manner than is required to support both our churches and schools, and all our charitable and religious institutions.

Given they worked 12 hours a day one wonders when the populace had time, let alone money, to spend on carousing.

An interesting consequence of the growing industrialisation, especially in the Clyde valley, was that wages for labourers began to increase. Farm workers worked from 6 am to 6 pm in summer and from 8 am to 4 pm in winter. But invariably the hours were governed by the season and the weather, with indoor jobs such as threshing done on dark and wet days and extra hours put in during manuring, sowing and harvest.

Orr Properties in Lochwinnoch 1818

From *A General Description of the Shire of Renfrew*. Geo Crawfurd 1710, updated Geo. Robertson 1818.

Barony	Lands	Proprietor	Valued rent £	s	d
Castlesempill	Part of Sheills	William Orr		10	10.1/2
Gavin & Risk	Risk	William Orr	45	6	8
Barr	Part Westhills	William Orr	29	6	
	Part Bridgend	Robert Orr	11	8	
Glen	Linthills	John Orr	34	13	4
	Auchinhean	Thomas Orr	33	6	8
	Kaim Hill	Robert Orr, writer	33	6	8
	Kaim	William Orr	32		
	Glenmill	Robert Orr	26	13	4
	Fairhills	James Orr	15		
	Lorabank	Robert Orr	20		
	Langyards	Robert Orr	63	6	8

Other properties in Renfrewshire

Paisley	Ralston	Robert Orr	265		
	High Parks	Charles Fox Orr	40		
	Lylesland	Robert Orr	66	13	4
Kilbarchan	Bankhead	Mr Orr`s reps.	167	9	

Land usage in the Parish of Lochwinnoch in 1818:

Arable, in cultivation	8000 acres
Pastures, natural grass	5750
Moss or muir of little value	4000
Roads, water, houses etc	500
Plantations, some extensive eg Castle Semple	1000
Total	19250 acres.

Part V

ORR IN IRELAND

There was much change in Scotland and Ireland as the populations moved about driven by political, economic and religious pressures. In Scotland there were a number of campaigns to force clearance of areas conducted directly by the English Crown and also by substantial landowners evicting the resident Highlander, Lowlander and Border people as they turned to large scale sheep farming in the mid to late 18th century. As long ago as 1513, when Henry VIII defeated James IV of Scotland at Flodden Field, there followed years of disruption and war as Henry sought control - including the defeat of James V at Hadden Rig near Berwick in 1542 and the `rough wooing` in 1544 and 1545, which drove the population out of southern Scotland. The accession of James VI of Scotland as James I of England in 1603 merged the two crowns and led to further political and especially religious pressures, that had a direct impact on migration to Ireland.

Life was difficult rather than dangerous for the Presbyterians under James VI/I, but dissension became more deadly with Charles I and his drive to impose his absolute supremacy and episcopacy (the rule of bishops) on the Kirk. Rebellion in Ireland in 1641 saw a reverse flow of refugees that hard pressed the mainland Scots who had to cope with a huge influx of essentially charitable cases. The firm hand of Cromwell in 1649-1650 saw some further disruption and reallocation of land in Ireland while the Irish bishops continued to harass the Presbyterians. The persecution that drove thousands of Scottish Presbyterians to Ulster followed from the Restoration of Charles II in 1660 through to the `Killing Time` in 1685.

But we get ahead of ourselves. It should be remembered that the West Coast of Scotland has very many lochs and two belts of islands; the Inner and Outer Hebrides. The coast of Ireland is very close to Scotland - a mere 21 miles at its nearest, and there was always the interplay between the local fishing industry and small-scale trading. In times of crisis, famine or war it was sometimes safer to move family and flocks to another and more economically attractive residence. Such escapes were often followed within a generation by a return to the original homeland once conditions had returned to normal.

My thanks to Barbara Holt in New Zealand for a new claimant for the first Orr in Ireland, who appeared in an Index of Wills (Appendix 9) in the Salt Lake City Library of the Latter Day Saints. This gives a Richard Orr having lodged a will (or his executors or family did) in 1563. His residence is given as Clontarf in the Diocese of Dublin, site of a famous victory by King Brian Boru over the Vikings in 1014. Richard is not a common name in Scotland and cannot rule out the possibility that he may well have a different origin. I remarked earlier on the possibility of a Norse origin from their word `Orri` meaning `blackcock` (a bird) and that a link appeared in the Lincolnshire Assize Roll of 1298 with reference to a Roger Orre in 1202. That the name Orre should turn up so early on the East coast of England where Norman knights from William the Conqueror's time had lands, raises all sorts of possibilities.

As for Richard, he may have been a merchant or trader or a dealer in cattle and horses from south west Scotland. Wigtownshire and the Mull of Kintyre is about 110 miles as the crow flies from Dublin but a mere 21 miles from northern County Down. Perhaps he was an adventurer from England as in 1556 Mary I, Queen of England, began a plantation scheme for most of the old counties of Leix and Offaly which were renamed Queens and King`s County. At this time some 160 families mainly from England and the Pale (the secure district around Dublin) were granted estates there. The settlers had to face resistance from the native Irish and a century of rebellions of varying degrees of seriousness. Whatever Richard`s origin he was a resident in 1563 and had an estate of some kind to pass on to his heirs.

Against this background came the opportunity of permanent settlement in Ireland with land on offer at reasonable rents on the estates of two Scottish landlords, Sir Hugh Montgomery and Sir James Hamilton ca 1606, and subsequently elsewhere under the Plantation of Ireland, 1610-1630. *The Montgomery Manuscripts*, (Ed. G.Hill 1873) compiled by William Montgomery ca 1696, gives a contemporaneous view of life in the early days of that settlement:

> I now go on with Sir Hugh Montgomery's plantation, which began about May, 1606, and thus it was, viz.:-Sir Hugh, after his return from Ireland to Braidstane, in winter 1605, as he had before his coming into Ireland, spoken of the plantation, so now he conduced his prime friends to join him therein, viz:-John Shaw of Greenock, Esq. and Patrick Montgomery of Black House. Sir Hugh also brought with him Patrick Shaw, Laird of Kelsoland and Hugh Montgomery, a cadet of the family of Braidstane with many others, and gave them lands in fee farm in Donaghadee parish under small chief rents.

> There came over also divers wealthy able men, to whom his lordship gave tenements in freehold, and parks by lease, so they being as it were bound, with their heirs, to the one, they must increase the rent for the other, at the end of the term or quit both which makes the park lands about towns give 10s. per acre rent now, which at the plantations the tenants had for 1s. rent, and these being taken, the tenants had some 2, some 3, and some 4 acres, for each of which they passed a boll of barley, rent. They built stone houses, and they traded to enable them to buy land, to France, Flanders, Norway. etc., as they still do.

> I desire that this brief account may serve as a sampler of Sir Hugh's first essay to his plantation, for it would be tedious (as it would be impossible for me) to enumerate all the substantial persons whom he brought or who came to plant in Grey Abbey. Newtown, and corner parishes. Therefore let us now pause awhile, and we shall wonder how this plantation advanced itself (especially in and about the towns of Donaghadee and Newtown), considering that in the

spring time (1606), those parishes were now more wasted than America (when the Spaniards landed there), but were not at all encumbered with great woods to be felled and grubbed, to the discouragement or hindrance of the inhabitants for in all those three parishes aforesaid, thirty cabins could not be found, nor any stone walls, but ruined roofless churches, and a few vaults at Grey Abbey, and a stump of an old castle in Newtown, in each of which some gentlemen sheltered themselves at their first coming over.

But Sir Hugh in the said spring brought with him divers artificers, as smiths, masons, carpenters, etc. I knew many of them old men when I was a boy at school, and had little employments for some of them, and heard them tell many things of this plantation which I found true. They soon made cottages and booths for themselves, because sods and saplings of ashes, alders, and birch trees (above thirty years old) with rushes for thatch, and bushes for wattles, were at hand. And also they made a shelter of the said stump of the castle for Sir Hugh, whose residence was mostly there, as in the centre of being supplied with necessaries from Belfast (but six miles thence), who therefore came and set up a market in Newtown, for profit for both the towns. As like wise in the fair summer season (twice, sometimes thrice every week) they were supplied from Scotland, as Donaghadee was oftener, because but three hours sail from Port Patrick, where they bespoke provisions and necessaries to lade in, to be brought over by their own or that town's boats whenever wind and weather served them, for there was a constant flux of passengers coming daily over.

I have heard honest old men say that in June, July, and August, 1607, people came from Stranraer, four miles, and left their horses at the port, hired horses at Donaghadee, came with their wares and provisions to Newtown, and sold them, dined there, stayed two or three hours, and returned to their houses the same day by bed-time, their land journey but twenty miles. Such was their encouragement from a ready market, and their kind desires to see and supply their friends and kindred, which commerce took quite away the evil report of wolves and wood-kerne, which enviers of planter's industry had raised and brought upon our plantations; but, notwithstanding thereof, by the aforesaid gentlemen's assiduity to people their own farms, which they did, (1607), after Sir Hugh and his Lady's example, they both being active and intent on the work (as birds, after pairing to make nests for their brood), then you might see streets and tenements regularly set out, and houses rising as it were out of the ground (like Cadmus's colony) on a sudden, so that these dwellings became towns immediately.

Yet among all this care and indefatigable industry for their families, a place of God's honour to dwell in was not forgotten or neglected, for indeed our forefathers were more pious than ourselves, and so soon as [the] said stump of the old castle was so repaired (as it was in spring time, 1606), as might be shelter for that year's summer and harvest, for Sir Hugh and for his servants that winter, his piety made some good store of provisions in those fair seasons, towards roofing and fitting the chancel of that church, for the worship of God; and therein he needed not withdraw his own planters from working for themselves, because there were Irish Gibeonets and garrons (ponies) enough in his woods to hew and draw timber for the sanctuary; and the general free contribution of the planters, some with money, others with handicrafts, and many with labouring, was so great and willingly given, that the next year after this, viz. in 1607, before winter it was made decently serviceable, and Sir Hugh had brought over at first two or three chaplains with him for these parishes. In summer, 1608, some of the priory walls were roofed and fitted for his Lady and children and servants (which were many) to live in.

Now the harvests 1606 and 1607 had stocked the people with grain, for the lands were never naturally so productive since that time, except where no plough had gone, and where sea oar (called wreck) is employed for dung, to that degree that they had to spare and to sell to the succeeding new-coming planters, who came over the more in number and the faster because they might sell their own grain at a great price in Scotland, and be freed of trouble to bring it with them, and could have it cheaper here. This conference gave occasion to Sir Hugh's Lady to build water mills in all the parishes, to the great advantage of her house, which was numerous in servants, of whom she stood in need, in working about her gardens, carriages, etc., having then no duty days' work from tenants, or very few as exacted, they being sufficiently employed in their proper labour and the public. The millers also prevented the necessity of bringing meal from Scotland, and grinding with quairn stones (as the Irish did to make their graddon) both which inconveniencies the people, at their first coming, were forced to undergo.

Her Ladyship had also her farms at Grey Abbey and Comber, as well as at Newtown, both to supply newcomers and her house; and she easily got men for plough and barn, for many came over who had not stocks to plant and take leases of land, but had brought a cow or two and a few sheep, for which she gave them grass and so much grain per annum, and an house and garden plot to live on, and some land for flax and potatoes, as they agreed on for doing their work, and there be at this day many such poor labourers amongst us; and this was but part of her good management, for she set up and encouraged linen and woollen manufactory, which soon brought down the prices of the breakens and narrow cloths of both sorts.

Now everybody minded their trades, and the plough, and the spade, building, and setting fruit trees, etc, in orchards and gardens, and by ditching in their grounds. The old women spun, and the young girls plied their nimble fingers at knitting, and everybody was innocently busy. Now the golden peaceable age renewed, no strife. contention, querulous lawyers, or Scottish or Irish feuds, between clans and families, and surnames, disturbing the tranquillity of those times; and the towns and temples were erected, with other great works done (even in troublesome years) as shall be in part recited, when I come to tell you of the first Lord Viscount Montgomery's funeral, person, parts, and arts; therefore, reader, I shall be the more concise in the history of the plantation I find that in a few years from the beginning of the Plantation. viz. in A.D. 1610, the Viscount brought before the King's muster master 1,000 able fighting men to serve, when out of them a militia should be raised. The said Sir Hugh (for the great encouragement of planters and builders) obtained a patent dated the 25th of March, 11th Jac. by which Newtown aforesaid is erected into a corporation, whereof the said Sir Hugh is nominated the first Provost, and the burgesses are also named.

The First Orrs from Scotland

James Orr and his wife Janet McClement, were the first documented settlers to come to the province of Ulster in about 1607 as part of the settlement by Hugh Montgomery in County Down. In the *Hamilton Manuscripts,* which refer to the family of the other Scottish settler Sir James Hamilton, there are two Orrs named as tenants in the accounts for Alice, Countess of Clanbassie in 1681. These were Patrick Orr in Ballywalter Town who was paying a rent of £2.9s.6d per annum; and Thomas Orr in Bangor Town who was paying rent of £16s.6d per annum. It is likely that other Orrs came to Ireland in the Plantation period, 1610-1630, and settled in County Donegal; Co Londonderry, and Co Tyrone. We know of John Orr of Raphoe who was granted denization in 1617 during the Plantation, and of an Orr family in Co Tyrone in 1655. John and James Orr of Letterkenny, Donegal were defenders in the siege of Londonderry and possibly came from the Raphoe family.

There are several Orrs mentioned in the Hearth Money Rolls (HMR) and Poll Tax Returns for County Antrim, 1660-1669. William Orr (2) Antrim Town 1666 and 1669 HMR. Widow Orr, Parish of Raloo, townland of Ballywillin. 1669 HMR Robert Orr, Parish of Raloo, townland of Ballyrickard More 1669. HMR. Pat Ore, Parish of Ballymoney, townland of Ballymoney. 1666 and 1669 HMR. John Ore, Parish of Ballymoney, townland of Greenshields; 1669 HMR. Pat Oar, Parish of Billy, townland of Liscolman. 1660 Poll Tax. John Ore, Parish of Kilwaughter, townland of Ballykeel, 1666 and 1669 HMR. John Oure, Parish of Larne, townland of Larne Town, 1669 HMR. John Orre, Parish of Finvoy, townland of Knockans. 1669 HMR. John Orr, Parish of Ballinderry, townland of New Park. 1669 HMR.

ORR in the Griffith Valuation and Tithe Applotments

A very valuable supplementary source for tracing ancestors are the Tithe Applotments and Griffiths Valuation which took a number of years to complete. The original records for Northern Ireland are in PRONI (ref VAL 1B/) and for the rest of Ireland in the National Archives, Dublin but they have been filmed by the LDS and an Index is also available on a commercial CD. The Index for Ireland shows that there were some 518 Orr households in the Valuation.

This source provides an indication as to the parishes and counties in the ancient province of Ulster (the 9 counties of Antrim, Armagh, Cavan, Donegal, Down, Fermanagh, Londonderry, Monaghan and Tyrone) where the surname is almost exclusively found. This may help in providing a focus for a search in a case where only the county of origin of an ancestor is known.

The report is based on the 'Index to Surnames' or 'Householders Index' that was compiled by the staff of the National Library of Ireland in the 1960's. Although this Index covers surnames only and gives no precise references to the documents for the parish where the surnames appear, it does record the occurrence of properties occupied by Orr's in each of the civil parishes of a county. It covers the surnames of farmers (usually leaseholders) in the Tithe Applotment books compiled 1823-1838 and also all names of property occupiers in the printed version of the tenement valuation, known as 'Griffith Valuation', covering all properties in Ulster, 1857-1864. Whilst it records the exact number of householders in the case of the Griffith Valuation, it provides only an indication of the presence or absence of a surname in the Tithe Applotment books.

County	Total	
Antrim	107	
Armagh	70	
Cavan	6	
Donegal	38	Total Householders recorded in
Down	122	Griffith`s Valuation: 518
Fermanagh	4	The breakdown by County to Townland is provided in Appendix 10
Londonderry	77	
Monaghan	15	
Tyrone	79	

The *Ulster Pedigree* by Gawin Orr tells us that descendents of Patrick Orr, son of James Orr and Janet McClement, went to Co Armagh and Co Donegal. This would have been about the 1630s. Unfortunately he did not investigate those lines in his pedigree. A Donnell Orr of Raphoe is listed in the 1630 Muster Rolls. Two Orrs, James and John, from Letterkenny, Co Donegal are included in the names of the defenders of Derry in *Fighters of Derry, their Deeds and their Descendents being a Chronicle of events in Ireland during the Revolutionary Period, 1688-91.* by William R Young. In Donegal there were Orrs also in Taughboyne and Muff, some of whom went to the United States, with Andrew Orr and Sarah Love located in Iowa. Londonderry locations include the parishes of Aghadowey, Glendermott, Eglinton and Magherafelt.

A well documented family from Strabane, Co Tyrone are the Orrs who founded Orrville, Wayne County, Ohio. – their story is separately told. Orrs were also located in Clogher, Omagh, Dungannon, Clonfeacle (who have descendants in Perth, Australia), and Castledergh.

Armagh had a fairly substantial number of Orrs until the early nineteenth century when they faded from the scene; many probably joining the exodus to the USA, Canada and Australia. They were for a while quite numerous around Loughgall, Kilmore, Tynan, Mullaghbrack, Market Hill, and Portadown. Joseph Orr and Sons, and William Orr, were large mill owners – linen manufacturers and finishers, at Loughgall; while James and William Orr were owners of a private hospital or institution at the Course Lodge, Rich Hill in 1861.

William Orr of Co Antrim was one of the larger bleachers of linen ca 1839 in all of Ulster, finishing some 15,000 pieces a year. Orrs were spread around Co Antrim but with some groupings around Ballymena, Antrim Town, the parishes of Kirkinriola and Ahoghill Increasing industrialisation and the growth of engineering and shipbuilding in Belfast inevitably drew workers to that locality. With it came a range of supporting services such as carriers – transporting materials to the mills, finished goods to the countryside or the docks for export. There were too, an increase in services including solicitors, accountants, book keepers, dress makers, tailors, merchants, grocers, wine and spirit retailers to provide for the increased population. This is illustrated by the Orrs listed in the 1841-2 *Martin`s Directory of Belfast*:

The Misses Orr, dressmakers, 1 James Place
Hamilton Orr, 130 Ann St.
Robert Orr, publican, 202 North St.
Mrs Orr, servant`s registry office (an employment office) 3 Academy St.
William Orr & Son, linen manufacturers, merchants, bleachmills, Glengall St.
Robert Orr, of Wm Orr merchants, residence, Glengall St.
Miss Orr, 9 Joy St.
William Orr, tailor, Townend St.
Hugh Orr, Clerk of Petty Sessions, 2 North Thomas St.
David Orr, cart maker, 20 West St.
William Orr, public carrier, 20 Francis St.
M. A. Orr, dressmaker, 108, Cromac St.
Mrs Orr, Ingram Place.
John Orr, blacksmith, 3 Back Lane.
Forsythe & Orr, flax spinners, Upper Falls Mill, Falls Rd.
William Orr, Solicitor, High St Ballymena and 76 Lower Gardiner St., Dublin.

Messrs Murphy & Orr of Ardoyne, Belfast, proudly declared (*Old Belfast*, R. M. Young, 1896) that their table linen was chosen for presentation by the Ladies of Belfast as a wedding present for H.R.H. The Duchess of York; and their house linen chosen for presentation by the Ladies of Ireland. Joseph Orr and Son were established as seed merchants and florists at 12/14 Ann Street in 1851 and were still trading in 1886 (*Bassetts Directory of Co Down*).

Co Down, perhaps regarded as the `home county`, has had a considerable number of Orrs and many especially around the north east corner at Newtownards, Bangor, and Donaghadee. They were also around Comber, Saintfield, Ballygowan, Kilkeel, Killinchy, Downpatrick and Dromore. The County Down Land Deeds in 1876 gave the following land owners:-

Charles Orr, address Greencastle, Kilkeel, owned 39 acres.
Gawn Orr, address Granshaw, Comber, owned 71 acres.
John Orr, address Ballymacasken, Killinchy, owned 70 acres.
Margaret Orr, address Ballymartin, Kilkeel, owned 6 acres.
Mary Orr, address Ballykeel, Comber, owned 24 acres.
William Orr, address Ballymartin, Kilkeel, owned 44 acres.
William Orr, address Ballykeel, Comber, owned 127 acres

The excellent book *Ulster Pedigrees. Descendants, in many lines, of James Orr and Janet McClement who emigrated from Scotland to Northern Ireland ca 1607.* was researched and published by Ray A Jones (1977) has a Library of Congress Catalog reference No. 77-82468. There are still copies available in the second hand book market but they are becoming quite rare. There is a copy in the LDS Library in Salt Lake City Catalog Reference: Call No 929.2415.Or7j; location JSMB British Book. It is also on fiche reference: FHL British Fiche 6036613.

It is a follow up on the work by Gawin Orr of Castlereigh (12 Jun 1756 - 7 June 1830) which is in the Linen Hall Library, Belfast. Ray Jones added information from the early volumes of Gravestone Inscriptions series (vols 1-12) by R. J. Clarke, and other data he compiled. It contains some 2,800 Orr connections although, unfortunately, it is sometimes rather short of dates. A list of the surnames of persons who married an Orr is at Appendix 8.

Part VI

A ONE NAME STUDY
Another Way of Researching Family History

A One Name Study is the research in depth and collection of <u>all</u> occurrences of a name worldwide as opposed to the more familiar research of a particular person or descendants of one person or couple. It may sound difficult or complicated but it isn't really. The people who undertake One Name studies are enthusiasts of course - and in many instances they may organise and run their "name" family history society. But you can be a One Name researcher without undertaking a family society

A One Name Study is the research of a particular name, not necessarily your own - perhaps your husband or wife's line, or even no one related to you at all. The collection together and linking up of all persons with your chosen name would, in an ideal world, result in the finite family tree with all the connections made and verified. There can be a great deal of work involved for a common name. No one has started Smith for example, and the current registered names are selective and quite rare with some having less than a thousand records. Nevertheless, some people have started work on larger studies with world populations in the tens of thousands and more. The Orr study is one such large undertaking that has turned out to be far larger than ever anticipated. There are simply too many of us to allow them all to be linked and verified. With regret therefore under the rules of the Society, the study has been discontinued. Limited work will however continue.

There is a need for commitment to undertake a study as it has a much wider scope and opens so many channels of communication with other researchers. If you do research a blood line you will inevitably come into contact with cousins. They may be several generations removed but they are cousins nonetheless. It is challenging to be an authority on your name and very rewarding to be able to help people find their family roots. It is also totally absorbing, as you will invariably go off at a tangent intrigued by the surrounding history and events that influenced your family, perhaps explaining why they migrated or emigrated when they did It is the ideal companion to researching your Clan. All clans have their septs - the smaller family groups associated with a clan. A One Name study is also an alternative when you reach the genealogists "brick wall". When you have gone as far as you can on your direct blood lines and just cannot find Uncle Fred who "went to America" and joined the Gold Rush. It provides the opportunity to continue with your interest in history and always with the hope that one day the brick wall will finally crumble to reveal your wealthy ancestor!

It is not difficult to start a One Name study, however, it is important to have some idea of how many people there might be - how rare is your chosen name. A look at telephone directories for the whole country at your local library is a good start or visit some websites that have the phone book on line such as White Pages. In the USA it is possible to find out how many of a given surname there are by visiting the US Census Bureau facility at http://www.census.gov/genealogy/www/freqnames.html And recently some of the larger sites, sunch as Ancestry.com have enabled facilities that produce distribution maps from the Census returns. Another useful guide for Scottish families is the Scottish General Records facility where the number of persons within the relevant records can be ascertained. This is at www.scotlandspeople.gov.uk

There are two organisations that register One Name studies. The purpose is to provide a network for similarly minded researchers and a reference list that can be checked to see if anyone is researching that name. A particular name or spelling of a name is only registered once, but if already registered your offer of help may be welcomed with open arms by that person. Registration is therefore a resource for any family historian to use and may provide a shortcut for your researches. Membership of an organisation carries with it the obligation to reply to enquiries relating to your registered name (Self addressed stamped envelope or two International Reply Coupons should be included with the request).

You can register a name with the Guild of One Name Studies (G.O.O.N.S.), an international society with a worldwide membership. Write to:

> Guild of One Name Studies
> Box G, Charterhouse Buildings
> Goswell Road
> London EC1M 7BA

Or you can visit the G.O.O.N.S website at http://www.one-name.org.

In the USA write to The American Association of One Name Studies, 2509 Placid Place, Virginia Beach, VA 23456-3743

Experience of the Orr One Name Study.

The Orr One Name Study began some 30 years ago when I had the good fortune to be able to talk to many relatives, including several elderly great aunts and a great grandmother who gave me access to a quantity of old wills, and insurance policies. But these were my wife's relatives from Lincolnshire and Staffordshire, my own immediate family residing in Australia. Thus at an early date I came up against the hurdle of researching my paternal line which is in Ireland. I resorted to using a local researcher which was moderately successful back to 1845 or so when registration was introduced, but tailed off when research was needed through the many subsidiary records such as Parish Registers, Griffiths Valuation; Tithe Applotments; Muster Rolls and the like.

At this juncture, I took to researching an old family story - told to my father in 1932 by an elderly great aunt of his (she was in her 80's and father 18 at the time) of an alleged connection with the family of William Orr of Farranshane. Family stories, as we all know, tend to be gilded in the re telling but may occasionally contain a grain of truth. The story of William Orr (1766-1797), a farmer in the townland of Farranshane, Co. Antrim was a focal point for Rebellion in 1798. He was a member of the 'United Irishmen'and accused of administering a treasonable oath. He was arrested, tried by an allegedly drunken jury, and executed for alleged treason.. His story is related later.

The researching of William Orr's life and times led to in depth reading and acquisition of works about the 1798 Revolution, thence back to The Plantation of Ireland ca 1610. I was fortunate to find a specialist book seller who kindly copied a manuscript 'family tree' of William Orr that he came across; and he found for me a copy of *Ulster Pedigrees*. This wealth of information did not, however, take me forward in the research of my paternal line but opened another area of interest - the Orr origins in Scotland. From reading about the Plantation and the history of the Montgomery and Hamilton families there was a lead directly to the West coast and Renfrewshire. In particular there have been Orrs around the Parish of Lochwinnoch for some 700 years. Orr is an acknowledged sept of Clan Campbell. Yet another knock on was the extent of the emigration from both Ireland and Scotland to the Colonies. We may think of North America, both Canada and the United States, as the main destination but there were other adventurers who went to the West Indies, South America - Argentina, Chile, and literally up the Amazon. Then of course, the deportation of prisoners to 'the Colonies ' and especially to Australia and New Zealand which is said to have led to the nickname "Pommie" from POHMIE - Prisoner of His Majesty in Exile.

Many of these emigrants and adventurers were not only fleeing poverty, religious and social persecution but were enticed by the thought of a better life and free or cheap land. To many anything was better than the environment from which they came; they were incredibly resolute and also remarkably mobile for their time. They went to Canada and the wilds of Prince Edward Island and Nova Scotia; to the humidity of Alabama, South Carolina and Georgia; to New York, Pennsylvania; and the Ohio valley. Some were in the Mormon trek to Utah. In all these places they made their mark by fighting off the native Indians, clearing land and establishing townships some bearing the Orr name - Orrville, Wayne Co. Ohio is such a place named after an early pioneer Judge Smith Orr, who went to America in 1801.

The Orrs also made their contribution to the emerging United States. They were undoubtedly involved in the slave trade and were slave owners. Indeed this is clearly evidenced in Black American families in the Southern USA bearing the surname Orr.. Alexander Ector Orr from Strabane, Co Tyrone was a pioneer of the subways in New York City. James Laurence Orr (1822-1873) was governor of South Carolina and Speaker of the House of Representatives. A later Orr - Andrew, was also Speaker.

In my rambles through history I accumulated a substantial amount of individual Orr data which was not of direct relevance to my blood line and I wondered what to do with it. I knew that it represented over 20 years of dabbling and would probably be of interest to other Orr researchers. How then could I continue my wider interests (as they had become) and build on what information I had. With some trepidation I joined the GOONS as my aims and objectives were consistent with those of the Society.

When I looked at the extent of some One Name Studies with perhaps only a couple of hundred individuals and their researcher burrowing away in a narrow geographical area I sometimes felt a fraud. The catchment area I had chosen was the world and the Orr population far greater than I anticipated - 90,000 in the USA (1990 Census statistics); 9730 in the UK (1997 Electoral Rolls) and several thousands more in Canada, Australia and New Zealand. I had over 100,000 entries in my Orr databases. Some may regard a study of this kind as 'stamp collecting' in another guise - perhaps it is, but I'm not proud, I will gladly accepted Orr information from anyone anywhere, any time. Who knows, a future Orr researcher just might be glad of my efforts. On the up side I have acquired a number of Orr family trees from Scotland, Ireland, Alabama, Indiana, Iowa, Ohio, Australia and New Zealand and made contact with very many 'cousins' around the world. I enjoy it and wish I had started sooner. So if there is a message in my tale, it is for those who 'hit the brick wall' - don`t give up, look around you, there are other ways of persuing your genealogical interests, why not a One Name Study ?

PART VII

THE ORRS AT WAR

John McCrae, the Canadian poet and army doctor, penned the
haunting poem `In Flanders Field`, which has at its end a poignant
cry to remember:

> In Flanders fields the poppies blow
> Between the crosses, row on row,
> That mark our place; and in the sky
> The larks, still bravely singing, fly
> Scarce heard amid the guns below.
>
> We are the Dead. Short days ago
> We lived, felt dawn, saw sunset glow,
> Loved, and were loved, and now we lie
> In Flanders fields.
>
> Take up our quarrel with the foe:
> To you from failing hands we throw
> The torch; be yours to hold it high.
> If ye break faith with us who die
> We shall not sleep, though poppies grow
> In Flanders fields.

The Commonwealth War Graves Commission, www.cwgc.org,
maintains the graves and memorials for 1.7 million soldiers, sailors
and airmen who died in both World Wars. The CWGC database is
on line and free. It also lists over 60,000 civilians who died from
enemy action in the UK. Many of the smaller graveyards that are
scattered throughout the former war zones have been consolidated
and now also contain the dead of World War II. It speaks volumes
that so many of our soldiers gave their lives in two wars at or near
the same places such that they lie together in a foreign field. The
opening of the CWGC web site afforded the opportunity to search
for relatives that hitherto been just "Uncle Fred died in WWI".

It is likely that Orrs met their maker from the earliest times through military service. As a West coast of Scotland family, some may well have been employed as "galloglass" (mercenaries) in Ireland as long ago as the 13th century. In the 16th, 17th and 18th centuries many disenchanted and jobless Scots sought military service with other European states and did so, often with great distinction, in France, Spain, Germany, Poland. Sweden, and Russia.

Orrs were prominent in a variety of ways in the burgeoning America and some 102 of their number have been found who served in the Revolutionary War or War of Independence (1774-1783). Hugh Orr from Lochwinnoch (1717-1798) manufactured 500 muskets in 1748, and in the war he was well established as an iron-founder and arms merchant. His son Colonel Robert Orr was armourer at Springfield, Massachusetts. Division occurred between and sometimes within emigrant families with many of the British supporters going to Canada during the conflict. The remainder supported the American cause of Independence. The story of the Empire Loyalists as these migrants to Canada became known, is of itself a fascinating story.

No less than 129 Orrs from 16 States are recorded as taking part in the 1812 War against Britain. The distribution of the volunteers is an interesting illustration of how mobile the immigrants were. It shows their spread across the country from Vermont, Massachusetts, Maryland, New Jersey and New York in the North East down the coastal plain through Virginia, North and South Carolina to Georgia; through Pennsylvania and the Ohio valley to Tennessee and Arkansas and all points west to Texas.

An excellent article by Walter B. Hill, Jr. on the African American Civil War Memorial web site relates the story of the Coloured Troops and their history.. It was surprising to learn that slavery and its abolition was not initially a major issue in the American Civil War. But the realisation that the Confederacy were using slave labour to further their war effort led to the Second Confiscation Act and Militia Act (July 1862) which authorised the enlistment of all able bodied citizens between the ages of 18 and 45, including "persons of African descent". A consequence of this was General Order 143, Adjutant General's Office, May 22nd, 1863, and the creation of the Bureau of Colored Troops. The first regiment of the United States Colored Troops was mustered in June 1863 and 24 black American Orrs, former slaves or sons of slaves served the Union cause.

By way of illustrating the way the wider Orr "family" was split, there were a total of 1411 Orrs in the Muster Rolls. Some served for years while others responded to alarms and only served a few days before they were stood down. They were divided 547 Confederate Army and 864 in the Union Army.

Among many regiments who fought with great courage and distinction was Orr's Rifles, the 1st Infantry Regiment, South Carolina Volunteers formed in July 1861. Made up to a thousand men they were sent to Virginia and fought in no less than 22 engagements between June 1862 – Seven Days Battle, through to Appomattox Court House April 1865. The regiment suffered dreadful casualties at Fredericksburg (170) and the second battle of Manassas (116).

Congressional Medal of Honour

Two Orrs were awarded the Medal of Honour for courageous action under fire.

Charles A. Orr.

Born in Holland, New York, he joined the Army at Bennington NY. As a Private, with Company G, of the 187th New York Infantry, he and two others rescued several wounded and helpless soldiers at Hatchers Run, Virginia, on 27 October, 1864.

Robert L Orr.

Born 28 March 1836 in Philadelphia, PA. He served as a Major in the 61st Pennsylvania Infantry. At Petersburg, Virginia on 2 April, 1865, he retrieved the colours which had twice fallen and carried them under fire at the head of the column.

In modern times many American Orrs have paid the highest price in World War I. WW II, Korea, Vietnam and now two wars in Iraq Records available in the US National Archives (http://aad.archives.gov) show that 1681 Orrs enlisted of which 45 were killed in action during WWII; 31 were taken prisoners of war. Eight American Orr's were killed in action in the Korean War with a further 14 who were casualties or wounded. In Vietnam 524 Orrs were in action there, of whom 14 are listed as killed and are commemorated at Arlington National Cemetery. Honours conferred on Orrs in Vietnam included 7 Bronze Stars, 1 Air Medal, 2 Army Commendations and three Joint Service Commendations. To this roll of honour we sadly add another young man doing his duty, Pfc Cody Orr, 2nd Battalion, 20th Field Artillery Regiment, killed in Iraq 17 January 2004.

Turning to the Commonwealth countries, there were Orrs in Australian and New Zealand units that took part in the Boer War 1899 – 1902. Three Orrs were among the Australian troops - D. Orr of New South Wales; H. Orr of Queensland. John Orr of Tasmania, was a Corporal in the Fourth Tasmanian Contingent, Second Imperial Bushmen, Colonial Military Force, who was killed in action 18 November, 1901. New Zealand had about 6,000 troops in South Africa of whom some 230 lost their lives. The First Contingent of the New Zealand Mounted Rifles went to South Africa in October 1899. James Orr a bugler and farmer of Johnsonville, went with the 5th Contingent He was the son of John Forbes Orr a Wellington hotel keeper. Thomas Henry Orr of Auckland joined the fray on 15 March 1902 with the 8th

Contingent., but the peace agreement ended hostilities on 31 May – his brother and son served respectively in WWI and II.

By the time of the Great War, 1914-1918, very many Orrs had emigrated, taken up citizenship and joined the military. There were those who had recently emigrated and returned to the land of their birth to join up, and those who signed up anyway, such as S. Orr and John Richard Orr from Downpatrick, Co. Down, who served in the Canadian Infantry; Thomas Orr from British Columbia, Canada who served in the 1st/5th Northumberland Fusiliers; and Wallace Orr of San Francisco, California who served with the 1st Bn. Canadian Machine Gun Corps. Australia was well represented in WWI with 106 Orrs identified as having taken part, 21 being killed in action or dying from their wounds. Among them was a recent immigrant Peter Clowes Orr, Private 3rd Bn. Australian Infantry, a native of Girvan he was the son of John and Mary Orr and just aged 22 when he died of wounds on the Somme, 4 March 1917. Three of the Australians were awarded the Military Medal for gallantry - Pvte Arthur Orr; Bombardier William Arthur Orr, and 2nd Lt James Campbell Orr.

The Canadian Orrs were also well represented with 236 of their number listed in the Canadian National Archives as serving in the Canadian Expeditionary Force of WWI. Sixty thousand Canadians died in WW I (11,000 with no known grave) and are commemorated at the Vimy Memorial, Pas de Calais, France.

401 UK and Commonwealth Orrs died for their country in the two World Wars, including two persons who adopted the Orr surname as an alias when joining up. Based upon the origin of the regiment or service that they served in, the distribution is:

Australia	36	Malta	1	Trinidad	1	
Canada	40	New Zealand	17	Wales	1	
Hong Kong	1	Scotland	132	England	134	
Ireland	33	South Africa	4	Unknown	1	

One death in a family is tragedy enough but there were occasions when brothers were lost. Two sets of brothers were among the New Zealand losses in WW I - Robert Charles Orr and John William Orr from Auckland and Ernest Orr and Henry William Orr from Hamilton. There were brothers Herbert Orr, and F. Orr from Oldham, Lancashire; and, from the tiny island of Malta brothers Arthur George Orr died in 1917 and David died 1945.

It is particularly sad to record the death of both father and a son in active service. Sapper James Orr, 6 Bomb Disposal Coy. Royal Engineers died 3 October 1940. His son, Robert John Dillon Orr, 2nd Bn Royal Ulster Rifles, aged 20, died at Caen, France on 19 July 1944. Neither were the civilian population spared from family disaster. In Glasgow Annie Orr aged 29 and her mother Annie Goodwin Orr were killed in their home at 2, Shiskine St., Maryhill, on 14 March 1941. Nine civilian Orrs were killed by enemy action.

In the UK, every town has its War Memorial and we are familiar with the sight of the Cenotaph in Whitehall, London, which features in every Remembrance Day parade. 1998 was the 80th anniversary of the Remembrance Day services and included poignant scenes on television from the Ypres (Menin Gate) Memorial. Those commemorated at these places are but a few of the whole; we should not forget that the roll call at other memorials runs into millions.

It was heartening to see the patriotism that caused young boys to lie about their ages in order to sign up, the stoicism of families who lost loved ones and suffered great hardships without a bread winner, and of the gallant acts by so many. On the other hand it is chastening to see the numbers of soldiers, sailors and airmen who emerged as having no known grave - whose only memorial, if any, is on a plaque somewhere. More than anything else, this absence of a known grave demonstrates the wanton obscenity of war - it also serves as a silent reminder that we must not forget those who gave their lives for our freedom. In modern times they continue to serve their country albeit the nature of war has changed dramatically.

Orrs who gave their lives in World War I, and their Regiments

Irish Regiments.

They served with the Royal Irish Rifles, the Royal Inniskilling Fusiliers, the Royal Ulster Rifles, and The Irish Guards. It is noteworthy that a number of those killed were amongst the first to join up as gauged by their low serial number - such as

Rifleman John Orr, Ser. No 358 11th Bn Royal Irish Rifles
Sergeant William Orr, Ser No. 432 10 Bn Royal Irish Rifles
Rifleman Nicholas Orr, Ser. No. 741, 15th Bn Royal Irish Rifles
Rifleman John Orr, Ser. No. 774, 12 Bn Royal Irish Rifles.
Sergeant James Orr, Ser. No 3777, 1st Bn Royal Inniskilling Fusiliers
Rifleman William James Orr, Ser. No 4735, 2nd Bn Royal Irish Rifles.
Rifleman R. Orr, Ser. No 5380, 6th Bn Royal Irish Rifles.
Rifleman Hamilton Orr, Ser. No 6795, 1st Bn Royal Irish Rifles.
Rifleman F Orr, Serial No. 8298 1st Bn Royal Irish Rifles.

The number killed in action, by Regiment, were:

Royal Irish Rifles.

1 Bn	2nd Bn	3rd Bn	6th Bn	10th Bn	11th Bn	12 Bn	13th Bn	15th Bn
4	2	1	1	1	2	1	2	1

Royal Inniskilling Fusiliers

1st Bn	9th Bn	10th Bn	11th Bn	70th Bn
2	5	2	2	1

Royal Ulster Rifles		Irish Guards
1st Bn	2nd Bn	2nd Bn.
1	3	1

The principal Scottish regiments in which Orrs served were:

Royal Scottish Fusiliers 21
Highland Light Infantry 17
Argyll & Sutherland Highlanders 13
Seaforth Highlanders 12
Black Watch 11
Gordon Highlanders 7
Scots Guards 6
Cameronians 5
Queens Own Cameron Highlanders 5
Kings Own Scottish Borderers 3

The English regiments in which they served were:

Royal Artillery 21
Royal Engineers 8
Dragoons/Royal Armoured Corp 5
Kings Regiment (Liverpool) 5
Northumberland Fusiliers 5
Royal Army Service Corps 5
Pioneer Corps 3
Kings Own Royal Lancaster Regiment 3
Royal Fusiliers 3
East Lancashire Regiment 2
Durham Light Infantry 2
Royal Army Medical Corps 2
Cheshire Regiment 2
Royal Marine Light Infantry 2
Machine Gun Corps 2
Hampshire Regiment 2

The Fliers were:

RAF/RAFVR 25
Royal Flying Corps 1
Army Air Corps 1
Royal Australian Air Force 4
Royal Canadian Air Force 8
Royal New Zealand Air Force 2

The Sailors were:
Merchant Navy 6
RN/RNVR 21
Royal Australian Navy 1

Other Commonwealth Forces in which they served were:
Australian Infantry 23
Australian Artillery 3
Australian Pioneers 1
Australian Army Medical Corps 1
Australian Army Service Corps 1
Canadian Infantry 23
Canadian Artillery 4
Canadian Army Medical Corps 2
Canadian Pioneers 1
Canadian Engineers 1
Black Watch of Canada 1
Cameron Highlanders of Canada 2
South African Infantry 2
South African Engineers 1
Pretoria Regiment 1

Memorials to the dead, missing and with no known grave.

As would be expected with the wide diversity of countries and branches of the armed forces in which they served, Orrs were in some of the famous battles. They feature too in many memorials throughout the world to those with no known grave, who died at sea in the Merchant Navy or the Royal Navy, those buried at sea, and the many gallant fliers, for whom their final resting place is known only to God. In collating this information it drives home just how many hundreds of thousands for whom their memorial is but an inscription on a wall somewhere. It shows too, the sheer stupidity of man and the inhumanity of one to another.

We are familiar with the sight of the Ypres (Menin Gate) Memorial from the Remembrance Day services but those commemorated there are but a few of the whole. Thousands more lie in unknown graves and are commemorated elsewhere - 35,000 with no known grave commemorated at Arras, 13,000 at Le Touret. At Vis en Artois, Pas de Calais - 9,000 from Great Britain Ireland and South Africa who died between 8 August and 11 November 1918. 20,000 at the Loos Memorial; 14,000 including 300 South Africans at Pozieres; and at Cambrai 7000 with no known grave. 10,000 Australians are commemorated at Villers Bretonneux, Somme. We forget that the conflict was also in Mesopotamia - Egypt, Iraq, Palestine and Gallipoli. The 40,000 Commonwealth troops commemorated at Basra, Iraq; 4228 Australians and 708 New Zealanders commemorated at Lone Pine, Gallipoli. 20,000 at Helles Memorial, Gallipoli; 24,000 at Kranji, Singapore; and the Rangoon Memorial with 6000 buried in the cemetery and 27,000 in unknown graves throughout Burma, Assam and Lauban (Borneo) - many the victims of Japanese savagery and murder while unarmed POWs. The list is seemingly endless.

Every town in the United Kingdom has its Memorial and there are national and international commemoration sites for the missing and with no known grave; these contain their share of Orrs.

Ypres (Menin Gate) Memorial, Iepers, West Vlaanderen, Belgium.

Capt. J. A. Orr, 1st Bn. Cameron Highlanders 22.10.1914
Pvte. Thomas Orr, 2nd Bn. Royal Scots 14.12.1914

Pvte. William Orr, 1st Bn Royal Dragoons 12.11.1914

Sgt. William Orr, 10 Bn Royal Irish Rifles 4. 8.1917

Lt. Walter Leslie Orr, attd. 2nd Bn Royal Irish Rifles 25. 9.1915

Pvte Frank Orr, 1st/5th Northumberland Fusiliers 24. 5.1915

Pvte John Orr, 1st Gordon Highlanders 28. 5.1915

L/Cpl Thomas Orr, 1st /4th Northumberland Fusiliers 26. 4.1915

Pvte John Erskine Orr, 87th Bn. Canadian Infantry (Quebec Reg) 17. 9.1916

Rfn. David Orr, 1st/8th London Regiment (Post Office Rifles) 28. 8.1917

Capt. James Barbour Orr, 4th Bn Royal Scots Fusiliers 31. 7.1917

Tyne Cot Memorial, Zonnebeke, Belgium

Rfn Robert James Orr, 11 Bn Royal Irish Rifles 16. 8.1917

Cpl. David Fairbairn Orr, 9 Bn Royal Scots 20. 9.1917

Pvte John William Orr, 2nd (Waikato Coy) 2nd Auckland Regt. 4.10.1917

Pvte Leslie Orr, 1st Bn Otago Regiment, NZEF 12.10.1917

Pvte Thomas Orr, 2 Bn Royal Scots Fusiliers 29. 4.1918

Pvte Archibald Orr, 5/5 Cameronians (Scottish Rifles) 8. 5.1918

Ploegsteert Memorial, Hainaut, Belgium

Pvte John Orr, 1st Bn East Yorkshire Regiment 28.10.1914

Capt. Robert Clifford Orr, 3rd Bn Somerset Light Infantry 19.12.1914

Pvte Thomas Orr. 1/5th Bn Northumberland Fusiliers 10.4. 1918

Messines Ridge (New Zealand) Memorial, Mesen, West Vlaanderen, Belgium.

Rfn Ernest Orr, 4th Bn, 3rd New Zealand Rifle brigade 7. 6.1917

L/Cpl Henry William Orr, 1st Bn, 3rd New Zealand Rifle brigade 8. 6.1917

Pvte James Orr, 1st Bn, Wellington Regiment, NZEF 29. 7.1917

Thiepval Memorial, Somme, France.

Pvte Reuben Orr, 10 Bn Royal Inniskilling Fusiliers 1. 7.1916
Pvte Robert Orr, 10 Bn Royal Inniskilling Fusiliers 1, 7.1916
Pvte William James Orr, 9 Bn Royal Inniskilling Fusiliers 1. 7.1916
Rfn. John Orr 11th Bn. Royal Irish Rifles 1. 7.1916
Rfn James Orr, 13 Bn. Royal Irish Rifles 1. 7.1916
Pvte Lionel Orr, 11th Bn Royal Inniskilling Fusiliers 1. 7.1916
L/Cpl Walter Orr,. 16th Bn Highland Light Infantry 1. 7.1916
Pvte William Orr, 2nd Bn Seaforth Highlanders 1. 7.1916
2 Lt James Kenneth Orr, 16th Bn Middlesex Regiment 1. 7.1916
Pvte Francis John Orr, 8th Bn Kings Own Yorkshire light Infantry 1. 7.1916
Capt. David Orr, 108 Coy Machine Gun Corps 1. 7.1916
L/Cpl James Miller Orr, 4th Regiment South African Infantry 10. 7.1916
Pvte William Robert Orr, 1st Bn East Surrey Regiment 29. 7.1916
Pvte John Orr, 1st The Kings (Liverpool) Regiment 8. 8.1916
L/Cpl William Orr, 2nd Bn Kings Own Scottish Borderers 23. 8.1916
Pvte Frank James Orr, 17th Bn Sherwood Foresters 3. 9.1916
Rfn Robert Orr, 7th Kings Royal Rifle Corps 15. 9.1916
Pvte George Orr 7/8th Bn Kings Own Scottish Borderers 15. 9.1916
Sgt Robert Orr, 1/7th The Kings (Liverpool) Regiment 25. 9.1916
Pvte John Orr, 20th Bn Durham Light Infantry 30. 9.1916
L/Cpl Thomas Orr, 7/8th Bn Kings Own Scottish Borderers 27.10.1916
Pvte John Orr 15th Bn Highland Light Infantry 18.11.1916
Pvte James Orr, 6/7th Bn Royal Scots Fusiliers 1. 2.1917

Pozieres Memorial, Somme, France

Rfn Nicholas Orr, 15 Bn Royal Irish Rifles 24. 3.1918
CSM Archibald Orr, 1/8th Bn Argyll & Sutherland Highlanders 21. 3.1918
Pvte David Orr, 8 Bn Black Watch (Royal Highlanders) 23. 3.1918

Pvte Henry Arthur Orr, 2/5th Bn East Lancashire Regiment 31. 3.1918

Pvte Walter Orr, 5th Dragoon Guards (Prin. Charlotte of Wales Regt) *25. 3.1918*

Villers - Bretonneux Memorial, Somme, France
(Australian Memorial)

Sgt. William Joseph Orr, 14 Bn Australian Infantry 11. 4.1917

Capt. Robert Wells Orr, 14 Bn Australian Infantry 11. 4. 1917

CSM Vincent William Orr, 23rd Bn Australian Infantry 3. 5.1917

Cpl. J Orr, 57 Bn Australian Infantry 25. 4.1918

Pvte Cuthbert Donald Orr, 42nd Bn Australian Infantry 12. 8.1918

Loos Memorial. Pas de Calais, France

Pvte John Orr, 5th Cameron Highlanders 25. 9.1915

Pvte Robert Orr. 7th Bn Seaforth Highlanders 25.9.1915

Lt Jack Alexander Anderson Orr, 2 Bn Seaforth Highlanders 12. 6.1918

Arras Flying Services Memorial, Pas de Calais, France

Lt Osborne John Orr, DFC, 204 Sqdn RAF 23.10.1918

Arras Memorial, Pas de Calais, France

Cpl Robert Orr, 1/6th Bn Argyll & Sutherland Highlanders 26. 3.1916

Pvte James Orr, 1 /8th Bn Argyll & Sutherland Highlanders 23. 4.1917

Pvte Robert Orr, 4th Bn Gordon Highlanders 23. 4.1917

Pvte Alfred Orr, 9th Bn Cameronians (Scottish Rifles) 3. 5.1917

L/Sgt. Herbert Orr, 2/7th Bn Duke of Wellingtons Regiment 3. 5.1917

Pvte Alexander Orr, 2nd Bn Gordon Highlanders 7. 5.1917
Pvte Hugh Orr, 2nd Bn Royal Scots 4. 6.1917
Sgt. David Orr, 20th (Tyneside Scottish) Northumberland Fusiliers
5. 6.1917
2 Lt Hugh Brian Orr, attd 10/11 Bn Highland Light Infantry 22.
3.1918
Sgt. Robert Orr, MM and bar, 6/7 Bn Royal Scots Fusiliers 22.
3.1918
L/Cpl William Orr, 2nd Bn Scots Guards 28. 3 1918

Vimy Memorial, Pas de Calais, France (Canadian Memorial)

Pvte George Syme Orr, 8 Bn Canadian Infantry (Manitoba Regt)
22. 5.1915
Pvte Ralph Orr, 5th Bn Canadian Infantry (Saskatchewan Regt) 22.
5.1915
Sgt David Chalmers Orr, 72nd Bn Canadian Infantry (B. C Regt)
22.11.1916
Pvte Charles Henry Orr, 3rd Canadian Infantry (Cen Ontario Rgt)
19. 8.1917
Pvte John Orr, 8 Bn Canadian Infantry (Manitoba Regt) 29. 4.1917
Pvte James Franklin Orr, 21st Bn Canadian Infantry (E Ontario Rgt)
15. 8.1917
Pvte Robert Calder Orr, 8 Bn Canadian Infantry (Manitoba Regt)
15.8.1917
Pvte Wallace Orr, 1st Bn Canadian Machine Gun Corps 1.10.1918

Cambrai Memorial, Louverval, Nord, France

Pvte Robert Sherlock Orr 9 Bn Royal Fusiliers 20.11.1917
Rfn. John Orr, 12 Bn Royal Irish Fusiliers 22.11.1917
Pvte Henry Orr, 9th (North Irish Horse) Royal Irish Fusiliers
23.11.1917
Sgt James Orr, 1st Bn Royal Irish Fusiliers 23.11.1917
L/Cpl John Orr, 2/7 Bn Duke of Wellingtons Regiment 27.11.1917

Capt. James Henry Orr, 210 Siege Bty, Royal Garrison Artillery 30.11.1917
Rfn Edwin Alfred Orr 11 Bn Rifle Brigade 3.12.1917

Le Touret, Pas de Calais, France

Pvte William Orr, 2nd Bn Scots Guards 12. 3.1915
Pvte Herbert Orr, 2nd Bn Highland Light Infantry 19. 3.1915
Pvte William Orr, 2nd Bn Black Watch (Royal Highlanders) 9. 5.1915
Pvte Joseph Smith Orr, 2nd Bn Gordon Highlanders 16. 5.1915
Pvte Hugh Orr, 2nd Bn Highland Light Infantry 17. 5.1915

La Ferte -sous-Jonarre Memorial, Seine et Marne, France (British Expeditionary Force Mons/Le Cateau, Aug - Oct 1914)

Pvte John Orr, 1st Bn Scots Guards 15. 9.1914
Pvte Thomas Orr, 1st Bn Black Watch (Royal Highlanders) 22. 9.1914

Vis en Artois, Pas de Calais, France.

Pvte Andrew Orr, 1st Bn Cameronians (Scottish Rifles) 21. 9.1918
Pvte John Orr, Hawke Division, RNVR 25. 8.1918

Memorials to the dead, missing and no known grave in the Far East, Iraq, Israel, Italy, Tasmania, Turkey, New Zealand.

Helles Memorial, Gallipoli, Turkey

Pvte David Edward Orr, Royal Marine Light Infantry 8.5.1915
AB Albert Ernest Orr, Collingwood Division, RNVR 4. 6.1915
Pvte John Orr, 1/5th Bn East Lancashire Regiment 13. 6.1915
Pvte David Orr, 1/th Bn Argyll & Sutherland Highlanders 12. 7.1915
Pvte Robert Orr, 7th Bn Highland Light Infantry 12. 7.1915

Pvte Robert Orr, 2nd (Lowland) Field Co, Royal Engineers. 12. 7.1915

L/Cpl Thomas Orr, 1/5 th Bn Argyll & Sutherland Highlanders 12. 7.1915

Lone Pine Memorial, Gallipoli, Turkey (Australian Memorial)

Pvte Joseph Orr, 15 Bn Australian Infantry 3. 5.1915

Basra Memorial, Iraq

Pvte John Young Orr 1st Bn Highland Light Infantry 11. 1.1917

Jerusalem Memorial, Palestine/Israel

Pvte Henry Orr, 1 /4th Bn Roya Scots Fusiliers 19. 4.1917

Tasmania (Hobart) Garden of Remembrance

Gunner William Robert Orr, Australian Field Artillery 15. 2.1916

Canterbury Provincial Memorial Christchurch, New Zealand (NZ forces buried at sea)

Pvte Gordon Hugh Orr, 40th Reinforcements NZEF 4. 9.1918

Memorials in WW II and those for both World Wars.

Cassino Memorial, Italy.

Sapper James Orr, 4 Field Co. Royal Canadian Engineers 5. 7.1943

Fusr. John Orr, 1st Bn Royal Irish Fusiliers 27.10.1943

Singapore Memorial, Krani Cemetery, Singapore

Pvte Hugh Orr, 2nd Bn Argyll & Sutherland Highlanders 13.1.1942

Sai Wan Memorial, Hong Kong

Gunner Terance Nolan Gibson Orr, 965 Defence Bty, Royal Artillery 1.10.1942

Rangoon Memorial, Burma

Pvte William Henry Orr, 13 Bn The Kings (Liverpool Regiment) 1. 5.1943

Lauban Memorial, (Borneo)

Pvte Edwin John Keith Orr, 8 Divn. Australian Army Service Corps. 20.3.1945
Pvte Jack Sidney Orr, 2/10 Field Amb. Australian Army Medical Corps 4.3.1945

Sydney Memorial
(Australian forces south of 20 Latitude)

Flying Offr. Neville Sinclair Orr, Royal Australian Air Force. 27.11.1943

Alamein Memorial, Egypt.

L/Cpl Frank Ernest Orr, 19 Bn New Zealane Infantry 28. 6.1942
Sgt. John Hamilton Orr, 260 Sqdn Royal New Zealand Air Force 21.3.1943

National Memorials for both Wars.

Runnymede Memorial (Air Force)

Sgt James Orr, RAFVR 14. 3.1941
Sgt Thomas Edward Orr, 224 Sqdn, RAFVR 6. 2.1942
F/Lt William Boyd Orr, 91 Sqdn RAFVR 22. 7.1942

Pilot/O Nathaniel Percy Orr, 521 Sqdn RAFVR 25. 2.1943
Sgt. Archibald Orr, RAFVR 17.5.1943
Flt Sgt Thomas Allan Orr, Royal Austalian Air Force 5. 8.1944
Flying/O George Davidson Orr, 514 Sqdn RAFVR 17. 1. 1945
Sgt. Thomas Orr, 433 Sqdn RAFVR 12. 3.1945

Portsmouth Naval Memorial

Stoker, George Thomas Orr H M S Queen Mary 31.5.1916
Gunner James Orr, 3/2 Maritime Regiment, Royal Artillery 26. 1.1942

Plymouth Memorial (Royal Navy/Marines)

Pvte. Ernest Francis James Orr H M S Invincible 31.5.1916
AB John Orr, H M S Drake 14. 7.1941
Stkr. Hugh Orr, H M S Jupiter 27. 2.1942
AB David Orr H M S Farouk 13. 6.1942
Cook, Nicholas Darcy Orr H M S Avondale 29. 1.1943
Teleg. George Ewing Orr H M M, Royal Navy 10. 4.1945

Brookwood Memorial, Surrey

Sgt James Orr, 88 Field Regt. Royal Artillery 30. 6.1941
Lt. William Jacob Orr, 1st Bn Royal Regiment of Canada 19. 8. 1942
2 Lt Charles Stewart Allan Orr, 194 Field Reg. Royal Artillery 26. 3.1943
AB Ralph Orr, H M S Lapwing 20.3.1945

Chatham Memorial, Chatham, Kent

Stoker William Orr, H M S Queen Mary 31. 5. 1916
Boy 1st Class, William Henry Orr, H M S Vanguard 9. 7.1917
AB Harry James Orr, H M S Avenger 15.11.1942
AB James Orr, HMLCI (L) 170, Royal Navy 21. 4.1943

Lee on Solent (Fleet Air Arm)

Air Mech. John Orr, H M S Hermes, RN 9. 4.1942
A/Sub Lt Peter Jardine Orr, H M S Ruler, RNVR 14. 5.1945

The Tower Hill Memorial, London (Merchant Navy)

Peter Orr M V Empire Statesman 5.12.1940
John Orr S S Lapwing 26.9.1941
William Orr S S Shuntien 23.12.1941
Nelson Joseph Orr SS Indura 30.3.1942
George Fulton Orr MV Warwick Castle 14.11.1942
Edward Orr M V Abosso 29.10.1942

They fell in the `big name` actions too:

Dunkirk

Robert Orr, Royal Army Service Corps. 17.6.1940

El Alamein & Western Desert

Alastair Graham Orr, 2 Bn Queens Own Cameron Highlanders
10.12.1940
James Alexander Orr, 2 Bn Queens Own Cameron Highlanders
31.1.1941
Walter Scott Orr 2/3 Bn Australian Infantry 21.6.1941
Robert Orr 1 Bn Gordon Highlanders 27.10.1942
H R E Orr South African Engineering Corps 17.7.1942
Frank Ernest Orr, 19 Bn New Zealand Infantry 28.6.1942
Tom McLaren Orr, Royal Electrical Mechanical Engineers
16.10.1942
Ralph Thomas Orr, 6 Field Regt, NZ Artillery 25.10.1942 A
separate article about this grave follows.

Tobruk

Harold Campbell Orr, 2/12 Field Regt, Royal Australian Artillery
15.9.1941
Thomas Orr 26 Bn New Zealand Infantry 27.11.1941

Four Orr brothers of Belfast.

The brothers theme continues in my immediate family where four
brothers - Charles, Bobby, Harold and Samuel, served during
WWII. They were the sons of Robert Orr, a veteran of WWI, in
which he served with the Royal Engineers and was wounded. He
later ran a shoe repair shop in the Shankhill Road, Belfast which he
called `The Old Contemptible`.

The record for Rifleman
Harold Smith Orr, 1st
Battalion London Irish Rifles,
Royal Ulster Rifles, is
recorded on the CWGC site.
Harold died aged 20 on 1
March 1944 on the beach at
Anzio, Italy. He is buried at
The Beach Head Cemetery,
Anzio, plot XXII, A. 3.

Rfn. Harold Smith Orr
Photo the author.

Brother, Robert, served with the Royal Ulster Rifles (1939-1946).
Tragedy in war can also strike at the extended family unit, as with
Bobby, who had a brother in law, William Kane, KIA at Cambes
Wood on 7 June 1944 and in law, Alex wounded the same day.

Rfn Robert Orr.
Photo the author.

Brother, Samuel Orr, a Sergeant in 40 Commando, Royal Marines, was killed in Malaya, 26 December 1950. His story is separately told. The eldest brother, Charles, joined the army in 1934 and saw action in 1939 on the North West frontier (India). During WW II he was in Iraq, Palestine, Egypt, Sicily, Italy and through Europe. He survived the war and then served in post war Italy, Trieste, Austria, and West Africa. The regiment was then pitched into the conflict in Korea, including the slaughter on the Imjin River in April 1951, before serving in Hong Kong. Subsequently he was in Germany, British Army of the Rhine (BAOR) at Munchen Gladbach and Wuppertal. After servce with the colours for over 21 years, he took a Commission. as a Lieutenant (Quartermaster) and was later a Captain in the Royal West Afican Frontier Force. He retired as a Captain (Quartermaster) in the Royal Ulster Rifles and emigrated with his family to Australia.

Captain C. V. Orr, 1st Bn. Royal Ulster Rifles
Photo by the author

Campaign medals Captain C. V Orr. Photo by the author

From L to R as they appear in the photo, the medals are:

India Medal with NW Frontier clasp (Waziristan Campaign)
1939-45 star
Africa star
Italy star
1939-45 Defence Medal
1939-45 Medal
Korea Medal
UN Korea Medal
Coronation Medal
Long Service and Good Conduct Medal

The cap badge is that of the Royal Ulster Rifles

Sgt. Samuel Orr, PO/X 127316 40 Commando, Royal Marines.

Please inform Charlie Sammy Killed in Malaya. Photo by the author

Samuel Orr was born 28 November 1924, son of Robert and Robertina Orr of Belfast. One of eight children, he was the third son to join the regular army. His elder brother Charles was a pre war regular. Another brother, Harold Smith Orr, just one year older than Sam was killed in action on the Anzio Beach Head, 1 March 1944. A fourth brother, Robert, served throughout WWII with the Royal Ulster Rifles (1939-46).

Sam was killed on Boxing Day 1950 while leading a patrol in support of local Police against Communist Terrorists in North Perak, Malaya. For many long years, over 30, Sam lay in a grave in the jungle of Malaya and not until the mid 1980s was he re interred with his parents in Belfast. Fifty years after his untimely death the story of how he died has come to light. I am grateful to Ken Guest, son of the police officer in overall charge of the district, for information about that ill fated day. The information comes from notes compiled by Peter J. D Guest, Royal Federation of Malaya Police, at the time officer in charge at Grik, North Perak, Malaya.

The story began with an enquiry from Ken Guest if I was the nephew of a Samuel Orr RM, killed in Malaya, who was mentioned in an article published on a web site.

Ken wrote on 14 August 2001 that:

> My Father, Peter J. D. Guest, also served in the RM (1945-47) and later (1948-63) with the Royal Federation of Malay Police. In 1950 he was the OCPD in Grik, an end of the road frontier town in N. Perak. In that capacity he led the jungle burial service near Kampong Temenggor for Sgt Orr when he was buried alongside Police Lieutenant M. R. Livingstone. It was the death of Livingstone in an ambush the previous day, Xmas day, that led the RM/Police follow up patrol on which Sgt Orr lost his life.

Ken later wrote 15 August 2001.

> Many thanks for your prompt response and offer to help source more information about Sgt. Orr. My father was actively involved in the campaign with Royal Federation of Malaya Police jungle squads from 1948 until his last jungle patrol in 1959. He remained in Malaya on other duties until 1963. Before my Father passed away I was slowly helping him put down notes about his experiences in Malaya during the Emergency. As I result of that effort I have known something of the story of Sgt Orr for many years. I am only too pleased to be able to pass back to the Orr family something of what happened all those years ago. I have transcribed the following from the my Father's note covering the period he was based at Grik in N. Perak (Sep 1950- Mar 1952).

From Peter J. D. Guest's unpublished notes: The Death of Police Lieutenant Livingstone (with permission).

About two months after the big 10th October 1950 ambush the Frontier Branch garrison out at Temenggor was changed or rather rotated. This time a European Police Lieutenant was sent up there as the O/C of the post. On 24th Dec 1950 the CTs. stopped and burnt a bus on the road out to Titi Gantong. I took a party out there and studied the scene. We found the tracks of the departing Communists and we followed these up to the top of an adjoining slope before the light failed. We then walked the four miles back to Grik that evening. I was approached by a chap named 'Jock' Storrier, who was at that time in charge of the Frontier Branch. He showed me a signal that had just come in from P/Lt. Livingstone, the Lieutenant out at Grik and a good friend.

It was transmitted from their post in kampong Temenggor, to where the post had been moved after the Tin Mine was closed by Government order. The signal said that he had just had a report that the Mine (about six miles away) was burning, and that he would go out the next morning to visit the scene. Both Storrier and I agreed that an isolated non-working Mine going up in flames was highly suspect and reeked of the bait with an ambush set. We endeavoured to signal back a message saying, "Don't go near the scene, suspect CT involvement and possible ambush". But the radio set at Temenggor had closed down and wasn't scheduled to open up again the next morning at about 8 am. On our instructions the night operator at Grik was told to try and raise Temenggor through the night to put the message across.

The next day was Christmas Day and I was called (on request) at 5 am to get geared up and have a breakfast snack before returning to the scene of the burnt bus at first light. We picked up the tracks and managed to follow them for about three more miles heading north. This was within three or four miles of the Siamese frontier. After we lost the tracks I did a square search of the area until we gave up and marched back to Grik. I reckon we had covered about fourteen or fifteen miles that morning and felt I had earned my Xmas lunch in the Rest House.

As I arrived at Grik there was frenzied activity going on. The message we had tried to send to Temenggor all night, had finally been passed at 8 am, when Temenggor came on air. The operator at Temenggor replied that a patrol under Lieutenant Livingstone had already left for the mine to investigate the fire. Storrier sent a message telling them to send a man after the patrol and recall them. The next message was that the patrol had been ambushed. Livingstone and four men had been killed and the remaining eight men all wounded. A patrol under another P/Lieutenant, David "Jock" Auld, was formed up and they were just leaving when I returned.

I gathered up my gear, organised an escort party and got away in mid afternoon to follow on after the others. I reckoned that they would get as far as the 10th mile on the track and would camp there overnight. Darkness arrived as we moved down the track but I kept my patrol going. I knew that Lieutenant Auld didn't know we were coming so as we approached the 10th mile I got my guys to call out in identification. We made contact to the surprise of the others and I asked my escort if they wanted to stay in the camp overnight. To my surprise they elected to go back in the dark and promptly left!

After sleeping overnight we set off at first light to march out to Temenggor. About half way we had to swim across the width of the Sungei Perak, making bamboo rafts to carry our weapons and gear. We got across OK and went on the last lap of about ten miles. Again, it went dark on the track but we pushed on to reach Kampong Temenggor after dark. I was dead beat, having done about fourteen to fifteen miles the previous day, followed by over ten miles extra the precious evening. Then twenty miles on this days march. We camped overnight in the Frontier Branch base of bamboo huts with palm leaved roofs.

Xmas Day 1950

The following morning a party under P/Lt. Auld's command was sent off whilst I remained to recover and brief the Marine party who were following up. I also had to arrange for the wounded men, some of whom had made their own way back to the kampong. In the course of the day our party came back with Livingstone's body and those of the four men killed in the fight at the ambush. The Marines arrived and sent out a patrol. Horror of horrors, their patrol returned with the body of their Sergeant (PO/X 127316 Sgt. Samuel Orr RM), a well known and liked character.

As burials are conducted fairly swiftly in the tropical climate for obvious reasons, we had to have graves dug for two Europeans (Police Lieutenant Livingstone and Sgt. Orr RM) and four Malayas Policemen. We arranged to hold the funerals the following morning and it was agreed with the Marines that I should conduct the burial service for the Europeans. We weren't sure of the denominations of the two chaps, so a signal was sent to the Marine Padre at Grik asking for appropriate guidance for a service acceptable to both Catholic and Protestant denominations. He duly signalled one out to us.

I remember that the Corporal involved in the accidental shooting was beside himself and we had to ensure he was accompanied at all times to safeguard him. It was quite a day.

The following morning I conducted the funeral service for the two Europeans. The Marines provided a guard of honour. Everybody gathered around and I read out the text supplied by the RM Padre and lead the Lords Prayer. The Marines fired three volleys and we left a party to fill in the graves, which we marked with two crosses made from planked wood with the names inscribed on them. We also set up a fence around the graves fashioned from bamboo. Just after that I lead the Marines to the Muslim funeral of the four Policemen at a nearby location. We remained to do patrols and help restore the morale of the kampong. After that came the long march back to Grik to complete our Xmas season. (end of note about this). More than forty years later the Royal Marines repaid this debt of honour by sending Bugler Hill in full blues uniform to play the last post at the funeral of my father.

In slowly researching events in areas my Father served in, I also heard from a former member of the Marines who was in the same

Commando unit as Sgt. Orr in N. Perak. He knew him and had this to say, "Sgt. Orr was a well known character in the Corps, a well liked SNCO".

A few months later on another operation in the same area Marine R.H.V. Eames (7792) also lost his life and my Father buried him too, next to Sgt. Orr and P/Lieut Livingstone. Some time later the graves were relocated. I believe P/Lt. Livingstone was later buried in Kumunting Rd Christian Cemetery, Taiping, Perak, West Malaysia. I do not at this point know the final location of Sgt. Orr's grave but am sure, as you have suggested, that the War Graves Commission should be able to resolve this. For your additional information my Father also had photographs both of the jungle burial service itself and the twin graves of Sgt Orr and Police Lieut. Livingstone. In the service photograph my father stands at attention centre frame back to camera looking over the graves, on the other side, facing the camera, stand the honour guard of Marines from Sgt. Orr's platoon dressed in their jungle green field uniforms.

The burial party at Temenggor led by Inspector P J D Guest
Photo courtesy of Ken Guest

A note from fellow Marine, James Robinson. RM

Having served with 40 Commando RM in Malaya, I can Remember 'Paddy' very well, He was not in my Troop, A troop, He was well known and respected member of the Commando with a wealth of experience under his belt and a credit to his unit, as with most of the casualties at that time, we did not have time to reflect, only to mourn the passing of another Good Marine, With the Commando units being widely dispersed and each Troop being out of touch for Months on end, it was a sad case when the casualty list's came through, And I have to say the only thoughts of most Marines at the time was 'lets get out there and finish it'. The Royal Marines have finally decided to erect a monument to all Marines who have been killed in Action since 1945 to the present day it's sad to say a total of 527 Marines have been killed since 1945, the monument stands by the Admiralty Arch, and is called 'The Graspan Memorial'. If I can be of any assistance please let me know.

All the best, ex Royal Marine James Robinson, 1947-1972.

Sometime in the 1980s Sam was brought home and re interred with his parents at the Belfast City Cemetery. None of the surviving family seem to know the exact circumstances in which Sam was apparently accidentally shot by one of his own men. It would have been investigated and reported at the time and efforts are being made to obtain whatever information may be available. Meanwhile I can but be sorry for the corporal involved who has had a terrible burden to carry since then. If forgiveness can lighten the load, then so be it, shed that load corporal.

It is worth recording that the Malaya campaign was a long, dreary, bloody, and largely unsung event, rather like the Korean War which was taking place at the same time. Even fifty years ago, the government's attitude to `small scale` campaigns was desultory and they did not like publicity in a post war rebuilding environment. Yet over fifty years on our servicemen are still the best and get sent to the world`s hotspots (often where their country has no direct interest) to get killed for the sake of political kudos. These

149

politicians are not worthy to lick the boots of those that fought and died with honour.

A few facts - from *Conflict and Violence in Singapore and Malaya, 1945-83* by Richard Clutterbuck provides the statistics for 1950, the bloodiest year of the entire campaign when the kill ratio of guerrilla to security force personnel was 2.5. In that dreadful year 314 police officers and 79 soldiers were killed and 1145 civilians killed or wounded. In addition 905 security force personnel were wounded. Further details about the Malaya campaign, and a memorial to those killed is to be found at http://britains-smallwars.com/malaya/

Sgt. Samuel Orr, Royal Marines   Photo by the author

Ralph Thomas Orr, (1912-1942) Bombardier, New Zealand Armed Forces.

When a friend went on holiday to visit family working in Egypt, I little realised that she would visit the El Alamein memorial. While there, and knowing of my genealogy interests, she photographed the grave of an Orr (below).

Grave of Ralph Thomas Orr, El Alamein. Photo courtesy Mrs M Gower

To my suprise not only was Bombardier Ralph Orr included in the casualties listed in an article I had written for the Guild of One Name Studies, but I was currently in contact with a New Zealand researcher, Barbara Holt, who is a relative. Ralph was a cousin to her mother and had volunteered to do his bit when war broke out. The story is further filled out, as after the end of the Boer War Thomas Henry Orr, Ralph`s father, decided to remain in South Africa where he married and raised a family. When he died in 1919 his widow and two children Doris Mildred Orr and Ralph Thomas Orr moved to New Zealand and rejoined the family there.

The First World War saw John (Jack) Clement Orr (younger brother of Thomas Henry) serving with the New Zealand Expeditionary Forces on the Somme in 1917. Born in Wellington in 1879 he was called up in 1916. Jack had the misfortune to be wounded and gassed on 22 February 1918. After hospitalisation and convalescence he returned to the front line in October 1918 in time for the armistice., finally getting home on 30 May 1919. Between 1927 and 1933 he and his wife Ruth, lived in London where Jack worked as a buyer for the clothing trade in New Zealand.

The family comes the full circle with Ralph Thomas Orr, the son of Thomas Henry. In 1939, aged 28 years, Ralph was single and worked for the Port Line Ltd in Wellington. Although declined for service at the first attempt (because he was the only son of a widow) he signed up on 7 February 1940.. By October he was with the 6th New Zealand Field regiment in Egypt. He was then shipped to Greece in 1941 before returning a few months later to Egypt. In February 1942 he was promoted to Lance Bombardier, then Bombardier in August. Sadly he was killed in action on 25 October 1942 during the second battle of El Alamein. While in Egypt he met up with a first cousin, Jack Clendon, whose mother was an Orr. They are shown with another (unnamed) soldier in the desert in 1942. The lower photograph shows Ralph as a young man, pre war, with his mother and sister. Thanks to Barbara it is possible to put a face to at least one young man who lies in a foreign field.

Three New Zealanders in the Desert 1942. Left unknown, centre Jack Clendon a cousin of (right) Ralph Thomas Orr (1912-1942)
Photo courtesy Merrilee Palmer

**Ralph with his mother
and sister**
Photo courtesy Merrilee Palmer

Part VIII

INVENTORS: Scottish Ingenuity and Entrepreneurship

My thanks to A. C. (Sandy) Orr of Scone, Perthshire, for this story of his family

"Scotch impudence and perserverance is beyond all"

History tells us that it was the ability to adapt and improve machinery and processes that saw the change from linen to cotton manufacture in the Paisley and Glasgow areas during the 1800s. With this grew a strong competition in the market place for so long enjoyed by the Lancashire cotton manufacturers. It was this competition that caused Samuel Oldknow, a Lancashire textile magnate, to utter the above comment. Concomitants of the industrial growth were more and better roads, and canals for the carriage of raw materials for the new iron works. These developments meant more employment, urban growth, higher standards of living and a demand for the conveniences of life - the consumer society and service industries began to emerge.

It was against the background of a demand from the middle classes for the `elegancies of life ` that a niche market for a carpet cleaning service was found and exploited by Alexander Orr (1839-1919) of Edinburgh. We tend to think of carpets merely as floor covering but in the 18th century it was commonly a thick woolen fabric used to cover tables and beds. The manufacture of hand made carpets as floor coverings was brought from France and it was not until the 19th century that power looms were introduced. During the 19th century homes were carpeted with free lying squares and when soiled were lifted and beaten with flails. Alexander Orr (Sr) was a cabinet maker and upholsterer who had premises in Pitt Street, Edinburgh. He started a carpet cleaning business and developed industrial machinery for the purpose which he patented in 1887. Very simply he improved the construction and way the machine beat and cleaned carpets, and the way the dust was collected. He produced his machines in three sizes, 15ft 17ft and 20ft long using Oregon pine for the casing.. On his death the rights passd to his son, Thomas (1864-1929) who had trained as an engineer and who continued production in Fettes Row, Edinburgh. These industrial machines were used by carpet cleaners, laundries, house furnishers and the like with well over a hundred in use throughout the UK and abroad.

The carpet cleaning side of the business was managed by another son, George Marshall Orr (1879-1939), who took over the manufacturing side in 1929. He continued manufacture and spent a

deal of time travelling at home and abroad supervising assembly and installation. During this period a modern dust extraction unit was added. A further son, Richard, had an interest in the busines and set up his own carpet cleaning business in Liberton, Edinburgh which closed down in 1986.

Carpet Cleaner. Photo courtesy A. C. Orr

In 1923 George Orr, now trading under his own name, moved from Fettes Row firstly to Drum Brae Road, Corstorphine and then to larger, more modern premises on the Glasgow Road, Corstorphine where he ran the business until his death in 1939. All types of rugs, carpets and tapestries were received for cleaning while repairs and alterations were carried out on traditional and oriental carpets. These services were carried out for the public and trade customers as well as for Insurance companies. A furnishing department offered an innovatory ` Home Selection Service ` where pattern books were delivered to peoples homes " for leisurely selection " From 1939 until 1959 the family of George continued to run the business before it passed to his son, Alexander C Orr. Now well into the 20th century the Orr Carpet Beating Machine was of sufficient significance to be included in the ` Design Review ` published by the Council of Industrial Design, for the 1951 Festival of Britain.

Change was, however, catching up with the market place as general standards of living improved and the introduction of fitted carpets with in situ cleaning, resulted in less lifting of carpets for cleaning. Sadly the call for the machines became less and the last two were produced in the 1960`s - a reconditioned machine for England and a final new machine with metal framework (another innovation) to South Africa. Regular orders were still executed for spares but continuation was not viable and the firm of George Orr (Machine Makers and Carpet Cleaners) ceased trading on 21 June 1968.

The invention may not rank in the public mind alongside those of some more famous Scots - John Logie Baird (TV), John Boyd Dunlop (car tyres), John Macmillan (the bicycle) or John Paul Jones (the US Navy) to mention just a few - but it did bring to many a better quality of day to day life for the best part of 100 years.

John Bryson Orr - Orr's Zinc White, a basic paint pigment.

The Industrial Revolution in Scotland did not happen overnight but the Scots already had a reputation for the design of agricultural implements and the improvement of machinery, such as Small's new plough design (1763) Andrew Meikle's power driven threshing machine (1786) and Patrick Bell's horse drawn reaper (1826). In America Hugh Orr (1717-1798) of Lochwinnoch was responsible for the introduction of the first tilt hammer, new ploughing tools - and guns for the American revolutionaries. The Scots also acquired a reputation for proactive thinking and the middle classes of the day were rapidly becoming entrepreneurs, developing new ways of manufacture and grasping the opportunities that arose from the Industrial developments in the Scottish Lowlands.

Following the American War of Independence there was an impetus to the cotton industry in Scotland and the use of new technology brought from Lancashire. This saw the likes of Neil Snodgrass of Glasgow inventing the scutching machine used in wool preparation (1792); William Kelly of New Lanark who applied power to Compton's mule (1790) and Archibald Buchanan who built the first integrated cotton mill (1807) This expansion led to other demands in bleaching, dying and printing thus the Vale of Leven enjoyed greater prosperity and saw the foundation of the St Rollox chemical works, the biggest chemical works in the world in its day, making bleaching powder.

From my perambulations round the internet I knew of the US patent Office index and had noted some six patents held by Orrs all in the field of industrial chemistry. I was therefore delighted when a fellow researcher gave me information of a privately printed book 'Orr's Zinc White - The First Fifty Years ` printed by the Imperial Smelting Corporation in 1948. and the story of an innovative home grown chemist. - John Bryson Orr (1840-1933) born in Blantyre, Lanarkshire.

J. B. Orr developed and patented a process for the manufacture of a paint pigment. ` Orr`s Zinc White ` (Patent 517 of 1874) which had a novel manufacture as it included a calcining process (heat treatment) of the basic chemicals. His process led to a major change in the pigment and paint industry. Perhaps older persons can recall with me the task of `whitewashing` or ` liming ` the walls of the detached toilet and the walls of the backyard because it brought a brightness and sense of space to it. J B Orr was the creator of `Duresco` the first washable distemper widely used on both internal and external walls.

J B Orr was the son of a dyer and was apprenticed to the firm of Lewis, McLellan and Co., Oil and Colourmen and Drysalters in Glasgow. where he studied chemistry at the Andersonian College. He travelled widely and was in Europe on the outbreak of the Franco German war so he acted as an unofficial war correspondent for a Glasgow newspaper. He returned to Glasgow and in 1872 set up a factory for the manufacture of ` lithopone ` which meant merely a white mineral product prepared artificially rather than occurring naturally.

Black is white.... sometimes

An amusing aspect of the earlier products was `a chameleon like behaviour in bright sunlight`. rather like the silver compounds used in photographic film. There is the case of a policeman on point duty in a supposedly white rubber coat but which was in fact black on the sunny side and white on the shady. And that of the farmer whose freshly painted white gate turned black at noon but was white again when the puzzled painter was brought to the scene in the late afternoon. J B Orr`s invention produced a lightfast product and in time became the basic pigment for the paint industry. In 1930 the company was merged with the Imperial Smelting Corporation Ltd of which he was a director until his death on 23 September 1933.

The significance of the invention to the town of Widnes was great. Until 1898 J B Orr had devoted himself to the colour trade but in that year he expanded into industrial development in Glasgow, then in Charlton, south east London, and then the Vine Works, Widnes. Workers of the area were long used to handling chemicals and with a good hinterland for raw materials, Widnes was a prime location for the manufacture of a product that grew to over a quarter of a million tons annually. The works was a significant employer and one renowned and way ahead of its time, for conferring benefits of pensions, welfare, forums for discussion, and opportunities for job enhancement and advancement.

Part IX

CLAIMS TO FAME

We all like to think there is someone famous in our ancestry, and in the broader family there some Orrs worthy of comment. Here are a few I have come across so far:

Congressional Medal of Honour.

The following are the citations for the awards:

Charles A. Orr.

Rank and organization: Private, Company G, 187th New York Infantry. Place and date: At Hatchers Run, Va., 27 October 1864. Entered service at: Bennington, N.Y. Birth: Holland, N.Y. Date of issue: 1 April 1898. Citation: This soldier and two others, voluntarily and under fire, rescued several wounded and helpless soldiers.

Robert L Orr.

Rank and organization: Major, 61st Pennsylvania Infantry. Place and date: At Petersburg, Va., 2 April 1865. Entered service at: Philadelphia, Pa. Born: 28 March 1836, Philadelphia, Pa. Date of issue: 28 November 1892. Citation: Carried the colors at the head of the column in the assault after two color bearers had been shot down.

USA Orrs

Very many Orrs became involved in local politics and served the community in various roles from teachers, Chief of Police, Fire Chief, Post Masters, magistrates and judges. Some went on to become Justices of the Supreme Court, others full time politicians including Alexander Dalrymple Orr (1761-1835) a great grandson of the Rev Alexander Orr of Beith, who served as Representative from Kentucky 1791-7. Benjamin G. Orr was Mayor of Washington, 1817-19; James Lawrence Orr, Governor of South Carolina 1865-8 and US Minister to Russia 1872-3; and Robert Dunkerson Orr, was Governor of Indiana, 1981-89.

Alexander Ector Orr (1831-1914). Born in Strabane, Co Tyrone, he was President of the New York Rapid Transit Commission, and Vice President of many financial institutions. He was the founder of the New York subway system.

Carey Orr (1916-1962) He joined the staff of the Chicago Examiner and had his first cartoons published in the Nashville Tennessean. He later moved to the Chicago Tribune where his work was often published on the front page, for over forty six years. His character of a tall, lean, bearded `Uncle Sam` adorned many bitingly critical cartoons. A crusader for public safety, he brandished his pen against gangsterism, waste and corruption in government, prohibition, communism, and President Franklin D. Roosevelt and the New Deal He was awarded the Pulitzer Prize in 1960. His niece was Martha Orr (1908-2001) who in 1934 created and drew the character "Apple Mary", a proud, independent lady selling apples from a pushcart during the dark days of the Depression of the 1930s.

William T. Orr (1917-2002) He began as an actor, having credits in many films of the 1930s and 1940s. But it was as an executive director that his skills blossomed and was responsible for many well known and liked television series including: Maverick (1957), 77 Sunset Strip (1958), Hawaiian Eye (1959), No Time for Sergeants (1964) and Mister Roberts (1967),

William Orr (1808-91), was a manufacturer and inventor, born in Belfast of Ulster Scot parentage. He was the first to manufacture merchantable printing paper with wood fibre in it, and made several other improvements and discoveries along similar lines.

Nathaniel Orr (b. 1822), of Scottish ancestry, retired in 1888 with the reputation of having brought the art of wood engraving to the highest perfection, and "the signature 'Orr,' cut in the block was always a sure guarantee of art excellence."

England

A William Orr, sometimes using the name Cunningham, was a highwayman in Northumberland. He was entenced to 14 years transportation but managed to escape. He was later caught and sentenced to transportation for life in September 1776.

Ireland

James Orr and John Orr of Letterkenny, Donegal, were in the Seige of Derry in 1689. They are listed on page 236 of the book called *Fighters of Derry Their Deeds and Descendants being a Chronicle of Events in Ireland during the Revolutionary Period, 1688-91,* by William R. Young, Eryre and Spottiswoode, London, (1932). They are also identified in an Act of Attainder of May 1689 when in a desperate last fling King James II declared named Protestants attainted and forfeit of goods and life. A Moore Orr was Sheriff of Londonderry in 1846.

William Orr of Farranshane (1766 – 1797). "The Patriot", was executed 14 October 1797 at Carrickfergus. He was tried by a jury that was detained overnight and well supplied with strong drink until a verdict was reached – he was convicted of being a United Irishman, and executed as an example to others. There is a separate story about him.

Convicts to Australia, 1791-1815

William "Rebel" Orr, was sentenced to transportation for life, and transported to Australia on the "Friendship". He subsequently escaped to the Sumatra islands, and later returned to Ireland. His travels and exploits are referred to in *Remember All the Orrs*, by R. H. Foy.

Edward Orr, b Antrim 1794 was a tailor in Antrim, who was sentenced to 7 years in 1814. He was transported on the "Canada".

John Orr, was sentenced to life and transported on the "Friendship".

Margaret Orr, b 1748 was sentenced to 7 years and transported in 1792 on the "Boddington".

James Orr, the Bard of Ballycarry. (1770-1816)

Although a relatively minor poet, James Orr was one of the group termed `folk` poets who often composed in the vernacular and contributed significantly to understanding the society of their day. He was born near Ballycarry in the parish of Templecorran (Broad Island) in County Antrim, in 1770. The only son of a weaver, he was said to be a spoilt child. A bachelor all his life, he was a supporter of the 1798 Rebellion and escaped to America. He soon returned under a general amnesty, and resumed farming and weaving. His first volume of poetry was published in 1804. He was a founding member of the Ballycarry Masonic Lodge and they were responsible for the erection of a large monument to him in 1831 (He died 24 April 1816). His poem "The Irishman", published in 1805, has been much quoted over the years (first verse below).

The savage loves his native shore,
Though rude the soil and chill the air;
Well then may Erin`s sons adore
Their isle, which Nature formed so fair!

What flood reflects a shore so sweet,
As Shannon great, or past`ral Bann?
Or a friend or foe can meet,
So gen`rous as an Irishman?

Rev. Robert Orr (1833-1915), Methodist Minister.

Robert Orr of Ballreagh was a prayer leader at his local church and had six sons who joined him there. Three of them - Robert, Thomas and James became preachers. The brothers featured large in the ministry of the Primitive Wesleyan Methodist church and later in the United Conference. Robert (the son) first started with itinerant preaching in 1861 until 1878 when he was appointed to Clones, then Rathdrum; Kingsland Park, Dublin; Clonakilty and Antrim. In all he completed 44 years service in the active ministry and a further 10 years in the University Road Circuit, Belfast.

There were several other Orr Minister`s, of various denominations including Rev Alexander Orr the son of James Orr of Holywood House, Co Down. He was rector of Lambeg Church of Ireland (1847-1860). His sister Jane married Gathorne Hardy, later 1st Earl of Cranbrook and his sister Catherine married Charles Hardy. Their father, James was one of the original partners in the Northern Banking Company. The Rev. John Henry Orr, DD was Moderator of the General Assembly in Belfast, 1887.

In Scotland

A Link to Robert the Bruce

An actual link back to Robert the Bruce exists in the case of the Rev Alexander Orr, minister at Hazelside, who married Barbara Crawford, a descendant of The Bruce. The Rev Alexander`s son, also a Rev Alexander, married Agnes Dalrymple of Waterside, Keir, Dumfries. Their daughter, Barbara Orr, married the Rev. John Craig. of Ruthwell. Their daughter Agnes Craig, married the Rev

Henry Duncan, saviour of the Ruthwell Cross, and founder of the Savings Bank movement in 1810.

Sheriffs

William Orr of Mitcheltoun, Lochwinnoch (d 1596) Sheriff of Renfrewshire.
Thomas Orr of Jaffraystock, Lochwinnoch (d 1598) Sheriff of Renfrewshire.
John Orr, Sheriff of Ayr (d 1609).
Marion Orr spouse of William Lightbody (d 1586), Sheriff of Lanark

Lord John Boyd Orr of Brechin (1880-1971) Born in Kilmaurs Lord Orr was Professor of Agriculture at Aberdeen University, an Independent MP; and Director General of the United Nations Food and Agriculture Organisation 1945-8. He was an eminent authority on food and nutrition and awarded the Nobel Preace Prize in 1949

Andrew Orr (1801-1872) was the son of a well known stationers in Glasgow, Francis Orr. After university he entered business and found an interest in local politics. He was soon a member of the Council from 1842-1860 and Lord Provost for three years in 1854. He received a knighthood in 1858. His particular achievements for which the residents of Glasgow were grateful was his drive to purchase land for public parks in Glasgow; and the scheme to replace the well system for water by a clean supply from Loch Katrine.

Links by Marriage in the Female Line

The Orr family have done well in their marriages as attested by the following links via the Penrose family (of Cornwall and Tasmania)

Dr Thomas Arnold.

Headmaster of Rugby School (1828 – 42) He was the son of a Customs officer and born on the Isle of Wight 13 June 1795. He was educated at Winchester College and at Corpus Christi College, Oxford where he met his lifelong friend John Taylor Coleridge. A first class honours degree followed and he became a teacher and ordained as deacon at Laleham. In 1827 he was invited to become a master at Rugby school and appointed headmaster in 1828. His impact on education was enormous, not only on his pupils at Rugby, but on the system itself. He introduced mathematics, modern languages and modern history and instituted the form system and prefects to keep discipline. Above all perhaps, he taught the pupils to think for themselves He wrote several books including *Principles of Church Reform* (1833) and was a strong campaigner for Catholic Emancipation. He married Mary Penrose ca 1820 and had five children, of whom Thomas was father of Mary Augusta and Julia Arnold.

Matthew Arnold (1822-1888).

Poet and critic. He was born in Laleham, Surrey, the eldest son of Dr Thomas Arnold. After Oxford he became a schools inspector from 1851-86. He published several volumes of poems which are highly regarded, also *Essays in Criticism* (1866, 1888), *Culture and Anarchy* (1869) and books on religion including *Literature and Dogma* (1872) and *Last Essays on Church and Religio"* (1877).

The Huxleys,

Julia Arnold, sister of Mary Augusta Arnold (Mrs Humphry Ward) married Leonard Huxley, sometime editor of *The Cornhill* magazine. Their children were:

- Julian, biologist, Director General UNESCO, author.

- Aldous, writer, born Godalming, Surrey in 1894. Educated at Eton and Balliol College, Oxford. He was a friend of D. H. Lawrence and author of *Brave New World* (1932), and *Eyeless in Gaza* (1936).

Mary Augusta Arnold aka Mrs Humphry Ward (1851-1920),

Born in Tasmania Mary came to England with her family, and in 1872 married Thomas Humphry Ward, an academic at Brasenose College, Oxford. She was a leading Victorian author writing for several periodicals. Her early work included *Robert Elsmere* a romance and spiritual story that was the basis for the setting up of a settlement for the poor of London in Tavistock Square in 1897. Her later novels were all on social and religous issues and included *Marcella* (1894), *Sir George Tressady* (1896), *The Case of Richard Meynell* (1911), *Helbeck of Bannisdale* (1898). Despite her concern for the poor She was a vehement anti suffragette and campaigned hard against the giving of votes to women. At Girton College when debating the issue she received a very torrid reception and later wrote novels that were critical of the suffragette movement including *The Testing of Diana Mallory* (1908) and *Delia Blanchflower* (1915).

Her son, Arnold Ward, MP for Watford supported her views in Parliament. When her sister Julia, died in 1908 she took her nephews, Julian and Aldous Huxley, under her wing. By 1914 she was very well known in America and was commissioned by the government to visit the Western Front and write a book about it. The object was to encourage American support for the World War that had broken out. As a result of her tour she wrote two books - *England's Effort* (1916) and *Towards the Goal* (1917). In her latter years she and her husband were beset by the debts of their son, a dissolute gambler, and they had to sell the family home to pay off his debts. She died on 26 March 1920.

Others in the Penrose family line include:

Admiral Charles Penrose (1759-1830).

Francis Cranmer Penrose (1817-1903), Astronomer, Surveyor of St Pauls.

Dame Emily Penrose, daughter of Francis Cranmer Penrose, was Principal of Somerville College, Oxford, and very influential in the campaign to admit women to degrees. In the 1890s the Somerville Council was prominent in an unsuccessful campaign to admit women to degrees; the success of the 1920 campaign owed much to the diplomatic skills and academic reputation of the then Principal, Miss (later Dame) Emily Penrose.

The commoner who really did marry her Prince was Marion Gordon Orr. She is a member of the family featured in the story of the inventor of an industrial carpet cleaner. Princess Marion d'Orleans, Comtesse de la Marche. Marion Gordon Orr was descended from John Orr (1786), Alexander (1839), and William Gordon Orr (1885). She married Thibault d' Orleans, son of Henri, Prince d' Orleans, Comte de Paris and Pretender to the throne of France. Her husband, Thiebault, was tragically killed in a hunting accident in Central Africa in 1983.

Canada

Bobby Orr - Canadian Ice Hockey player.
What more can be said than probably one of the greatest ice hockey player of all time. There are several dedicated web sites that record his playing career in sumptuous detail.

Wesley Fletcher Orr, 1831-1898. Mayor of Calgary. Wesley Fletcher Orr was born in Lachute, Quebec and married Priscilla Miller in 1861. They had three children, Addie (Wood), Maggie (Beattie) and Albert Lorne Clark. Wesley invested in Calgary property in 1883, and was assistant editor of the Calgary Herald in 1888, but left in 1889 to spend more time with his property interests and the development of Calgary. He was a very active politician and was first elected as alderman in 1888. He served no less than five terms and as Chairman of Public Works he oversaw the development of Calgary's water, sewer and electric lighting systems. He was elected mayor in 1894, shortly after Calgary was incorporated as a city, and further terms in 1895 and 1897. He was an assiduous promoter of agricultural and industrial development of the Calgary area, including railways and coal mining.

WILLIAM ORR of Farranshane, Co. Antrim. Irish Patriot

THE FIRST VICTIM

They led him forth from his prison cell!
They swung him high on the gallows tree
And the people wept as the brave man died-
Died for his faith and counterie.- Old Ballad

The execution of William Orr, Carrickfergus 14 October 1797
Reproduced from *The Northern Leaders of `98*. F. J. Bigger (1906)

William Orr was the son of a farmer and bleach-green proprietor, of Farranshane, in the county of Antrim. The family were in comfortable circumstances and there were several Orr homes in the district. William resided at Farranshane, and his brother James at Cranfield. His father, Samuel, succeeded to Kilbegs (the home farm) from his father, also Samuel, about 1796 while uncles were farmers in the area - James Orr at Creavery and John Orr at The Folly. Another uncle, William, had died young and a fifth uncle, Joseph, went to England.

F J Bigger (author of *The Northern Leaders of `98 (No. 1) William Orr* was an a great admirer of William Orr and gives a rather rosey account of events. He says that the young William received a good education, which he afterwards turned to account in the

service of his country. We know little of his early history, but we find him, on growing up to manhood, an active member of the society of United Irishmen, and remarkable for his popularity amongst his countrymen in the north. His appearance not less than his principles and declarations, was calculated to captivate the peasantry amongst whom he lived.

William Orr in prison.
Reproduced from *The Northern Leaders of `98*. F. J. Bigger (1906)

He is said to have stood six feet two inches in height, was a model of symmetry, strength, and gracefulness, and the expression of his countenance was open, frank, and manly. He was always neatly and respectably dressed - a prominent feature in his attire being a green necktie, which he wore even in his last confinement.

The original aim of `United Irishmen` was to obtain equality for all under the law, regardless of religious persuasion. However, these noble aims were soon distorted as the society became exposed to more extreme views. After about 1795 the leader of the United

Irishman, Wolfe Tone, was in France and the aims of the society turned to the use of force in order to achieve its objectives and, importantly, sought the aid of the French. In the turmoil of those times and fear of war with France, it was inevitable that the government brought in an Insurrection Act under which it was deemed a treasonable act to administer the oath of membership for the United Irishman.

The home of William Orr at Farranshane, looted and burned by the military in 1798. Reproduced from *The Northern Leaders of `98*, F.J. Bigger (1906)

William was alleged to have administered the Oath to two soldiers who informed on him, he was arrested and tried. There was great sympathy for William and many considered it a trumped up charge. Indeed the jury was locked in a room overnight and were copiously supplied with food and whiskey until they reached a decision. The judge apparently cried when handing down the mandatory sentence of death. The `guilty` verdict was followed by attempts to have it overturned - the foreman was an elderly man who was so confused he did not know what he was doing and one of the two soldiers who were witnesses was of unsound mind. Appeals were made to the powers that be but it is clear that the government wanted to make an example of William and he was executed at Carrickfergus, Co

Antrim on 14 October 1797. A a contemporary letter from Mary McCracken to her brother, Henry Joy McCracken (a leading figure in the United Irishmen) is cited in *The Life and Times of Mary Ann McCracken* by Mary McNeill, and gives a clear picture of events.

"Sept. 27, 1797

We are informed [wrote Mary to Harry] that Bills of Indictment were found at Carrick Assizes against all the State Prisoners who are present confined in Dublin, and all those who have been liberated on bail except Wm Davidson, but are not sorry to hear that the Trials cannot come on before Feby, as that of Mr. Orr's trial has clearly proved that there is neither justice nor mercy to be expected, even the greatest Aristocrats here join in lamenting his fate, but his greatness of mind renders him rather an object of envy and admiration than of compassion. I am told that his wife is gone with a letter from Lady Londonderry to her brother [Lord Camden, the Viceroy] on his behalf, if this be true I think it shows her to be equal in firmness and energy of character to her husband. If you have not already heard it you will be surprised when I tell you that old Archd Thompson of Cushendall was foreman of the Jury, and it is thought will loose his senses if Mr. Orr's sentence is put in execution, as he appears already quite distracted at the idea of a person being condemned to die thro' his ignorance, as it seems he did not at all understand the business of a juryman. However he held out from the forenoon till six o'clock in the morning tho' it is said he was beat and threatened with being wrecked and not left a sixpence in the world on his refusal to bring in the verdict guilty, neither would they let him taste of the supper or drink which was sent to the test, and of which they partook to such a beastly degree. Was it therefore to be much wondered at if an infirm old man should not have sufficient resolution to hold out against such treatment? It will not much surprise you I suppose to hear that two Attorneys have turned Informers Downpatrick, one of them cousin to Charles Brett, a doctor also has acted the same worthy part which is extraordinary from the liberal education they in general receive, but if we live long enough I suppose we will not be surprised at anything."

The cry "Remember Orr" was a watchword in the Rebellion that broke out in 1798. His speech from the dock is a humbling address:

"My friends and fellow-countrymen-In the thirty first year of my life I have been sentenced to die upon the gallows and this sentence has been in pursuance of a verdict of twelve men who should have been indifferently and impartially chosen. How far they have been so, I leave to that country from which they have been chosen to determine; and how far they have discharged their duty, I leave to their God and to themselves. They have, in pronouncing their verdict, thought proper to recommend me as an object of humane mercy. In return, I pray to God, if they have erred, to have mercy upon them. The judge who condemned me humanely shed tears in uttering, my sentence. But whether he did wisely in so highly commending the wretched informer, who swore away my life, I leave to his own cool reflection, solemnly him and all the world, with my dying breath, that that informer was foresworn.

The law under which I suffer is surely a severe one-may the makers and promoters of it be justified in the integrity of their motives, and the purity of their own lives ! By that law I am stamped a felon, but my heart disdains the imputation.

My comfortable lot, and industrious course of life, best refute the charge of being an adventurer for plunder; but if to have loved my country-to have known its wrongs-to have felt the injuries of the persecuted Catholics, and to have united with them and all other religious persuasions in the most orderly and least sanguinary means of procuring redress-if those be felonies, I am a felon, but not otherwise. Had my counsel (for whose honorable exertions I am indebted) prevailed in their motions to have me tried for high treason, rather than under the insurrection law, I should have been entitled to a full defence, and my actions have been better vindicated; but that was refused, and I must now submit to what has passed.

To the generous protection of my country I leave a beloved wife who has been constant and true to me, and whose grief for my fate has already nearly occasioned her death. I have five living children, who have been my delight. May they love their country as I have done, and die for it if needful

I trust that all my virtuous countrymen will bear me in their kind remembrance, and continue true and faithful to each other as I have been to all of them. With this last wish of my heart-nothing doubting of the success of that cause for which I suffer, and hoping for God`s merciful forgiveness of such offences as my frail nature may have at any time betrayed me into - I die in peace and charity with all mankind."

The scene on the fateful day was described thus.

Saturday morning, the 14th of October, 1797, dawned clear and bright upon the old town of Carrickfergus. Blinds were drawn, shops were closed, everywhere signs of sorrow and mourning were visible. At the prescribed hour the condemned man emerged from his prison cell and declined to use a coach, fearing that he might be separated from his friends and that soldiers might be his companions. He expressed the wish to have the company of the Rev. Mr. Stavley and the Rev. Mr. Hill upon his journey to the scaffold, and these gentlemen were permitted to sit with him in the carriage.

The authorities evidently feared an attempt at rescue as there was a strong military guard, from different regiments in Belfast and Carrickfergus. At the place of execution the infantry were drawn up in the form of a triangle round the gallows; on the outside of the infantry the cavalry continued to move; while at some distance two cannons were planted, commanding the Carrickfergus and Belfast roads. But these precautions were unnecessary. The people shunned the sight of this unpardonable butchery, and, shutting themselves up in their houses, prayed for the painless death and eternal happiness of the martyr William Orr.

When the gallows had been reached, Orr shook hands with his friends, and with an heroic attempt at cheerfulness which he could not have felt, told them to bear up bravely. With a firm step he mounted the fatal ladder, and drawing up his fine manly figure to its full height, looked unflinchingly upon the dangling rope and the bristling arms of the soldiery. The hangman stealthily advanced and slipped the noose round the neck of the condemned man. As he did so an indignant flush spread over Orr's features, and in a loud voice he exclaimed -

I am no traitor! I am persecuted for my country. I die in the true faith of a Presbyterian.

The next moment the ladder was kicked away, and the soul of the first victim stood before his God. Such was the fate of William Orr, one of the noblest men who ever breathed, and thus he died by the hand of a wicked and blood stained Government.

Dr. William Drennan, the son of a Presbyterian clergyman was a founding member of the Dublin Society of United Irishmen and later its secretary and president. He advocated " a constitutional conspiracy " which is what most of the United Irishmen had in mind until roughly 1795. He penned the famous poem *Wake of William Orr*. There is more about Dr William Drennan and the early days of the United Irishmen is in the following note about The Volunteers..

WAKE OF WILLIAM ORR.
by William Drennan

Here our worthy brother lies;
Wake not Him with women's cries;
Mourn the way that manhood ought
$it in. silent trance of thought.
Write his merits on your mind'
Morals pure and manners kind
On his head, as on a bill.
Virtue placed her citadel.
Why cut off in palmy. youth?
Truth he spoke, and acted truth.
"Countrymen, UNITE!" he cried,
And died, for what his Saviour died!
God of peace, and God of love,
Let it not thy vengeance move,

Let it not thy lightnings draw
A nation guillotined by law.
Hapless nation, rent and torn,
Early wert thou taught to mourn
Warfare of six hundred years,
Epochs marked by blood and tears.
Hunted thro' thy native grounds,
A flung REWARD to human hounds;
Each one pulled and tore his share,
Emblem of thy deep despair.
Hapless nation-hapless land,
Heap of uncementing, sand;
Crumbled by a foreign weight;
And by worse, domestic hate.
God of mercy, God of peace,
Make the mad confusion cease;
O'er the mental chaos move,
Through it speak the light of love.
Monstrous and unhappy sight,
Brother's blood will not unite;
Holy oil and holy water,
Mix, and fill the earth with slaughter.
Who is she with aspect wild?
The widowed mother with her child,
Child new stirring in the womb,
Husband waiting for the tomb.
Angel of this sacred place
Calm her soul and whisper, peace,
Cord, nor axe, nor guillotine
Make the sentence-not the sin.
Here we watch our brother's sleep,
Watch with us, but do not weep;
Watch with us through dead of night,
But expect the morning light.
Conquer fortune-persevere--
Lo! it breaks-the mornin clear!
The cheerful COCK awakes the skies,
The day is come-arise, arise
FEMINIS LUGERE HONESTUM ES VIRIS ME MINISSE."

Ballymore, October, 1797.

The Volunteers

The Treaty of Limerick in 1691 saw thousands of Jacobite supporters leave the country and the soldiers (the " Wild Geese ") take up service with France and Spain. This was of itself ominous but it left the vast majority (4/5ths) of the population, Roman Catholic, excluded from the political process. It led to the creation of a virtual church state and a Catholic `nation` was born.

The Protestants of the Church of Ireland were the only ones to be called `Protestant` and they had a monopoly on power. Neither the Catholics or the Dissenters - mainly the Presbyterians, were represented in the Irish Parliament and were subject to penal laws. They paid tithes to the Established church - the Church of Ireland, and the Catholics also paid to their own church by tradition and loyalty. The only option open to Catholics was trade and industry and they made the provisioning trade virtually their own. This led to a strong middle class and a potential ally for the aggrieved Protestant middle class.

A turning point for the movement was the decision to parade in Dublin on 4 November 1779, William III`s birthday, and declare their support for `Free Trade` ie to trade direct with the British Colonies. Their protest succeeded and a new voice in Ireland was born.

The first Convention at Dungannon 15 February 1782 saw some 250 delegates from 143 Ulster Volunteer Companies joined in debate and producing resolutions that Poynings Law (the supremacy of the Privy Council over Parliament) was unconstitutional; sought relaxation of penal laws against Catholics and repeal of the Declaratory Act which prevented service under the Crown. On 16 April1782 Henry Grattan moved a Declaration of Rights to Parliament and it was unanimously agreed; this was ratified by the English Parliament 27 May 1782. The Declaratory Act was repealed and Bills were presented to repeal Poynings Law, the Perpetual Mutiny Act and to secure the independence of the judiciary.

There was further debate that the repeal of the Declaratory Act was just that and not acceptance of the right of the Irish to legislate for Ireland. This led to a second Convention on 21 June 1782 and support for Henry Flood who had pursued the point against the de facto leader Lord Charlemont. The British Parliament finally passed a Renunciation Act explicitly giving up the right to legislate for Ireland. But the damage was done; first there was division in the leadership and thus its policies. Second, there was a growing awareness of the Volunteer Conventions which seemed to be giving instruction to the Irish Parliament.

Bitten by the power and results they had achieved, a third Convention at Dunmurry met on 8 September 1783. Here the main issues became parliamentary reform and political rights for Catholics (the latter another cause for division in the Volunteers ranks). The main resolution was that specific details of a plan to reform Parliament be brought to a National Convention in Dublin on 10 November 1783.

On 29 November Henry Flood and other MPs took a draft Bill to Parliament; this they did dressed threateningly in their Volunteer uniforms. This colossal error of judgment was their downfall. For six years Parliament had acceded to popular proposals and cooperated although they were always wary of military threat. Now, however, the American War was over and General Burgoyne was back in Ireland with 20,000 troops under his command. Parliament rejected the demands by 157 votes to 77. William Drennan later wrote that the fall of the British Empire began from that day.

The American War, repeal of the Sacramental Test, independence for the Irish Parliament, the renunciation dispute and the subsequent parliamentary and Catholic emancipation were all burning issues to the Presbyterians. It was against this backcloth that the young Dr

William Drennan graduated from medical school in Edinburgh. On his return to Belfast in August 1778 he joined the Blue Company of Belfast Volunteers where he took a keen interest in politics. He moved to Newry where he helped form the Newry Union Volunteers that included Catholics, in 1784.

A sea change in membership of the Volunteers began as more members from the lower classes, including Catholics, were recruited and the nature of the Volunteers changed. Such that in letters to Dr Bruce in February 1784, May 1785 and August 1785 Drennan was proposing that there ought to be an inner circle of radical reformers. Things came to a head as a result of proposals for a Grand Parade to celebrate Bastille Day, 17 July 1791 and a civic commemoration of the French Revolution.

By 1791 Drennan 's views and that of others, including Wolfe Tone, had become more radical and they wished to reconstruct the Volunteers. Both Tone and Drennan were approached and asked for a set of resolutions suitable for the occasion. In 1794 Drennan was charged with seditious libel that his Address to the Volunteers incited armed rising. Fortunately he had the services of John Philpot Curran as his lawyer and he was acquitted.

Tone was elected to honorary membership of the Belfast Volunteers and invited to come to Belfast " in order to assist in framing the first club of United Irishmen". The first meeting was at Barclays Tavern on 1 April 1791. Three weeks after this Napper Tandy and Drennan founded the Dublin Society of United Irishmen. Whether it was Drennan or Tone or someone else who coined the title of the United Irishmen is still debated, but the society`s existence was self evident.

At this juncture there was the influence of the French Revolution and the fear of the British government of French invasion; changing views on courses of action, the creation and involvement of the Catholic Committee; dissent amongst themselves and a pervading influence in the Volunteer movement of Freemasonry. Official perceptions were that the Volunteers were potentially dangerous and they were forbidden to parade in uniform and disbanded by Proclamation of the Lord Lieutenant in 1794. This led the Society of United Irishmen to go underground and Wolf Tone becoming resident in Paris where French assistance to join in a Revolution was his goal.

Drennans letter to Dr William Bruce 7 February 1784:
(PRONI.D553/20)

> I should like to see the institution of a society as secret as the Freemasons, whose object might be by every practicable means to put into execution plans for the complete liberation of the country. The secrecy would surround the proceedings of such a society with a certain awe and majesty, and the oath of admission would inspire enthusiasm into its members. Patriotism is too general and on that account weak. We want to be condensed into the fervent enthusiasm of sectaries, and a few active spirits could, I should hope, in this manner greatly multiply their power for promoting public good. The laws and institutes of such a society would require ample consideration: but it might accomplish much.

By 1791 his views had hardened: (PRONI. D553/70)

> It is my fixed opinion [he wrote to Bruce], that no reform in parliament, and consequently no freedom, will ever be attainable by this country but by a total separation from Britain; I think that this belief is making its way rapidly, but as yet silently, among both protestants and catholics, and I think that the four quarters of the kingdom are more unanimous in this opinion than they themselves imagine. It is for the collection of this opinion (the esoteric part, and nucleus of political Doctrine) that such a society, or interior circle, ought to be immediately established, around which another circle might be formed, whose opinions are still halting between, who are for temporizing expedients and patience, and partial reform.

Wolf Tone's credo ran thus: (Tone: Autobiography pp 50-51)

To subvert the tyranny of our execrable government, to break the connection with England, the never-failing source of all our political evils, and to assert the independence of my country - these were my objects. To unite the whole people of Ireland, to abolish the memory of all past dissensions, and to substitute the common name of Irishman in place of the denominations of Protestant, Catholic and Dissenter - these were my means.

And over 200 years later the squabbling and injustice on all sides goes on.......

Mary Allan's letter about Samuel Redmond Orr.

An interesting letter from a Mary Allen in 1899 describes a possible connection with William Orr. This has subsequently been validated in Bob Foy's book *Remembering all the Orrs*. William had a brother Samuel (1774-1831) who married Mary Redmond (1761-1836). They had ten children some of whom died as infants, but six went to America including Samuel Redmond Orr b 1793.

This is a typed version of the letter from Mary A Allen and the connection via Samuel brother to William Orr of Farranshane, 1761-1797.

"Erie, Whiteside Co, Dec 26th 1899

Mr Samuel Redmond Orr

My Dear Sir,

You will pardon my addressing you; my excuse is a letter from your brother Daniel Orr of Ogdenburg, Lawrence Co, NY, who informed me of your personality and place of residence. I am the daughter of John Orr who died at Sidney the County of Hastings, Province of Ontario about AD 1870 whom I can barely remember; he came not far from 1820 and remained until the close of his life; he was the son of Samuel Orr of Belfast, Ireland

and nephew of William Orr who was wickedly executed at Carrickfergus on the 14th of October 1797 for an alleged political offence charged as a felony. Your brother kindly furnished information that yourself and he are the sons of Hugh Orr, who was a son of Samuel Orr and nephew of William Orr who was excecuted at Carrickfergus as above stated. His further information is that his father Hugh had a brother John who settled, lived and died on Quente Bay, Hastings Co, Ontario also a brother William who lived at Prescott, Canada. A third brother Joseph who always remained in Ireland, although one sister (whose name he does not give) who always lived in Ireland, but who visited his and your father in AD 1844 and at the same time, or occasion visited "John" (or his family) on Quente Bay; he knows of no other brother or sister of his father than the foregoing. It was current in my family with my mother (who died) when I was fifteen years of age) her brothers and sisters, my grandmother and my older brothers and sisters, that our father (Johns) family (all sons and daughters of Samuel Orr and nephews and nieces of William Orr above mentioned) consisted of Hugh, Mary and John (my father) by the first wife of Samuel Orr; and Joseph, James and Margaret by Samuels second marriage which was with a Miss Redmond; that Hugh visited my father once about 1823 or 4 and returnd to Ireland; that James visited him at Sidney, Hastings Co., after the visit of Hugh returned to Ireland and afterwards came back to America and was for a time at Montreal and permanently remained in America. but did not see John after his visit to the latter. That Margaret visited America three times and resided at Johns house twice. I have very vivid recollection of her last visit to us, it was about the year AD 1844 - I sat upon her lap- her tears fell on my face and she plead with my mother to take me with her back to Ireland. I remember this very distinctly, my father was then dead. Mary whom I have always understood was the full sister of my father, John, never visited him though my family heard she once came to America, and the talk in our family was that the half sister Margaret, had more affection for John than his full sister Mary. I was told by my mother that John was fonder of Margaret than Mary, who always understood that Joseph remained in Ireland and never heard that Hugh settled in this country, nor that our father John had a brother William, and I am without any doubt that my father John was visited by a brother, known to my mother and the older children of my father as James. - my mother liked James well and frequently mentioned him as a fine care less boy. Your brothers family history has striking points of resemblance to my knowledge of my own, you will perceive the differences. William Orr certainly can not be duplicated; William Orr was certainly my great uncle, bitterness against the English government in consequence of his execution was rife in our family from my earliest recollection. I venture to hope that you being the senior of your brother Daniel, might aid me with further knowledge that you might have. Last summer for the first time for many years, I visited my birthplace in Hastings Co, Ontario and was told by the widows of my brothers that about six or seven years ago an acquaintance of theirs who had just then returned from Ogdensburg, told them that he had met a gentleman who said he was the son of Hugh Orr and had known the descendants of his uncle John, living round the Bay of Quente, and to say to them that it was not his place to visit them but if they would write to him he would give them "family information" that would be of much interest to them. On my return home I caused correspondence to be had with Ogdensburg and the result is the information which your brother has given me. Would it be asking too much of you to write me what you know of the subject on which I have written ?

Most respectfully yours,
Mary A Allen.

Hugh Orr of Lochwinnoch, Renfrewshire and Bridgewater, Massachusetts, USA.

Hugh Orr was born in Lochwinnoch in Renfrewshire on 13 January 1717. His father, Robert, was a maltster, meaning he made malt for brewing beer and probably operated a public house. His mother was Margaret and possibly also with the maiden name Orr. Lochwinnoch was for a very long time a centre for the Orrs in Scotland and marriage with cousins was very common.

Hugh was brought up to be a tradesman - variously described as a locksmith, door lock filer, a gunsmith. and manufacturer of agricultural tools such as plough shears and scythes. As was typical of the day he was able to turn his hand to most things and this he demonstrated in later life. In 1737 he left Scotland and went to America where he eventually settled about 1740 in East Bridgewater, Massachusetts. In Bridgewater he set up the first tilt or trip hammer in the area and began to produce the new agricultural implements, the metal shears for ploughs as well as other edge tools such as axes and scythes. In 1753 he made a machine for dressing flax and became an exporter of flax seed His initiative and industry led to a spread of tool manufacturers in other states, including nearby Connecticut and Rhode Island.

By the time of the conflagration with Britain he was well established as an iron founder and a manufacturer of arms. In 1748 he produced 500 muskets for the province of Massachusetts Bay which were the first of their kind manufactured in America; these were carried away by the British when they abandoned Boston. During the Revolutionary War he was much involved in manufacturing of iron and brass cannon and cannon balls and set up a foundry with a Frenchman. In *Colonial and Revolutionary Families of Pennsylvania, Vol 1 (Kent family)* there is a note that

> May 15 1777, Colonel Hugh Orr is directed to complete twenty cannon, twelve - pounders, for the Continental ship "Raleigh", to

be sent by Captain Thompson to Province, where he was to receive a quantity of pig iron from the ship "Columbus".

Hugh Orr later extended his business interests to agricultural produce and flax seed which he exported to his father in Scotland.

In 1786 he employed two fellow Scots, brothers Robert and Alexander Barr to build him carding, roping and spinning machines. These were probably the first "jenny" and "stock-card" machines made in the United States. With the growth of his business interests Hugh began to purchase land, mainly in the Bridgewater area and, it transpires, largely from his relatives by marriage. It is quite likely that his increasing prosperity meant that he was able to help less well off relatives. The *Native Soil Manuscripts Index* provides several examples of his initiative and possibly philanthropy.

Hugh Orr was an entrepreneur, a Senator, a patriot and, moreover, a diligent worker for his family and his new country.

Year	Location	Comments
1742	Bridgewater, MA	bought of Timothy Edson, ninety rods and a quarter.
1752	Mendon, MA	bought 5 acres of Ebenezer Byrom for eight pounds.
1759	Bridgewater, MA	bought of Ebenezer Byram 227 acres for £968.
1760	Bridgewater, MA	bought of William Allan, 10 acres and dwelling house for £80.
1760	Bridgewater, MA	bought 1.1/2 acre from Byram for six pounds.
1766	Newton, MA	bought 6 acres and 98 rods for £8.6s.8d.
1769	Milton, MA	bought 28 acres of Mary Cargill, for £100.

1769	Plymouth, MA	bought 24 acres of Jonathan Orcutt with dwelling house.
1770	Bridgewater, MA	land from Eleazor Washburn - inheritance or forfeiture ?
1770	Bridgewater, MA	bought late John Carey, cornmill £52.13s.4d
1770	Ashfield, MA	bought of Jonathan Edson, 1.1/2 acres 26 rods for six shillings.
1771	Bridgewater, MA	acquired 6 acres of Eunice Cary. Settlement of some kind.
1772	Claremont, NH	bought property of late John Alden for twenty four pounds.
1775	Bridgewater, MA	bought of Alden land for twenty four pounds.
1779	Claremont, NH	bought of Benjamin Alden 60 acres for £150.
1794	Hartford, CT	bought 1.1/3 acres of Timothy Edson for twenty shillings.
1798	Falmouth, MA	bought of Sara Crosswell land in Plymouth $269.17
1799	Bridgewater, MA	bought 32 acres for £245.11.0d.

Hugh Orr married Mary Bass (b 21 March 1724) in East Bridgewater on 4 August 1742 and had at least three children: Jannet Orr, Susanna Orr (b 1752 d 20 December 1836) and Robert (b1746 d 5 Feb 1811) As Colonel Robert Orr this son was the master-armourer at the US Arsenal at Springfield, Massachusetts. Robert is alao credited with inventing an improved method of making scythes and was the first manufacturer of iron shovels in New England. Other children named by varying sources are: Hugh, James, Charlotte, Matilda, Rosanna, Jean/Jane, Bethia, Margaret, Bathsheba.

Links to the Pilgrim Fathers through Marriage

Mary Bass was the daughter of Captain Jonathan Bass (1697-17 May 1750) and Susanna Byram (15 Jan 1649-19 Sep 1783). Captain Bass was the son of Samuel Bass and Mary Adams and Susanna was the daughter of Nicholas Byram and Mary Edson. Going back a further generation, Samuel Bass was the son of John Bass and Ruth Alden. This lady was the daughter of Pilgrim John Alden.

Nicholas Byram was the son of Nicholas Byram and Susannah Shaw. Samuel Bass was the son of Samuel Bass and Anne Saville of Saffron Walden, Essex, England.

A second line links to Pilgrim William Bradford through Jannet Orr, the daughter of Hugh and Mary Bass. Jannet married Cushing Mitchel who was the son of Edward Mitchel and Elizabeth Cushing. Edward Mitchel married Alice Bradford, daughter of John Bradford and Mercy Warren. John Bradford was the son of William Bradford Jr and Alice Richards. William Jr. was the son of Pilgrim William Bradford and Alice Carpenter.

With a growing position and status in society Hugh Orr entered politics and for several years was Senator for Plymouth County, MA. He died in Bridgewater on 6 December 1798 in his 82nd year.

Some Orrs in Corstorphine, Edinburgh

This is a family group that was collated during general research of the Orr name and provided a link to the McCullough family in Queensland, Australia.

First Generation

1. John ORR.

John married Christian GORDON. Christian died in 1784.

They had the following children:

2	i.	James (1742-)
	ii.	Patrick. Born on 13 Nov 1748.
	iii.	John. Born on 5 Aug 1751.
	iv.	Margaret. Born on 16 Aug 1745.
3	v.	Helen (1739-)

Second Generation

2. James ORR. Born on 22 Oct 1742.

In 1773 when James was 30, he married Agnes BISSET, in Kirkliston,.
They had the following children:

4	i.	James (1786-<1861)
	ii.	John. Born in 1774.
	iii.	Anne. Born in 1776.
	iv.	Janet. Born in 1777.
	v.	Eupham. Born in 1780.
	vi.	E. Born in 1785.
	vii.	Peter. Born in 1789.
	viii.	William. Born in 1793.
	ix.	Ian ? Born in 1791.

3. Helen ORR. Born on 16 Sep 1739.

On 2 Aug 1760 when Helen was 20, she married Robert YOUNG, in Kirkliston,. Robert died on 12 Oct 1821.

They had the following children:

	i.	John. Born on 5 Dec 1760.
	ii.	Robert. Born in 1778.
5	iii.	Elizabeth (1780-)

Third Generation

4. James ORR. Born in 1786 in Kirkliston, Midlothian. James died bef 1861, he was 75. Occupation: Agricultural labourer; ploughman.

In 1806 when James was 20, he married Barbara BISHOP, in Kirkliston,. Born in 1786 in Ratho, Midlothian.
They had the following children:

6	i.	Agnes (1815-)
7	ii.	James (1812-)
8	iii.	John (?1821-)
9	iv.	William (1821-)
	v.	Alexander. Born in 1827 in Corstorphine.

Alexander married WILDE.

	vi.	Christian. Born in 1808.
	vii.	Robert.
	viii.	Ian ?.

5. Elizabeth YOUNG. Born on 6 May 1780 in Colinton, Midlothian.

On 17 Feb 1803 when Elizabeth was 22, she married Alexander SUTHERLAND, in Canongate, Edinburgh.

They had the following children:

| 10 | i. | Helen (Ellen) (1804-1882) |
| | ii. | William. Born on 6 Jun 1806. |

Fourth Generation

6. **Agnes ORR.** Born in 1815 in Kirkliston,. Occupation: Laundress, previously general servant.

On 29 Aug 1841 when Agnes was 26, she married Robert SMITH, son of John SMITH, in Corstorphine. Born in 1813 in Midlothian.

They had the following children:

11	i.	John (1844-)
	ii.	James. Born in 1849 in Corstorphine. Occupation: Joiner.
	iii.	Barbara. Born in 1852 in Corstorphine. Occupation: Laundress.

7. **James ORR.** Born in 1812 in Kirkliston,. Occupation: Turnpike labourer.

On 16 Oct 1837 when James was 25, he married Mary BROWN, in Edinburgh St Cuthberts. Born in 1816 in Inveresk.

They had the following children:

12	i.	James (1839-)
13	ii.	William (1841-)
	iii.	Barbara. Born on 21 May 1845 in Corstorphine.
14	iv.	John (1848-)
	v.	Helen. Born on 21 Jan 1854 in Corstorphine, Midlothian.
	vi.	Jane. Born on 14 Dec 1855 in Corstorphine, Midlothian.
	vii.	Hettler/Heather.

8. John ORR. Born ? 1821 in Cramond, Edinburgh.

On 12 Dec 1847 when John was 26, he married Jane STARK, in Corstorphine. Born in 1824 in Coulter, Lanarks.

They had the following children:

   i.   William. Born in 1853 in Corstorphine.
       Occupation: Nursery gardener.

William married Helen. Born in 1857 in Leith, Edinburgh.

   ii.   James. Born on 21 Jun 1855 in Corstorphine.
       Occupation: 1881 Census unemployed
       footman.
   iii.   Grace. Born on 7 May 1857 in Corstorphine.
   iv.   Alexander. Born on 25 Jan 1859 in
       Corstorphine.
   v.   Barbara Bishop. Born on 3 Sep 1861 in
       Corstorphine.
   vi.   Marion Henderson. Born on 19 Sep 1865 in
       Corstorphine.

9. William ORR. Born in 1821 in Corstorphine, Meadowhouse.

On 27 Nov 1854 when William was 33, he married BONNAR Elizabeth, daughter of Elizabeth MONTEITH, in Edinburgh. Born in 1831 in Dunfermline, Fife.

They had the following children:

   i.   James Leslie. Born on 7 Nov 1855 in
   Colinton, Midlothian. Occupation: Accountants Clerk.
   ii.   Elizabeth Monteith. Born on 11 Feb 1861 in
       Corstorphine.
   iii.   William Bonnar. Born on 31 Oct 1863 in
   Edinburgh St Cuthbert. Occupation: Apprentice grocer.
   iv.   Elizabeth Monteith. Born on 24 Jul 1857 in
       Colinton, Midlothian.

10. Helen (Ellen) SUTHERLAND. Born on 6 May 1804 in Slateford. Helen (Ellen) died in 2 Heriot Mt., Edinburgh on 3 May 1882, she was 77.

On 8 Oct 1824 when Helen (Ellen) was 20, she married James MUIRHEAD, son of Hugh MUIRHEAD & Margaret JOHNSTON, in Corstorphine. Born on 16 Jan 1801 in Currie, Midlothian. James died in 3 Lower Brand Place. on 12 Jul 1876, he was 75.

They had the following children:

	i.	James. Born in 1825.
	ii.	Alexander. Born in 1827.
	iii.	Margaret. Born in 1830.
	iv.	Hugh. Born in 1833.
15	v.	Elizabeth (1836-1918)
	vi.	Helen. Born in 1839.
	vii.	Marion. Born in 1845.

Fifth Generation

11. John SMITH. Born in 1844 in Corstorphine. Occupation: Gardener.

John married Isabella MORRISON, daughter of MORRISON & Jane. Born in 1837 in Foveran.

They had the following children:

i.	Isabella. Born in 1866 in Foveran. Occupation: servant 1881.
ii.	Agnes. Born in 1868 in Corstorphine.
iii.	Robert. Born in 1869 in Corstorphine. Occupation: Railway surfaceman.
iv.	Alexander M. Born in 1871 in Corstorphine. Occupation: Joiner.

12. James ORR. Born on 12 Feb 1839 in Corstorphine. Occupation:

Labourer in oil works. 1891 Census roadman.

On 17 Nov 1868 when James was 29, he married Margaret CORSTORPHINE, daughter of James CORSTORPHINE and Isabella MILLAR, in Corstorphine.[14] Born in 1837.

They had the following children:

- i.   Isabella. Born on 6 Feb 1870 in West Calder.[15]
- ii.   James. Born in 1875 in West Calder. Occupation: Butcher.
- iii.   John Henry. Born in 1877 in Corstorphine. Occupation: 1891 Census scholar.
- iv.   Alfred T. Born in 1879 in Corstorphine. Occupation: 1891 Census scholar.
- v.   Margaret. Born on 31 Aug 1871 in West Calder.
- vi.   Rachel. Born on 3 Apr 1873 in West Calder.

13. William ORR. Born on 17 Jan 1841 in Corstorphine. Occupation: Labourer in oil works in 1881.

On 7 Jun 1861 when William was 20, he married Elizabeth GOODALL, in Leith, Edinburgh. Born in 1838 in Edinburgh.

They had the following children:

- i.   William. Born in 1860 in Linlithgow.
- ii.   James. Born on 11 Nov 1861 in Edinburgh Parish, Edinburgh. Occupation: Labourer in oil works.
- iii.   Agnes. Born on 5 Jan 1865 in Edinburgh Parish, Edinburgh.
- iv.   John. Born on 11 Dec 1866 in Corstorphine. Occupation: Waggon greaser.
- v.   Elizabeth. Born on 11 Apr 1869 in Corstorphine.

vi.   Hannah. Born on 8 May 1871 in Corstorphine.

vii.   George Brown. Born on 4 Aug 1873 in West Calder, Edinburgh.

viii.   Alexander. Born in 1876 in West Calder, Edinburgh.

ix.   infant. Born on 4 Dec 1863.

14. John ORR. Born in 1848 in Corstorphine, Midlothian. Occupation: Labourer.

John married Janet. Born in 1847 in Corstorphine.

They had the following children:

i.   Jane. Born in 1875 in St Cuthberts, Edinburgh.

ii.   James. Born in 1878 in St Cuthberts, Edinburgh.

iii.   Barbara. Born in 1880 in St Cuthberts, Edinburgh.

15. Elizabeth MUIRHEAD. Born on 4 May 1836 in Borthwick, Midlothian. Elizabeth died in Monkton Hall Tce. on 27 Mar 1918, she was 81.

On 3 Dec 1858 when Elizabeth was 22, she married David WHITELAW, son of David WHITELAW & Elizabeth CAIRNS. Born on 3 Mar 1835 in Seton, Elgin. David died on 7 Jun 1890, he was 55.

They had one child:

i. James Muirhead (1863-1944)

Sixth Generation

16. James Muirhead WHITELAW. Born on 26 Jul 1863 in Mansfield Cottage. James Muirhead died in 26 Bernhard St., Paddington, Qld. Australia on 25 Aug 1944, he was 81.

On 6 Jan 1887 when James Muirhead was 23, he married Esther Belcher HINTON, daughter of Henry HINTON & Elizabeth BELCHER, in Christ Church, Milton, Queensland, Australia. Born on 19 Dec 1863 in 2 Frederick St.. Wales. Esther Belcher died in 26 Bernhard St., Paddington, Qld. Australia. on 21 Mar 1940, she was 76.

They had one child:
  17 i.   Edna Rose (1903-1981)

This links to the McCulloch line.

Index

Esther Janice	19
Gail Andrea	23
Heather Marie	21
James Hamilton	spouse of 17
MORRISON	
Isabella	spouse of 11
MUIRHEAD	
Alexander	child of 10
Elizabeth	15
Helen	child of 10
Hugh	child of 10
James	spouse of 10
James	child of 10
Margaret	child of 10
Marion	child of 10
ORR	
Agnes	6
Agnes	child of 13
Alexander	child of 4
Alexander	child of 13
Alexander	child of 8
Alfred T.	child of 12
Anne	child of 2
Barbara	child of 7
Barbara	child of 14
Barbara Bishop	child of 8
Christian	child of 4
E	child of 2
Elizabeth	child of 13
Elizabeth Monteith	child of 9
Elizabeth Monteith	child of 9
Eupham	child of 2
George Brown	child of 13
Grace	child of 8
Hannah	child of 13
Helen	child of 7

Helen	3
Hettler/Heather	child of 7
Ian ?	child of 2
Ian ?	child of 4
infant	child of 13
Isabella	child of 12
James	4
James	7
James	12
James	child of 12
James	child of 13
James	child of 8
James	child of 14
James	2
James Leslie	child of 9
Jane	child of 7
Jane	child of 14
Janet	child of 2
John	8
John	14
John	child of 13
John	child of 2
John	1
John	child of 1
John Henry	child of 12
Margaret	child of 12
Margaret	child of 1
Marion Henderson	child of 8
Patrick	child of 1
Peter	child of 2
Rachel	child of 12
Robert	child of 4
William	9
William	13
William	child of 13
William	child of 8

William	child of 2
William Bonnar	child of 9
SMITH	
Agnes	child of 11
Alexander M	child of 11
Barbara	child of 6
Isabella	child of 11
James	child of 6
John	11
Robert	spouse of 6
Robert	child of 11
STARK	
Jane	spouse of 8
SUTHERLAND	
Alexander	spouse of 5
Helen (Ellen)	10
William	child of 5
WHITELAW	
David	spouse of 15
Edna Rose	17
James Muirhead	16
YOUNG	
Elizabeth	5
John	child of 3
Robert	spouse of 3
Robert	child of 3

William Orr, Lochwinnoch. Ten "Bonnet Lairds"

A `bonnet laird` was a farmer who physically worked his land ie he was not an absentee landlord relying on the labour of others.

This file is a 10 generations line of William Orr, compiled from copy notes which seem to be extracts from the Cairn of Lochwinnoch, Andro Craefurd [Andrew Crawford] 1837; and the Kaim Orr Genealogy by William Hogarth Kerr. pub Scottish Genealogist Vol 17 #2, 1970. There are obvious place name links ie farm names, but it is difficult to interpolate this with other files because of the repetitive christian names of William, Robert. James, Mary, Elizabeth etc. used by the families.

The source document gives some dates (year) and where a date is clearly identified the full dates have been entered as shown in the IGI (Note: these dates have not been further verified). This file was cross checked with a descendant of William Orr, Auldyard, in October 1999.

First Generation

1. William ORR.

William ORR married Margaret BIGGART, daughter of Thomas BIGGART of Brigend. Margaret died in 1601.

They had the following children:

	i.	Janet. Born in 1601.
	ii.	Robert.
2	iii.	William (-1685)
	iv.	John.

Second Generation

2. William ORR. Born in before 1601. William died in 1685.

ca 1630 William first married Isobel AITKEN. Isobel died in 1651 in Lochwinnoch.

They had one child:

      3   i.   William (ca1630-)

In 1674 William second married Isobel or Janet Orr MONTGOMERY.

Third Generation

3. William ORR. Born ca 1630. Occupation: Farmer.

On 12 11 1657 when William was 27, he married Jenet ADAMS, in Lochwinnoch.

They had the following children:
               i.   Janet. Born in 1677.
               ii.   William (-1710)

Fourth Generation

4. William ORR. William died in 1710. Occupation: Farmer in Kame. Religion: Covenanter. Refused to take Test confined Tollbooth. Relented and released 1685.

William married Issobell DOWNY/DOWNIE.

They had one child:

5   i.   William (ca1680-)

Fifth Generation

5. William ORR. Born ca 1680. Occupation: Farmer Kame.

On 2 9 1698 when William was 18, he first married Margaret ROBISON/ROBINSON, in Kilbirnie.

They had the following children:

6	i.	William (ca1701-)
7	ii.	Margaret
	iii.	Jean.
		On 20 6 1722 Jean married Hugh BRYDINE.
8	iv.	Isobel (1707-)
9	v.	James (1710-)
	vi.	Janet. Born in 1713. Janet married John AITKEN.
	vii.	John. Born in 1715.
	viii.	Ann. Born in 1718.
		On 5 1 1751 when Ann was 33, she married Robert BURNS, in Dunlop.
	ix.	Mary. Born in 1721.
		On 12 9 1739 when Mary was 18, she married David HENDERSON, in Paisley.
	x.	Agnes. Born in 1724.
		Agnes married James WHITE.

On 30 6 1731 when William was 51, he second married Jean ORR, in Lochwinnoch.

Sixth Generation

6. William ORR. Born ca 1701. Occupation: Farmer in Kame; portioner.

On 14 11 1732 when William was 31, he married Janet ORR, daughter of James ORR, in Lochwinnoch.

They had the following children:

10 i.   William (1736-ca1800)
    ii.   Margaret. Born in 1733. Margaret died in Died young.
    iii.   Janet. Born in 1735. Janet died in Died young.
    iv.   James. Born in 1738. James died in Died young.
    v.   Margaret. Born in 1740. On 23 6 1761 when Margaret was 21, she married Robert ADAM, son of Robert ADAM, in Lochwinnoch.
    vi.   James. Born in 1743. On 5 8 1780 when James was 37, he married Janet AITKEN, daughter of John AITKEN, in Lochwinnoch.
    vii.   Jean. Born in 1745. On 13 4 1771 when Jean was 26, she married William CAMPBELL, son of William CAMPBELL, in Lochwinnoch.
    viii. Mary. Mary first married Matthew CLARK. Mary second married Hugh FAIRSERVICE.
    ix.   John. John married Margaret EWING.
    x.   Robert. Born in 1753.

7. Margaret ORR.

In 1721 Margaret married William (?) CRAWFORD, son of George CRAWFORD.

They had the following children:

    i.   John. Occupation: Weaver, in Paisley.
    ii.   Janet.
    iii.   Margaret. Margaret married Matthew CRAWFORD. Born in Lochwinnoch.

8. Isobel ORR. Born in 1707.

On 11 4 1730 when Isobel was 23, she married Gavin COCHRANE, son of James COCHRANE.

They had one child:

    i.   UNNAMED who married BOAG.

9. James ORR. Born in 1710. Occupation: Farmer, Kame and Fairhill.

James married WYLLIE Janet, daughter of John WYLLIE.

They had the following children:

    i.   John. Born ca 1732. In 1753 when John was 21, he married Margaret GLEN, in Greenbrae.
    ii.   William. Born in 1744. Occupation: Farmer, Auldyards. On 22 8 1772 when William was 28, he married Mary HOLM/ HOME, daughter of Robert HOLM/HOME, in Lochwinnoch.
    iii.   John. Born in 1746. John married.
    iv.   James. Born in 1751. On 6 7 1793 when James was 42, he married Margaret POLLOK, in Lochwinnoch.

Seventh Generation

10. William ORR. Born in 1736. William died ca 1800, he was 64.

William married Agnes POLLOK, daughter of Matthew POLLOK.

They had the following children:

    i.   William. Born in 1772. William died young.

	ii.	Janet. Born in 1774. On 12 1 1793 when Janet was 19, she married William BARBOUR, in Lochwinnoch.
	iii.	Jean. Born ca 1776. On 13 5 1797 when Jean was 21, she married James KER(R), in Lochwinnoch.
	iv.	Mary. Born in 1778. Mary died in Died young.
11	v.	William (1780-)
	vi.	Agnes. Born in 1781. On 4 6 1803 when Agnes was 22, she married William ORR, son of James ORR, in Lochwinnoch.
12	vii.	Robert (1783-)
	viii.	John. Born in 1785. In 1807 when John was 22, he married TODHILL.
	ix.	Mary. Born in 1787. On 31 8 1805 when Mary was 18, she married William BARBOUR, in Lochwinnoch.
	x.	Matthew. Born in 1789. On 27 3 1811 when Matthew was 22, he married Elizabeth " Bethia " SEDGWICK, in Paisley.
	xi.	Margaret. Born in 1791. On 6 11 1819 when Margaret was 28, she married William LOGAN, in Lochwinnoch.

Eighth Generation

11. William ORR. Born in 1780.

On 3 8 1805 when William was 25, he married Janet BRODIE, daughter of James BRODIE, in Lochwinnoch.

They had the following children:

13	i.	William (1806-1868)
	ii.	Margaret. On 2 2 1828 Margaret married Robert CAMPBELL, in Lochwinnoch.
	iii.	Agnes. Born in 1809.

iv.	Janet. Born in 1813.
v.	Marion. Born in 1815.
vi.	Jacobina. Born in 1818. On 17 11 1846 when Jacobina was 28, she married John Buchanan NEWLANDS, in Lochwinnoch.
vii.	Elizabeth. Born in 1820.
viii.	Ann. Born in 1822.
ix.	James. Born in 1826.

12. Robert ORR. Born in 1783. Occupation: Weaver, Lochwinnoch.

On 4 7 1807 when Robert was 24, he married Jean HENDRY/HENRY, daughter of Robert HENDRY, in Lochwinnoch.

They had one child:

| | i. | Agnes. Born on 6 5 1810. |

Ninth Generation

13. William ORR. Born in 1806. William died on 1 2 1868, he was 62.

On 4 4 1846 when William was 40, he first married Margaret CONNEL, in Lochwinnoch. Margaret died on 15 8 1862 in Lochwinnoch.

They had one child:

| 14 | i. | Margaret (1851-) |

On 10 10 1865 when William was 59, he second married Christina Sophia McBRIDE, in Locranza, Isle of Bute.

They had one child:

| | i. | William. Born in 1866. William died in 1919, he was 53. |

206

Tenth Generation

14. Margaret ORR. Born in 1851.
On 8 11 1869 when Margaret was 18, she married James DICKIE, in Lochwinnoch.

They had the following children:

<ul>
<li>i.   Eliza Constance.</li>
<li>ii.   Mabel Margaret. She married James STEVENSON.</li>
<li>iii.   Janet.</li>
<li>iv.   Robert.</li>
<li>v.   Margaret. Margaret died before 1920.</li>
</ul>

Index

|---|---|
Janet	child of 1
WYLLIE Janet	spouse of 9
John	child of 1
Robert	child of 1
William ORR	1
ADAMS	
Jenet	spouse of 3
AITKEN	
Isobel	spouse of 2
BIGGART	
Margaret	spouse of 1
BRODIE	
Janet	spouse of 11
COCHRANE	
UNNAMED	child of 8
Gavin	spouse of 8
CONNEL	
Margaret	spouse of 13
CRAWFORD	
Janet	child of 7
John	child of 7
Margaret	child of 7

William (?)	spouse of 7
DICKIE	
Eliza Constance	child of 14
James	spouse of 14
Janet	child of 14
Mabel Margaret	child of 14
Margaret	child of 14
Robert	child of 14
DOWNY DOWNIE	
Issobell	spouse of 4
HENDRY HENRY	
Jean	spouse of 12
McBRIDE	
Christina Sophia	spouse of 13
MONTGOMERY	
Isobel or Janet Orr	spouse of 2
ORR	
Agnes	child of 5
Agnes	child of 10
Agnes	child of 12
Agnes	child of 11
Ann	child of 5
Ann	child of 11
Elizabeth	child of 11
Isobel	8
Jacobina	child of 11
James	9
James	child of 9
James	child of 6
James	child of 6
James	child of 11
Janet	child of 3
Janet	child of 5
Janet	spouse of 6
Janet	child of 6
Janet	child of 10
Janet	child of 11
Jean	spouse of 5
Jean	child of 5

Jean	child of 6
Jean	child of 10
John	child of 5
John	child of 9
John	child of 9
John	child of 6
John	child of 10
Margaret	7
Margaret	child of 6
Margaret	child of 6
Margaret	child of 10
Margaret	child of 11
Margaret	14
Marion	child of 11
Mary	child of 5
Mary	child of 6
Mary	child of 10
Mary	child of 10
Matthew	child of 10
Robert	child of 6
Robert	12
William	4
William	5
William	6
William	child of 9
William	10
William	child of 10
William	11
William	13
William	child of 13
William	2
William	3

POLLOK

Agnes	spouse of 10

ROBISON or ROBINSON

Margaret	spouse of 5

The descendants of the Rev. Alexander Orr of Dumfries

First Generation

1. Rev Alexander ORR. Born ca 1650. Alexander died in 1710, he was 60. Occupation: Minister at Beith, Ayrshire 1689 and 6 May 1693 at St Quivox. Education: University of Glasgow degree 13 July 1671. Religion: Presbyterian and a Covenanter.

In 1677 when Alexander was 27, he married Barbara CRAWFURD, daughter of William C CRAWFURD & Anna LAMONT.

They had the following children:

2	i.	Alexander (1686-1767)
	ii.	Archibald. Born on 24 Jul 1691.
	iii.	Anna. Born ca 1688.

Second Generation

2. Rev Alexander ORR. Born in 1686. Alexander died in Hoddam, Dumfries on 19 Jun 1767, he was 81. Occupation: Minister at Muirkirk 1717 and 1729 at Hoddam, Dumfries.

On 25 Jan 1722 when Alexander was 36, he married Agnes DALRYMPLE, daughter of John DALRYMPLE & Agnes COPLAND. Born ca 1697. Agnes died on 21 May 1760, she was 63.

They had the following children:

3	i.	Alexander (1725-1774)
	ii.	Patrick. Born on 12 Oct 1727 in Waterside, Dumfries.
	iii.	William. Born in 1729. William died in Mar 1760, he was 31.
4	iv.	John (1726-)

5   v.   Barbara (1723-1804)
        vi.   Susan.

In 1768 Susan married William MURRAY, son of William M. MURRAY.

6   vii.   Agnes (1722-1809)

Third Generation

3. Alexander ORR. Born on 23 Mar 1725 in Muirkirk. Alexander died in Nov 1774, he was 49. Occupation: Writer to the Signet (lawyer).   He   resided   mainly   in   Edinburgh.

On 1 Jul 1761 when Alexander was 36, he married Elizabeth CANT, daughter of Ludovick CANT. Elizabeth died in Mar 1811.

They had the following children:

        i.   Alexander. Born on 8 Apr 1764 in
                Edinburgh. Alexander died in at sea with his
                family. Occupation: Colonel East India Co.
7   ii.   John (-1813)
        iii.   Elizabeth. Born on 3 Jun 1762 in Edinburgh.
                Elizabeth married John BALFOUR.
        iv.   Agnes. Born on 3 Apr 1767 in Edinburgh.
                Agnes died in 1846, she was 78.
        v.   Louisa. Born on 23 Apr 1769 in Edinburgh.

4. John ORR. Born in 1726 in Waterside, Dumfries. Occupation: Merchant in Whitehaven then in London County, Virginia, USA.

Children:
        i   Alexander Dalrymple. Born ca 1765. He became a
                long serving Congressman for Kentucky (p189).
        ii.   Benjamin. Born ca 1768.
        iii.   John Dalrymple.

iv.   William. Born ca 1783.
v.   Ann. She married Hugh STEWART.
vi.   Elizabeth. Born ca 1780.
vii.   Susanna. Born in 1784.
viii.   Eleanor. Born in 1773.

5. Barbara ORR. Born on 10 Oct 1723 in Waterside, Dumfries.
Barbara died in 1804, she was 80.

On 5 Oct 1767 when Barbara was 43, she married Rev John
CRAIG. John died in 1798.

They had one child:
        8   i.   Agnes

6. Agnes ORR. Born on 9 Nov 1722 in Waterside, Dumfries. Agnes
died in Canongate, Edinburgh. on 11 Jun 1809, she was 86.

In 1750 when Agnes was 27, she married Rev William YOUNG.
William died in 1761.

They had one child:
        9   i.   Agnes (-1812)

Fourth Generation

7. John ORR. Born in Edinburgh. John died on 2 Jun 1813.
Occupation: Surgeon East India Co.

In 1807 John married Mary Ann WILLIAMS. Born ca 1790.
Mary Ann died on 9 Apr 1883, she was 93.

They had the following children:

      i.   John Balfour. Born in Apr 1810.

      ii.   Elizabeth. Born in 1809 in 18 Jan 1809.

Elizabeth who died on 1 Sep 1882, she was 73.

In Jun 1839 when Elizabeth was 30, she married Commander Alexander AITKIN RN

      iii.   Louisa. Born on 8 Nov 1811. Died on 14 Mar 1847, she was 35. She married Charles Heath WILSON.

      iv.   Frances. Born on 18 Feb 1813. Frances died in Nov 1836, she was 23.

8. Agnes CRAIG.

In 1804 Agnes married Rev Henry DUNCAN. Founder of the Savings Bank movement. He was responsible for saving the unique eighteen foot high, 7 C Ruthwell Cross, now restored within Ruthwell Kirk.

They had the following children:

              i.   George John Craig.

    10   ii.   William Wallace (-1836)

9. Agnes YOUNG. Agnes died in 1812.

In 1780 Agnes married Rev Thomas HARDY DD, son of Rev Henry HARDIE & Anne HALKERSTON. Born in 1748. Thomas died in 1798, he was 50.

They had the following children:

    11   i.   Sophia (1792-1845)

           ii.   Henry. Born in 1783. Henry died in 1807, he was 24. Occupation: Law student.

          iii.   William. Born in 1785. William died ca 1824. Occupation: East India Co.

William married Jane HUNTER, daughter of James HUNTER RN. Jane died ca 1877.

	iv.	Charles. Born in 1788. Charles died in 1814, he was 26. Occupation: Minister of Dunning, Perthshire.
12	v.	Thomas (1794-1836)
	vi.	Hugh Blair. Born in 1796. Hugh Blair died in 1797, he was 1.
	vii.	Agnes. Born in 1782. Agnes died in 1805, she was 23.
	viii.	Ann. Born in 1787. Ann died in 1857, aged 70.
	ix.	Janet. Born in 1790. Janet died in 1847, aged 57.

Fifth Generation

10. Rev William Wallace DUNCAN. William Wallace died in 1836.

In 1836 William Wallace married Mary LUNDIE, daughter of Rev Robert LUNDIE.

They had one child:

| | | |
| 13 | i. | Henry Robert |

11. Sophia HARDY. Born in 1792. Sophia died in Reading. on 8 Jan 1845, she was 53. Buried in Reading.

In 1819 when Sophia was 27, she first married Robert ALLAN FRCS, son of John ALLAN & Ann ORMSTON. Born on 6 Feb 1777 in Scotts Close, Edinburgh. Robert died in Edinburgh. on 26 Dec 1826, he was 49.

They had the following children:

14	i.	Agnes (-1890)
	ii.	James. Born on 16 May 1826 in Edinburgh.

James died in Sheffield on 19 Mar 1866, he was 39. Buried in Sheffield.

iii.   John. He died in infancy.

Sophia second married Gilbert BERTRAM. Gilbert died in 1817.

They had the following children:

i.   Thomas Hardy. Born on 21 Feb 1813. Thomas Hardy died ca 1889, he was 75. Occupation: Engineer Gt Western Railway Co.

Thomas Hardy married Helen McCALL, daughter of William McCALL.

ii.   William. who died young.

12. Thomas HARDY FRCS. Born in 1794. Thomas died in 1836, he was 42. Occupation: Surgeon in Edinburgh.

Thomas married Robina FORRESTER, daughter of Robert FORRESTER & Henrietta PORTEOUS. Robina died in 1877.

They had the following children:

15	i.	Thomas
16	ii.	Robert Forrester (-1883)
	iii.	Henry.
	iv.	William Forrester.

William Forrester married Emma Brent COONS.

	v.	Henrietta Porteous.
	vi.	Agnes Young. She died in 1852.
	vii.	Robina Forrester.

Sixth Generation

13. Rev Henry Robert DUNCAN. Occupation: Minister of Seville.

In 1875 Henry Robert married Catherine CHERRY, daughter of Alexander Inglis CHERRY ICS.

They had one child:

    17   i.   William Wallace

14. Agnes ALLAN. Agnes died on 13 Oct 1890.

On 24 Apr 1847 Agnes married John McCALL.

They had the following children:
    18   i.   William
           ii.   John. John died in 1870.
    19   iii.   Hardy Bertram
    20   iv.   Allan
           v.   Janet Sophia.

Janet Sophia married Ransome WALLIS.

15. Rev Thomas HARDY. Occupation: Minister of Fowlis Wester, Perthshire.

Thomas married Helen Isabella LISTON, daughter of Rev William LISTON & Mary FORBES.

They had the following children:

           i.   Mary Forbes. She died in 1875.
           ii.   Robina Forrester. She married William REID.

iii.   Henrietta Porteous. She married Rev Frank
SCOTT.

iv.   Helen Liston.

16. Robert Forrester HARDY. Robert Forrester died on 19 Apr
1883.

Robert Forrester married Janet WALKER, daughter of Rev James
WALKER.

They had the following children:

i.   Robert Forrester. He married Kitty Augiusta
JUDD.

ii.   Phillip.

Seventh Generation

17. William Wallace DUNCAN. Occupation: Minister at
Worcester.

In 1908 William Wallace married Violet Mary CLARKE, daughter
of Col. Henry Stephenson CLARKE.

They had one child:
i.   Henry Lundie.

In 1934 Henry Lundie married Diana Ethel INKSON, daughter of
Col. E. T. INKSON VC.

18. William McCALL.

William married Leonora Emily WHITTINGHAM.

They had the following children:

i.   Winifred Marion.
ii.   Janet Leonora.
iii.   Agnes Helen.

19. Hardy Bertram McCALL.

Hardy Bertram married Vida Mary ANDERSON.

They had one child:

i.   Vida Mary.

20. Allan McCALL.

In 1883 Allan married Ruth Helen SHOOBRIDGE.

They had the following children:

i.   William George.
ii.   Charles Howard Gibson.
iii.   John Lloyd.
iv.   Dorothy Ruth.

Index

CANT
Elizabeth   spouse of 3
CHERRY
Catherine   spouse of 13
CLARKE
Violet Mary   spouse of 17
CRAIG
Agnes   8
Rev John   spouse of 5
CRAWFURD
Barbara   spouse of 1
DALRYMPLE
Agnes   spouse of 2
DUNCAN
George John Craig   child of 8
Rev Henry   spouse of 8
Henry Lundie   child of 17
Rev Henry Robert   13
William Wallace   17
Rev William Wallace   10
FORRESTER
Robina   spouse of 12
HARDY
Agnes   child of 9
Agnes Young   child of 12
Ann   child of 9
Rev Charles   child of 9
Helen Liston   child of 15
Henrietta Porteous   child of 12
Henrietta Porteous   child of 15
Henry   child of 9
Henry   child of 12
Hugh Blair   child of 9
Janet   child of 9
Mary Forbes   child of 15
Phillip   child of 16

Robert Forrester	16
Robert Forrester	child of 16
Robina Forrester	child of 15
Robina Forrester	child of 12
Sophia	11
Rev Thomas DD	spouse of 9
Thomas FRCS	12
Rev Thomas	15
Captain William	child of 9
William Forrester	child of 12
LISTON	
Helen Isabella	spouse of 15
LUNDIE	
Mary	spouse of 10
McCALL	
Agnes Helen	child of 18
Allan	20
Charles Howard Gibson	child of 20
Dorothy Ruth	child of 20
Hardy Bertram	19
Janet Leonora	child of 18
Janet Sophia	child of 14
John	spouse of 14
John	child of 14
John Lloyd	child of 20
Vida Mary	child of 19
William	18
William George	child of 20
Winifred Marion	child of 18
ORR	
Agnes	6
Agnes	child of 3
Rev Alexander	2
Alexander	3
Col. Alexander	child of 3
Rev Alexander	1

Alexander Dalrymple	child of 4
Ann	child of 4
Anna	child of 1
Archibald	child of 1
Barbara	5
Benjamin	child of 4
Eleanor	child of 4
Elizabeth	child of 3
Elizabeth	child of 7
Elizabeth	child of 4
Frances	child of 7
John	4
John	7
John Balfour	child of 7
John Dalrymple	child of 4
Louisa	child of 3
Louisa	child of 7
Patrick	child of 2
Susan	child of 2
Susanna	child of 4
William	child of 2
William	child of 4
SHOOBRIDGE	
Ruth Helen	spouse of 20
WALKER	
Janet	spouse of 16
WHITTINGHAM	
Leonora Emily	spouse of 18
WILLIAMS	
Mary Ann	spouse of 7
YOUNG	
Agnes	9
Rev William	spouse of 6

The Dalrymple connection to Orr of Dumfries.

First Generation

1. John DALRYMPLE. Born in 1560. John died on 25 Mar 1625, he was 65. Buried in Keir Dumfries.

Children:

2	i.	John
	ii.	Malcolm.

Second Generation

2. John DALRYMPLE.

John married Katherine THOMSON.

They had one child:

3	i.	John

Third Generation

3. John DALRYMPLE.

John married Elizabeth HERRIES, daughter of William HERRIES & Marion McGILL.

They had the following children:

4	i.	John (1668-1731)
5	ii.	Robert
	iii.	Nicholas.

Nicholas married John FAIRGRAVE.

6   iv.   Isobel (-1770)

        v.   Katharine. Born in 1677. She died on 19 Jan 1752, she was 75. Katharine married but her spouse is not known.

Fourth Generation

4. John DALRYMPLE. Born in 1668. John died in 1731, he was 63. Buried in Keir Dumfries. Occupation: Chamberlain to the Duke of Queensberry.

John married Agnes COPLAND, daughter of John COPLAND & Agnes HAIRSTANES.

They had the following children:

    7   i.   Agnes (ca1697-1760)

        ii.   Elizabeth. She married William MURRAY.

        iii.   Susan. On 9 Jun 1737 she married Dugald MAXWELL.

        iv.   William. Born in Waterside, Dumfries. he died in 1760. Buried in Keir, Dumfries. Occupation: Chamberlain to Duke of Queensberry.

        v.   Hugh. Born in 1699. died on 26 Mar 1722, he was 23. Buried in Keir, Dumfries.

5. Robert DALRYMPLE. Occupation: Writer to the Signet (Lawyer). agent for the Stair family.

Children:

        i.   Hugh. Occupation: Lawyer, Gov. General of Grenada; also author and poet.

        ii.   Primrose. Occupation: Captain (? Navy ?).

6. Isobel DALRYMPLE. Isobel died on 4 Dec 1770. Buried in Keir Dumfries.

In 1721 Isobel married Rev Alexander BAYNE, son of John
BAYNE. Alexander died on 15 May 1776.

They had the following children:
- i.   Mary. Born on 4 Apr 1722. On 11 Aug 1793
  when Mary was 71, she married Rev William
  FORRESTER.
- ii.   Elizabeth. Born on 3 Jun 1723. On 26 Apr
  1750 when Elizabeth was 26, she married
  James ALISONE.
- iii.   Herries. On 19 Dec 1739 Herries married
  Alex BROWN.

Fifth Generation

7. Agnes DALRYMPLE. Born ca 1697. Agnes died on 21 May
1760, she was 63.

On 25 Jan 1722 when Agnes was 25, she married Rev Alexander
ORR, son of Rev Alexander ORR & Barbara CRAWFURD. Born
in 1686. Alexander died in Hoddam, Dumfries on 19 Jun 1767, he
was 81.

They had the following children:
- 8   i.   Alexander (1725-1774)
-    ii.   Patrick. Born on 12 Oct 1727 in Waterside,
  Dumfries.
-    iii.   William. Born in 1729. He died in March
  1760, aged 31.
- 9   iv.   John (1726-)
- 10   v.   Barbara (1723-1804)
-    vi.   Susan. In 1768 she married William
  MURRAY, son of William M. MURRAY.
- 11   vii.   Agnes (1722-1809)

Sixth Generation

8. Alexander ORR. Born on 23 Mar 1725 in Muirkirk. Alexander died in Nov 1774, he was 49. Occupation: Writer to the Signet (lawyer). Resided mainly in Edinburgh. On 1 Jul 1761 when he was 36, he married Elizabeth CANT, daughter of Ludovick CANT. Elizabeth died in Mar 1811.

They had the following children:

	i.	Alexander. Born on 8 Apr 1764 in Edinburgh. Alexander died in at sea with his family. Occupation: Colonel East India Co.
12	ii.	John (-1813)
	iii.	Elizabeth. Born on 3 Jun 1762 in Edinburgh. She married John BALFOUR.
	iv.	Agnes. Born on 3 Apr 1767 in Edinburgh. Agnes died in 1846, she was 78.
	v.	Louisa. Born on 23 Apr 1769 in Edinburgh.

9. John ORR. Born in 1726 in Waterside, Dumfries. Occupation: Merchant in Whitehaven then in London County, Virginia, USA.

Children:	i.	Alexander Dalrymple. Born ca 1765.
	ii.	Benjamin. Born ca 1768.
	iii.	John Dalrymple
	iv.	William. Born ca 1783.
	v.	Ann. She Hugh STEWART.
	vi.	Elizabeth. Born ca 1780.
	vii.	Susanna. Born in 1784.
	viii.	Eleanor. Born in 1773.

10. Barbara ORR. Born on 10 Oct 1723 in Waterside, Dumfries. Barbara died in 1804, she was 80.

11. Agnes ORR. Born on 9 Nov 1722 in Waterside, Dumfries. Agnes died in Canongate, Edinburgh. on 11 Jun 1809, she was 86.

On 5 Oct 1767 when Barbara was 43, she married Rev John CRAIG. John died in 1798.

They had one child:

    13   i.   Agnes

In 1750 when Agnes was 27, she married Rev William YOUNG. William died in 1761.

They had one child:

    14   i.   Agnes (-1812)

Seventh Generation

12. John ORR. Born in Edinburgh. John died on 2 Jun 1813. Occupation: Surgeon East India Co.

In 1807 John married Mary Ann WILLIAMS. Born ca 1790. Mary Ann died on 9 Apr 1883, aged 93.

They had the following children:

        i.   John Balfour. Born in Apr 1810.
        ii.   Elizabeth. Born in 1809 in 18 Jan 1809. Elizabeth died on 1 Sep 1882, she was 73.

In Jun 1839 when Elizabeth was 30, she married Commander Alexander AITKIN RN.

        iii.   Louisa. Born on 8 Nov 1811. She died on 14 Mar 1847, aged 35. Louisa married Charles Heath WILSON.
        iv.   Frances. Born on 18 Feb 1813. Frances died in Nov 1836, she was 23.

13. Agnes CRAIG.

In 1804 Agnes married Rev Henry DUNCAN.

They had the following children:

     i.   George John Craig.
     ii.   William Wallace (-1836)

14. Agnes YOUNG. Agnes died in 1812.

In 1780 Agnes married Rev Thomas HARDY DD, son of Rev Henry HARDIE & Ann HALKERSTON. Born in 1748. Thomas died in 1798, he was 50.

They had the following children:

     i.   Sophia (1792-1845)
     ii.   Henry. Born in 1783. Henry died in 1807, he was 24. Occupation: Law student.
     iii.   William. Born in 1785. William died ca 1824, he was 39. Occupation: East India Co.

William married Jane HUNTER, daughter of James HUNTER RN. Jane died ca 1877.

     iv.   Charles. Born in 1788. Charles died in 1814, he was 26. Occupation: Minister of Dunning, Perthshire.
     v.   Thomas (1794-1836)
     vi.   Hugh Blair. Born in 1796. Hugh Blair died in 1797, he was 1.
     vii.   Agnes. Born in 1782. Agnes died in 1805, she was 23.
     viii.   Ann. Born in 1787,she died in 1857, aged 70.
     ix.   Janet.Born in 1790,she died in 1847, aged 57.

Index

CANT
   Elizabeth   spouse of 8

COPLAND
   Agnes   spouse of 4

CRAIG
   Agnes   13
   Rev John   spouse of 10

DALRYMPLE
   Agnes   7
   Elizabeth   child of 4
   Hugh   child of 4
   Hugh   child of 5
   Isobel   6
   John   4
   John   2
   John   3
   John   1
   Katharine   child of 3
   Malcolm   child of 1
   Nicholas   child of 3
   Primrose   child of 5
   Robert   5
   Susan   child of 4
   William   child of 4

DUNCAN
   George John Craig   child of 13
   Rev Henry   spouse of 13

HARDY
   Agnes   child of 14
   Ann   child of 14
   Rev Charles   child of 14
   Henry   child of 14
   Hugh Blair   child of 14
   Janet   child of 14
   Rev Thomas DD   spouse of 14

Captain William	child of 14
HERRIES	
Elizabeth	spouse of 3
ORR	
Agnes	11
Agnes	child of 8
Rev Alexander	spouse of 7
Alexander	8
Col. Alexander	child of 8
Alexander Dalrymple	child of 9
Ann	child of 9
Barbara	10
Benjamin	child of 9
Eleanor	child of 9
Elizabeth	child of 8
Elizabeth	child of 12
Elizabeth	child of 9
Frances	child of 12
John	9
John	12
John Balfour	child of 12
John Dalrymple	child of 9
Louisa	child of 8
Louisa	child of 12
Patrick	child of 7
Susan	child of 7
Susanna	child of 9
William	child of 7
William	child of 9
THOMSON	
Katherine	spouse of 2
WILLIAMS	
Mary Ann	spouse of 12
YOUNG	
Agnes	14
Rev William	spouse of 11

The link to King Robert The Bruce.

The link to King Robert the Bruce runs thus:
Robert the Bruce married Isabella daughter of Donald, Earl of Mar

Their daughter Marjorie married Walter Stewart, High Steward of
Scotland.

Their son King Robert II married Elizabeth, daughter of Sir Adam
Mure of Abercorn.

Their 2nd son, Robert Stewart, Duke of Albany, Regent of Scotland
married Margaret Stewart, Countess of Monteith.

Their daughter Marjory Stewart married Sir Duncan Campbell of
Lochow.. Their son was Colin Campbell, 1st Earl of Argyll.

He married Isabel, daughter of John Stewart, Lord Lorn, Earl of
Athol

Their daughter, Lady Helen Campbell married Hugh Montgomerie
1st Earl of Eglinton.

Thir son John Montgomerie, Master of Montgomerie, married
Elizabeth daughter of Sir A. Edmonston, of Duntreath.

Their son. Hugh, 2nd Earl Eglinton, married Mariota daughter of
George Seton, 4th Lord Seton.

Their son. Hugh, 3rd Earl Eglinton, married Margaret Drummond,
daughter of Sir John Drummond of Innpeffrey.

Their daughter. Lady Ann Montgomerie, married Robert Semple
4th Lord Semple.

Their daughter, Barbara married Sir Colin Lamont of Inneryne,.

Their daughter Anna, married William Crawfurd, son of Patrick Crawfurd and Jean Craufurd. William died in 1674.
They had the following children:

i.   Barbara
ii.   Jean who married Patrick Craufurd.
iii.   Anna who married James Bruce.
iv.   Margaret who married James Young.
v.   Archibald

Barbara Crawfurd married Rev Alexander ORR. of Hazelside, qv Dumfries on 25 May 1683.

The Honourable Judge Smith Orr - Orrville, Wayne Co., Ohio

Judge Smith Orr   Photo courtesy Deb Spano

Orrville, Wayne Co. Ohio is a pioneer town named after Judge Smith Orr, son of Ulster Scot Samuel Orr, who went to America in 1801. Living a hard frugal, life the family managed to buy small plots of land and gradually accumulated some 300 acres. Some of this land was used to found the township that bears the family name.

The family originated from Talliard, Parish of Donoghkiddy, barony of Strabane, Co. Tyrone. The townland is associated. with Lisconbuy, Cloghogie and Benelealy in the *Civil Survey of Donegal, Londonderry and Tyrone* (Simmington, Irish Manuscripts Commission). Smith Orr was the youngest child of 8 born in 1797 but at the cost of a mother, Sarah, who died in childbirth. Following the 1798 Rebellion and its aftermath the family sailed for a new life in America in 1801. They settled first in New Castle, Delaware and it was not until 1812 that Samuel decided to take his family West. They took a stage coach to Cumberland, Maryland, which was the end of the line, and then joined a wagon train along the Old National Pike. They left the wagon train at Wheeling on the Ohio River and went forward pushing hand carts to arrive in the late Spring of 1812 in East Union Township, Wayne Co. and settled on a farm at Apple Creek. Samuel died in 1818 and is buried in the old cemetery there.

Smith Orr was reared in the wilderness that was all about them and learnt to read and write at home; importantly he also learnt mathematics and was subsequently a surveyor in the community and the state for 40 years. He married Maria Foreman in 1818 and began married life in a log cabin on Apple Creek. They bought a small farm in Baughman Township in 1821 and in 1825 they bought the 160 acre `home farm` one mile south of where Orrville now stands. They lived here until 1854 and their only child, William, was born there in 1826.

Over the years Smith Orr saw opportunities with the coming of the railroad and set up a saw mill for supplying railway ties and fuel logs as well as buying several small plots of land, The plots were subsequently set out as those for the new town that would become Orrville. He was elected a justice of the peace at a young age and re elected for over 25 years; and was selected to be a judge of the Common Pleas Court which he held until abolished by the Constitution of Ohio in 1853. Smith took an active part in politics and was a member of the Union Convention which met in

Baltimore in 1864 and re nominated President Abraham Lincoln. He died in 1865 and is buried in the old cemetery in Orrville.

The Orr monument, Orrville

Orrville is a hub for the family in Ohio and some excellent work was done by a local inhabitant, L G Weiss, who constructed a substantial family tree in 1968 and amended it in 1972. The family tree that follows is in the form of a Register Report, and has been updated from my own research and contacts with descendants; my special thanks to Deb Spano in New York and Vinson Tate in Ohio for their help and contribution.

Close up, the Orr memorial, Orrville. Photo courtesy Deb Spano

The Orr family, founders of Orrville, Wayne Co., Ohio

Much of the early work on this tree was done by L Weiss of Orrville (1972). Additional information has been supplied by Debora Spano, Vinson Tate and the author. For the purpose of this tree, dates of birth and marriages after 1899 are omitted, except when the person is deceased.

First Generation

1. Samuel ORR. Born abt 1725 in Coleraine.

Samuel married and had one child:

      2   i.   Samuel (c1750-1818)

Second Generation

2. Samuel ORR. Born abt 1750 in the Parish of. Donoghkiddy, Strabane, Co Tyrone. Samuel died in Apple Creek, Ohio in 1818, he was 68. He is buried in Apple Creek Cemetery, Wayne Co., Ohio. Tallord is mentioned which is almost certainly Tullyard near Strabane. There are two Tullyards within ca 6 miles of one another a) Donaghedy Parish, b) Desertcreat Parish. Abt 1776 when Samuel was 26, he married Sarah (SMITH), probably in Co Tyrone. Sarah died on 23 Nov 1797 In childbirth.

They had the following children:

3	i.	Smith (1797-1865)
4	ii.	Hugh (1779-1853)
	iii.	Sarah. Born in 1784 in Antrim.
5	iv.	James (1789-1873)
6	v.	Samuel (1791-1865)
7	vi.	Robert (~1777-1856)
	vii.	Margaret
	viii.	William

Third Generation

3. Smith ORR. Born on 22 Nov 1797 his mother d in childbirth, N Ireland (Tyrone). Smith died in Orrville, Ohio on 23 Apr 1865, he was 67. He is buried in Old Cemetery, East Church St, Orrville, Ohio. Occupation: Judge.

On 1 Feb 1821 when Smith was 23, he married Maria FOREMAN, daughter of David FOREMAN, in Wayne Co. Ohio. Born in 1799. Maria died in Orrville, Ohio in 1865, she was 66.

They had one child:

     8   i.   William M (1826-1893)

4. Hugh ORR. Born in 1779 in Antrim. Hugh died in Canaan Township, Ohio in 1853, he was 74. Buried in Wayne Presbyterian Cemetery.

On 14 Jul 1814 when Hugh was 35, he married Nancy STEEL, in Wayne Co. Ohio. Born in 1794. Nancy died in Canaan Township, Ohio in 1862, she was 68.

They had the following children:

     9   i.   Robert (1818-1866)
   10   ii.   James (1820-1891)
           iii.   Sarah. Born in 1824. Sarah died in Canaan Township, Ohio in 1873, she was 49. She married Cyrus STRATTON. Cyrus died in Canaan Township, Ohio.
           iv.   Samuel. Born in 1828 in Canaan Township and died there in 1846, he was 18.

5. James ORR. Born in 1789 in Antrim. James died in Apple Creek/Orrville, Ohio in 1873, he was 84. Buried in Apple Creek Cemetery, Ohio.

James first married Maria. Born in 1800. Maria died in Apple Creek in 1832, she was 32.

They had the following children:

	i.	Sarah A..
	ii.	William M.
11	iii.	Elizabeth
	iv.	Henry C.
	v.	Thomas B.
12	vi.	Samuel S (1819-1849)
	vii.	Barr.
	viii.	Joseph.
	ix.	Maria. She married SLEIGHMAN.

James second married Roseltha KENDRICK.

They had the following children:

	i.	Amanda.
	ii.	Martha.
	iii.	Emma.
	iv.	Ella.
	v.	Cordella.
	vi.	Charles.
	vii.	Davis.
13	viii.	James T (1828-?1860)

6. Samuel ORR. Born in 1791 possibly in Antrim. Samuel died in Apple Creek Ohio in 1865, he was 74.

Samuel married Mary BURNETT.

They had the following children:

14	i.	Thomas B (1821-1894)

15	ii.	Samuel (1825-1904)
16	iii.	Jane Anderson (1815-1904)
17	iv.	Smith (1826-1902)
	v.	David.
	vi.	Alfred.
18	vii.	Levi C (1830-1899)
19	viii.	William C (1833-1909)
	ix.	James T. Born in 1827.

7. **Robert ORR.** Born abt 1777. Robert died in Salt Twp. OH in 1856, he was 79. He is buried in Fredericksburg Cem.

Robert married Catherine ??. Born in 1784. Catherine ?? died in Salt Twp OH in 1855, she was 71.

They had the following children:

20	i.	John (1828-1910)
	ii.	Christina. Born in 1816. She died in Fredericksburg, OH in 1896, aged 80.
	iii.	Mary. Born in 1820. She died in Fredericksburg, OH in 1899, aged 79.
21	iv.	William (1828-1859)
22	v.	Elizabeth
	vi.	Macy. She married Allen RICHESON.

Fourth Generation

8. **William M ORR.** Born on 7 Jan 1826 in Baughman Twp. William M died in Orrville, Ohio in 1893, he was 66. Occupation: Lawyer and Judge. Education: Dalton, Wadsworth Academies. Washington & Jefferson Coll. Grad 1847. Qual. lawyer 1849. Wooster till 1865 then to Orrville.

On 4 Jul 1849 when William M was 23, he married Charlotte McFARLAND. Born in 1824. Charlotte died in Orrville, Ohio in 1862, she was 38.

They had the following children:

     i.   John. Born on 20 Jul 1851 in Orrville, Ohio. He died in Orrville, Ohio in 1883, he was 31.

     ii.   William S. Born on 4 Feb 1856 in Orrville, Ohio. He died in Orrville, Ohio on 3 Aug 1877, he was 21.

     iii.   Smith. Born in 1849 in Wooster, Ohio. Smith died in Orrville, Ohio in 1912, he was 63. Occupation: Doctor, MD; Graduated at Rush Medical Coll. Chicago 1876. On 16 Nov 1871 when Smith was 22, he married Martha RICHARDS[3], in Wayne Co. Ohio.

23   iv.   Maria (1858-1909)

9. Robert ORR. Born in 1818. Robert died in Canaan Township, Ohio in 1866, he was 48.

On 5 Mar 1846 when Robert was 28, he married Castilla DAWSON, in Wayne Co. Ohio. Born in 1819. Castilla died in Canaan Township.

They had one child:

24   i.   Wilson (1846-1888)

10. James ORR. Born in 1820 in East Union Twp. James died in Canaan Township, Ohio in 1891, he was 71.

On 11 Aug 1853 when James was 33, he married Melissa Jane BARNES, in Wayne Co. Ohio. Born in 1828. Melissa Jane died in Canaan Township, Ohio in 1900, she was 72.

They had the following children:

     i.   Meroa. Born in 1854 in Canaan Township, Ohio. Meroa died in Creston, Ohio in 1908, she was 54. Meroa married John WHONSETTLER. John died in Creston, Ohio.

ii.   Sarah. Born in 1855 in Canaan Township, Ohio. Sarah died in Hermanville, Ohio in 1919, she was 64.
Sarah married Daniel FETZER. Daniel died in Hermanville, Ohio.

iii.   Emma (Mary ?). Born in 1856 in Canaan Township, Ohio. Emma (Mary ?) died in Canaan Township, Ohio in 1928, she was 72.

iv.   Sophronia. Born in 1858 in Canaan Township. Sophronia died in Hermanville, OH in 1936, she was 78. Sophronia married John MENSCHING.

v.   Hugh. Born in 1859 in Canaan Township, Ohio. Hugh died in Medina in 1932, he was 73.

vi.   Robert. Born in 1860 in Canaan Township, Ohio. Robert died in Canaan Township, Ohio in 1863, he was 3.

25   vii.   Levi (1862-1936)

viii.   Florence Naomie. Born in 1864 in Canaan Township. Florence Naomie died in Canaan Township, Ohio in 1924, she was 60.

ix.   George. Born in 1866 in Canaan Township, Ohio. George died in Canaan Township, Ohio in 1867, he was 1.

26   x.   Charles (1869-1939)

xi.   William. Born in 1872 in Canaan Township, Ohio. William died in Creston, Ohio in 1960, he was 88.

xii.   Clinton. Born on 9 Nov 1873 in Canaan Township, Ohio. Clinton died in Canaan Township, Ohio in 1955, he was 81.
In 1903 when Clinton was 29, he married Daisy HAWK, daughter of Isaac HAWK and Emily LEITER. She was born in Stark Co.

11. Elizabeth ORR.

Elizabeth first married BONEWITZ.

Elizabeth second married Hugh HANNA, son of James HANNA.

They had one child:

27   i.   James (1804-1890)

12. Samuel S ORR. Born in 1819. Samuel S died in Applecreek.
OH in 1849, he was 30.

Samuel S married Mary McCLELLAND, in Wayne Co, OH. Born
on 2 Apr 1810 in Franklin Co., PA. Mary died in Seneca Co. on 10
Nov 1896, she was 86.

They had the following children:
        28   i.   William H (1847-1933)
                ii.   Ann Eliza.

13. James T ORR. Born in 1828 in Orrville, OH. James T died in
Orrville, OH ? 1860, he was 32.

On 15 Nov 1860 when James T was 32, he married Sophronie
BOYDSTONE, in Orrville, Wayne Co. OH.

They had one child:

        i.   Charles B. Born in 1864 in Orrville, OH.
Charles B died in Orrville, OH in 1904, he was 40.

On 18 Nov 1886 when Charles B was 22, he married Lillie A
FISCHER, in Wayne Co., OH. Born in 1867 in Orrville, OH. Lillie
A died in Orrville, OH in 1938, she was 71.

14. Thomas B ORR. Born on 31 Oct 1821. Thomas B died in Apple
Creek, Ohio in 1894, he was 72.

On 5 Oct 1848 when Thomas B was 26, he married Nancy
GADDIS, in Wayne Co., Ohio. Born in 1823. Nancy died in Apple
Creek, Ohio in 1867, she was 44.

They had the following children:

	i.	Martha. Born in Apple Creek, Ohio. Martha married Albert HUGHES.
	ii.	Mary. Born in Apple Creek, OHIO. Mary married Abram ESHLEMAN.
29	iii.	Abner G. (1856-1912)
30	iv.	Emma (1880-1957)
31	v.	William J (1859-1934)
32	vi.	Alice

15. Samuel ORR. Born in 1825. Samuel died in Apple Creek, Ohio in 1904, he was 79.

On 7 Sep 1848 when Samuel was 23, he married Eleanor CHAPMAN, in Wayne Co, Ohio. Born in 1825. Eleanor died in Apple Creek, Ohio in 1910, she was 85.

They had the following children:

33	i.	William S
34	ii.	Levi J (1852-1935)
	iii.	Mary Jane. Mary Jane died in Orrville, Ohio. Mary Jane married HUNTER. died in Orrville, Ohio.
	iv.	Elizabeth. Elizabeth died in Missouri. Elizabeth married Albert CHAFFIN. Albert died in Missouri.
	v.	Harvey. Harvey died in Smithville, Ohio.

16. Jane Anderson ORR. Born in 1815. Jane Anderson died in East Union Twp. OH in 1904, she was 89.

Jane Anderson married ARMOUR.

They had the following children:

	i.	Mary Emeree. Mary Emeree died in Michigan.
	ii.	Sarah Ellen Stauffer. Sarah Ellen Stauffer married LEWIS.

      iii.   Samuel David Anderson. Born in 1846.
                         Samuel David Anderson died in Orrville, OH
                         in 1890, he was 44.

17. Smith ORR. Born in 1826. Smith died in Apple Creek, Ohio in 1902, he was 76.

On 9 Jan 1845 when Smith was 19, he married Elizabeth ANDERSON, daughter of David ANDERSON & Elizabeth, in Wayne Co. Ohio. Born in 1826. Elizabeth died in Apple Creek, Ohio in 1870, she was 44.

They had the following children:

                i.   James Leander. Born in 1855 in Apple Creek,
                           Ohio. James Leander died in Portland,
                           Oregon.
                ii.   Ellen M. Born in 1858 in Apple Creek, Ohio.
                iii.   Samantha Jane. Born on 12 Mar 1848.
                iv.   Samuel C. Born in 1846.
                v.   Elizabeth. Born in 1851.
                vi.   David. Born in 1853.

18. Levi C ORR. Born in 1830. Levi C died in Apple Creek, Ohio in 1899, he was 69.

On 14 Feb 1867 when Levi C was 37, he married Ellen HACKETT, in Wayne Co. Ohio. Born in 1835. Ellen died in Apple Creek, Ohio in 1911, she was 76.

They had one child:

      35   i.   Willis (1870-1943)

19. William C ORR. Born in 1833 in East Union Twp., Ohio. William C died in Apple Creek, Ohio in 1909, he was 76.

On 19 Feb 1868 when William C was 35, he married Mary BOTT, in Wayne Co. Ohio. Born in 1836. Mary died in Apple Creek, Ohio in 1909, she was 73.

They had the following children:

36	i.	Laura A (1870-1948)
37	ii.	Ida (1872-1907)
38	iii.	Dudley S (1874-1957)

20. John ORR. Born in 1828 in Mt Eaton, OH. John died in Mt Eaton, OH in 1910, he was 82.

John first married Agnes LISLE, daughter of Robert LISLE. Born in 1830. Agnes died in 1870, she was 40.

They had the following children:

	i.	Calvin.
	ii.	Newton.
39	iii.	Thomas W (1861-1928)
	iv.	Quintilla.

Quintilla married Edward FERRIS.

On 18 Apr 1872 when John was 44, he second married Mary Jane ROBINETTE, in Holmes Co. OH. Born in 1836. Mary Jane died in 1913, she was 77.

They had the following children:

| 40 | i. | John Orlando (1873-1964) |
| 41 | ii. | Edward (1878-1953) |

21. William ORR. Born in 1828. William died in Mt Hope, OH in 1859, he was 31.

Children:

	i.	Thomas Allen. Born in 1848. On 17 Nov 1863 when Thomas Allen was 15, he married Margaret JAMESON, in Wayne Co., OH.
	ii.	Margaret.
	iii.	Martha.
	iv.	John.
	v.	Josiah.
	vi.	William.
	vii.	Mariah.

22. Elizabeth ORR.

Elizabeth married RICHESON.

They had one child:

        i.   Margaret Orr. Born in 1827. Margaret Orr died in Fredericksburg, OH in 1910, she was 83.

Margaret Orr married a Mr GEORGE.

Fifth Generation

23. Maria ORR. Born on 8 Jan 1858 in Orrville, OH. Maria died in Orrville, Ohio on 5 Jan 1909, she was 50.

Maria married Samuel M BRENNEMAN. Samuel M died in Orrville, Ohio.

They had the following children:

42	i.	Charlotte (1889-1948)
43	ii.	Maud (1890-1981)

24. Wilson ORR. Born in 1846 in Canaan Township. Wilson died in Canaan Township in 1888, he was 42.

On 2 Oct 1872 when Wilson was 26, he married Martha J CRANE, in Wayne Co. Ohio. Born in 1846. Martha J died in Canaan Township in 1936, she was 90.

They had the following children:
  i.   Ethel. Born in Canaan Township.
  ii.   Gertrude. Born in Canaan Township, Ohio.
  iii. Robert. Born in Canaan Township.

25. Levi ORR Dr. DVM. Born in 1862 in Canaan Township, Ohio. Levi died in Lodi, Ohio in 1936, he was 74.

On 24 Dec 1889 when Levi was 27, he married Flora GARVER, in Wayne Co. Ohio. Flora died in Lodi, Ohio.

They had the following children:

  i.   Emery. Born in 1890. Emery died in Lodi, Ohio.
  ii.   Merle. Born in 1892. Merle died in Lodi, Ohio.
  iii. Ray. Born in 1894. Ray died in Burbank, Ohio in 1963, he was 69.
44 iv.   Fern N (1898-)
  v.   Mary. Born in 1903. Mary died in Burbank, Ohio. Mary married Merle GERBER. Merle died in Burbank, Ohio.

26. Charles ORR. Born in 1869 in Canaan Township, Ohio. Charles died in Wadsworth, Ohio in 1939, he was 70.

Child:

  i.   Madge. Madge died in Wadsworth, Ohio.

27. James HANNA. Born on 28 Jan 1804 in Cumberland Co., PA. James died in Sugar Creek, Wayne Co. Ohio on 30 Dec 1890, he was 86. Occupation: Farmer.

In 1829 when James was 24, he married Sarah McCLELLAND, daughter of Samuel McCLELLAND & Ellen CROOKS. Born in PA.

They had the following children:

i.	Hugh R.
ii.	Samuel McClelland.
iii.	William. Occupation: Farmer, IL.
iv.	Sylvanis. Occupation: Farmer, Paulding Co., OH.
v.	Thomas S. Occupation: Farmer, home farm 1886.
vi.	John. Occupation: Farmer, Wood Co., OH.
vii.	Martha E. She married George HULL.
viii.	Sarah. She married Frank FEE.
ix.	Elizabeth. She married Thomas WEBSTER.

28. William H ORR. Born in 1847 in Orrville, Wayne Co. OH. William H died in Warsaw, IN in 1933, he was 86.

Child:

45 i.   William A (1898-)

29. Abner G. ORR. Born on 3 Feb 1856 in East Union Twp., OH. Abner G. died in Orrville, Ohio in 1912, he was 55. Occupation: Teacher for 7 years before farming.

On 27 Feb 1890 when Abner G. was 34, he married Sarah M BECHTEL, daughter of Jacob BECHTEL, in Wayne Co. Ohio. Born on 26 Jul 1861 in Greene Twp. OH.

They had the following children:

i.   Emily A. Born on 23 Jan 1899 in Orrville, OH. Emily A married John BAAB.

ii.   Mary E. Born on 10 Jul 1896. Mary E died in Orrville, OH in 1940, she was 43.

iii.   Walter B. Born on 16 Apr 1894.

iv.   Sarah Lucille. Born on 17 Mar 1906. Sarah Lucille died on 24 Aug 1907, she was 1.

v.   Charlotte K. Born on 27 Sep 1901.

30. Emma ORR. Born in 1880 in Apple Creek, Ohio. Emma died in Orrville, Ohio in 1957, she was 77.

Emma married Charles SWAINGART.

They had the following children:

i.   Carson. Born in 1905 in Orrville, Ohio. Carson died in 1905.

ii.   John Clair. Born in 1906 in Orrville, Ohio.

iii.   Charles O. Born in 1908 in Orrville, Ohio.

iv.   Russell. Born in 1910 in Orrville, Ohio. Russell died in Orrville, Ohio in 1912, he was 2.

v.   Viola. Born in 1913 in Orrvile, Ohio. She married Merle FEICHTER.

vi.   Orr Arlo. Born in 1915 in Orrville, Ohio.

31. William J ORR. Born in 1859 in Apple Creek, Ohio. William J died in Apple Creek, Ohio in 1934, he was 75.

On 28 Dec 1882 when William J was 23, he married Emma A BRENNEMAN, in Wayne Co. Ohio. Born in 1863. Emma A died in Apple Creek, Ohio in 1930, she was 67.

They had the following children:

    i.   Alta. She died in Lattasburg, Ohio. Alta married Earl MARTIN. Earl died in Lattasburg, Ohio.

    ii.   Clarence B. Born in 1885 in Apple Creek, Ohio. He died in Apple Creek, Ohio in 1961, aged 76.

    iii.   Celia Mae. Born in 1891 in Apple Creek, Ohio. She died in Apple Creek, Ohio in 1960, aged 69. Celia Mae married E Clifford SMITH who died in Apple Creek, Ohio.

32. Alice ORR. Born in Apple Creek, Ohio.

Alice married C N BADGER. C N died in Orrville, Ohio.

They had one child:

    i.   C E. Born in Orrville, OH.

33. William S ORR. William S died in Doylestown, Ohio.

On 7 Oct 1879 William S married Florence DIETRICK, in Wayne Co. Ohio.

They had the following children:

    i.   John.

    ii.   Oda.

34. Levi J ORR. Born in 1852. Levi J died in Wooster, Ohio in 1935, he was 83.

On 3 Oct 1875 when Levi J was 23, he married Sarah WALTER, in Wayne Co. Ohio.

They had the following children:

 i. Sarah. Born in 1878 in Wooster, Ohio. Sarah died in Orrville, Ohio in 1971, she was 93. Sarah married David DOUGLAS. David died in Orrville, Ohio.

 ii. Nettie. Born in 1879 in Wooster, Ohio. Nettie died in Barberton, Ohio. Nettie married Clyde KUNKLER. Clyde died in Barberton, Ohio.

 iii. Isa. Born in Wooster, Ohio. Isa married GAMENSFELTER.

 iv. Ida. Born in Wooster, Ohio. Ida died in Elyria, Ohio. Ida married DEVINNEY. died in Elyria, Ohio.

 v. Eva. Eva died in Arizona. Eva married HIXON. died in Arizona.

 vi. Walter. Born in 1892 in Wooster, Ohio. Walter died in Avon, Ohio.

35. Willis ORR. Born in 1870 in Apple Creek, Ohio. Willis died in Apple Creek, Ohio in 1943, he was 73.

Willis married Maude V n k. Born in 1874. She died in Apple Creek, Ohio in 1929, aged 55.

They had one child:

 i. Florence E. Born in 1906 in Apple Creek, Ohio. Florence E died in Apple Creek, Ohio in 1920, she was 14.

36. Laura A ORR. Born in 1870 in Apple Creek, Ohio. Laura A died in Apple Creek, Ohio in 1948, she was 78.

Laura A married Harry G. JAMESON. He died in Apple Creek, Ohio.

They had the following children:

      i.   Grace. Born in 1904 in Apple Creek, Ohio. She married Joseph A JOSEPH.

      ii.   Charlotte. Born in 1907 in Apple Creek, Ohio. She married Lawrence MANN.

      iii.   John R. Born in Apple Creek, Ohio.

37. Ida ORR. Born in 1872 in Apple Creek, Ohio. Ida died in Apple Creek, Ohio in 1907, she was 35.

Ida married David A McCULLOUGH. David A died in Apple Creek, Ohio.

They had one child:

      i.   Mary. Born in Apple Creek, Ohio.

38. Dudley S ORR. Born on 20 Dec 1874 in East Union Twp., Ohio. Dudley S died in Apple creek, Ohio in 1957, he was 82.

On 28 Sep 1895 when Dudley S was 20, he married Bertha L CARSON, daughter of John CARSON, in Wayne Co. Ohio. Born in 1876 in PA. Bertha L died in Apple Creek, Ohio in 1949, she was 73.

They had the following children:

      i.   Donald C. Born in 1895 in Apple Creek, Ohio.

Donald C died in Apple Creek, Ohio in 1918, he was 23.

	ii.	Ross J. Born in 1897 in Apple Creek, Ohio.
	iii.	Velma. Born in Apple Creek, Ohio. She married Arlo G GRABER.
	iv.	Wilbur. Born in Apple Creek, Ohio.
	v.	Cloyce E. Born in Apple Creek, Ohio.
46	vi.	Rene P
47	vii.	Ross J (1897-)

39. **Thomas W ORR.** Born on 18 Feb 1861 in Salt Creek Township, Wayne Co., OH. Thomas W died in Orrville, OH in 1928, he was 66. Occupation: Teacher, lawyer, Judge of the Probate Court, Ohio.

Thomas W married Emma J SMITH, daughter of Cyrus SMITH.

They had the following children:

48	i.	Ruth
	ii.	Maynard S.
	iii.	Lucil.
	iv.	Walter S.
	v.	Paul S.

40. **John Orlando ORR.** Born in 1873 in Fredericksburg, OH. John Orlando died on 13 Jan 1964, he was 91.

On 25 Mar 1896 when John Orlando was 23, he married Flora May SHOOK, daughter of SHOOK. Born in 1874. Flora May died in 1952, she was 78.

They had the following children:

	i.	Harold. Born in Youngstown, OH. Harold died in Youngstown, OH. Harold married Mildred CUTTER.

49	ii.	Quintilla Merle (1898-1989)
50	iii.	Vinson (1901-)

41. Edward ORR. Born in 1878. Edward died in Fredericksburg, OH in 1953, he was 75.

Edward married Lena MARTIN, in Fredericksburg, OH.

They had the following children:

	i.	George.
	ii.	Fern. She married Ted McCOY.
51	iii.	Martha

Sixth Generation

42. Charlotte BRENNEMAN. Born in 1889 in Orrville, Ohio. Charlotte died in Orrville, Ohio in 1948, she was 59.

Charlotte married a Mr CHAMBERLAIN. She died in Orrville, Ohio.

They had one child:

    i. Margaret. Born in 1918. Margaret died in New York City.

43. Maud BRENNEMAN. Born in 1890 in Orrville, Ohio. Maud died in Orrville Ohio in 1981, she was 91.

Maud married Carl CONGDON.

They had the following children:

    i. Carl Jr. Born in 1920 in Orrville, Ohio. he died in Orrville in 1992.
    ii. Rowland

44. Fern N ORR. Born in 1898. Fern N died in Wooster, OH.

Children:

        i.   Mary.
        ii.   Donald.

45. William A ORR. Born in 1898 in Warsaw, IN.

Child:

        i.   William F.

46. Rene P ORR. Born in Apple Creek, Ohio.

Children:

        i.   Donald.
        ii.   Judy.
        iii.   Robert.

47. Ross J ORR. Born on 9 Sep 1897.

On 18 Jan 1919 when Ross J was 21, he married Ethel May Hofacre, daughter of Alonzo Lawrence (Hoffacker) Hofacre & Daisy Anna Eyman Born on 21 Jul 1902. This is the link, via the Hofacre marriage, to Orrs in Mercer Co, PA and elsewhere in OH. See the separate register report.

They had the following children:

52	i.	Clayton Leroy
53	ii.	Delno Donald
54	iii.	Norma Jean
	iv.	Alonzo Dudley. He married Agnes Regina BRUMPTER.

v.	John William. He married May Lou STINE.
vi.	Harlow Ross. He married Shirley Ann Beechey.

48. Ruth ORR.

Ruth married Nicholas WEISS.

They had the following children:
	i.	Robert..
	ii.	William.

49. Quintilla Merle ORR. Born on 12 Dec 1898. Quintilla Merle died in Alliance, OH in Jun 1989, she was 90.

On 29 Jun 1917 when Quintilla Merle was 18, she married Jacob Marks TATE. Born in Moreland. Jacob Marks died in Dec 1968.

They had the following children:
	i.	Jean
55	ii.	Helen June
56	iii.	John Marks
57	iv.	Vinson Harold

50. Vinson ORR. Born in 1901. Vinson died in Fredericksburg, OH.

Vinson married Clarinda RAYLE.

They had one child:

58	i.	Kenneth

51. Martha ORR. She married Maynard BRENNERMAN.

They had one child:

      i.   Karen.

Seventh Generation

52. Clayton Leroy Orr. He married Mabel Marie Schnell.

They had the following children:

      i.   Susan Kay, she married Robert William Bleyle.
      ii.   James Walter, he married Susan Ann Hughes.
      iii.   Gary Lerr
      iv.   Jan Marie
      v.   Steven Paul

53. Delno Donald Orr. He first married Nettie Marvaline. Born on 18 Jul 1924. Nettie died on 18 Apr 1966, she was 41.

They had the following children:

   59   i.   Karen Lee
          ii.   Richard Delno
          iii.   Marcia. She married Dan Carpenter.
          iv.   Karla
          v.   Paula

Delno Donald second married a lady named Florence (surname not known).

54. Norma Jean Orr. She married Robert Wayne Knoble.

They had the following children:

   60   i.   Julia
          ii.   Ronald
          iii.   Laraine

55. Helen June TATE She married Edward CROSS.

They had the following children:

        i.   Mark.
        ii.   Matthew.

56. John Marks TATE. He married Elda LAPP.

They had the following children:

        i.   Deborah.
        ii.   Diane.
        iii.   Donna.

57. Vinson Harold TATE. He is a retired teacher and married Jo DONALDSON

They had the following children:

61   i.   Scott Vinson
62   ii.   Stephanie Caroline
        iii.   John Marks.

58. Kenneth ORR. He married Ruth HAHN, in Orrville.

They had the following children:

63   i.   Larry
64   ii.   Lynn
65   iii.   Stanley

Eighth Generation

59. Karen Lee Orr. She married Alan HITEPOLE.

They had the following children:

      i.   Marley Catherine.
      ii.   Nathan Alllen.

60. Julia Knoble. She married Larry YATES, in Orrville.

They had the following children:
      i.   Matthew Robert.
      ii.   Joel Allen.
      iii.   Adam Michael.

61. Scott Vinson TATE.

Scott Vinson married Kathleen SMITH.

They had the following children:
      i.   Elizabeth.
      ii.   Ethan.

62. Stephanie Caroline TATE. She married James HYNDS.

They had one child:

      i.   Caroline Jo.

63. Larry ORR. He married a lady named Sue. (Suirname unklnown)

They had the following children:

      i.   Brian.
      ii.   Carrie.

64. Lynn ORR. He married a lady named Linda (surname unknown)

They had one child:

i.   Jerod.

65. Stanley ORR married and then divorced. They had the following children:

i.   Ben.
ii.   Diana.

Index

BECHTEL
    Sarah M   spouse of 29

BONEWITZ
    UNNAMED   spouse of 11

BOTT
    Mary   spouse of 19

BOYDSTONE
    Sophronie   spouse of 13

BRENNEMAN
    Charlotte   42
    Emma A   spouse of 31
    Maud   43
    Samuel M   spouse of 23

BRENNERMAN
    Karen   child of 51
    Maynard   spouse of 51

BURNETT
    Mary   spouse of 6

CARSON
    Bertha L   spouse of 38

CHAMBERLAIN
    UNNAMED   spouse of 42
    Margaret   child of 42

CHAPMAN
    Eleanor   spouse of 15

CONGDON
    Carl   spouse of 43
    Carl Jr   child of 43
    Rowland   child of 43

CRANE
    Martha J   spouse of 24

CROSS
    Edward   spouse of 55
    Mark   child of 55

Matthew	child of 55
DAWSON	
Castilla	spouse of 9
DIETRICK	
Florence	spouse of 33
DONALDSON	
Jo	spouse of 57
FOREMAN	
Maria	spouse of 3
GADDIS	
Nancy	spouse of 14
GARVER	
Flora	spouse of 25
HACKETT	
Ellen	spouse of 18
HAHN	
Ruth	spouse of 58
HANNA	
Elizabeth	child of 27
Hugh	spouse of 11
Hugh R	child of 27
James	27
John	child of 27
Maude V	spouse of 35
Martha E	child of 27
Samuel McClelland	child of 27
Sarah	child of 27
Sylvanis	child of 27
Thomas S	child of 27
William	child of 27
HITEPOLE	
Alan	spouse of 59
Marley Catherine	child of 59
Nathan Allen	child of 59

HOFACRE
    Ethel May   spouse of 47
HYNDS
    Caroline Jo   child of 62
    James   spouse of 62
JAMESON
    Charlotte   child of 36
    Grace   child of 36
    Harry G   spouse of 36
    John R   child of 36
KENDRICK
    Roseltha   spouse of 5

KNOBLE
    Julia   60
    Laraine   child of 54
    Robert Wayne   spouse of 54
    Ronald   child of 54
LAPP
    Elda   spouse of 56
LISLE
    Agnes   spouse of 20

MARTIN
    Lena   spouse of 41
MARVALINE
    Nettie   spouse of 53
McCLELLAND
    Mary   spouse of 12
    Sarah   spouse of 27
McCULLOUGH
    David A   spouse of 37
    Mary   child of 37
McFARLAND
    Charlotte   spouse of 8

ORR

Abner G.	29
Alfred	child of 6
Alice	32
Alonzo Dudley	child of 47
Alta	child of 31
Amanda	child of 5
Ann Eliza	child of 12
Barr	child of 5
Ben	child of 65
Brian	child of 63
Calvin	child of 20
Carrie	child of 63
Celia Mae	child of 31
Charles	26
Charles	child of 5
Charles B	child of 13
Charlotte K	child of 29
Christina	child of 7
Clarence B	child of 31
Clayton Leroy	52
Clinton	child of 10
Cloyce E	child of 38
Cordella	child of 5
David	child of 6
David	child of 17
Davis	child of 5
Delno Donald	53
Diana	child of 65
Donald C	child of 38
Dudley S	38
Edward	41
Elizabeth	11
Elizabeth	child of 15
Elizabeth	22
Elizabeth	child of 17

Ella	child of 5
Ellen M	child of 17
Emery child of	25
Emily A	child of 29
Emma	child of 5
Emma	30
Emma (Mary ?)	child of 10
Ethel	child of 24
Eva	child of 34
Fern	child of 41
Fern N	44
Florence E	child of 35
Florence Naomie	child of 10
Gary Lerr	child of 52
George	child of 10
George	child of 41
Gertrude	child of 24
Harlow Ross	child of 47
Harold	child of 40
Harvey	child of 15
Henry C	child of 5
Hugh	4
Hugh Dr DVM	child of 10
Ida	child of 34
Ida	37
Isa	child of 34
James	5
James	10
James Leander	child of 17
James T	13
James T	child of 6
James Walter	child of 52
Jan Marie	child of 52
Jane Anderson	16
Jerod	child of 64
John	child of 8

John	20
John	child of 33
John	child of 21
John Orlando	40
John William	child of 47
Joseph	child of 5
Josiah	child of 21
Karen Lee	59
Karla	child of 53
Kenneth	58
Larry	63
Laura A	36
Levi Dr. DVM	25
Levi J	34
Levi C	18
Lucil	child of 39
Lynn	64
Macy	child of 7
Madge	child of 26
Marcia	child of 53
Margaret	child of 2
Margaret	child of 21
Maria	23
Maria	child of 5
Mariah	child of 21
Martha	child of 5
Martha	child of 14
Martha	51
Martha	child of 21
Mary	child of 25
Mary	child of 14
Mary	child of 7
Mary Jane	child of 15
Mary E	child of 29
Maynard S	child of 39
Merle	child of 25

Meroa	child of 10
Nettie	child of 34
Newton	child of 20
Norma Jean	54
Oda	child of 33
Paul S	child of 39
Paula	child of 53
Quintilla	child of 20
Quintilla Merle	49
Ray	child of 25
Rene P	46
Richard Delno	child of 53
Robert	9
Robert	child of 24
Robert	child of 10
Robert	7
Ross J	child of 38
Ross J	47
Ruth	48
Samantha Jane	child of 17
Samuel	6
Samuel	child of 4
Samuel	15
Samuel	1
Samuel	2
Samuel C	child of 17
Samuel S	12
Sarah	child of 2
Sarah	child of 4
Sarah	child of 10
Sarah	child of 34
Sarah A.	child of 5
Sarah Lucille	child of 29
Smith	3
Smith Dr MD	child of 8
Smith	17

Sophronia	child of 10
Stanley	65
Steven Paul	child of 52
Susan Kay	child of 52
Thomas B	child of 5
Thomas Allen	child of 21
Thomas B	14
Thomas W	39
Velma	child of 38
Vinson	50
Walter	child of 34
Walter B	child of 29
Walter S	child of 39
Wilbur	child of 38
William Dr. DVM	child of 10
William	21
William	child of 21
William	child of 2
William C	19
William F	child of 45
William S	33
William A	45
William H	28
William J	31
William M	8
William M	child of 5
William S	child of 8
Willis	35
Wilson	24

RAYLE
Clarinda	spouse of 50

RICHESON
UNNAMED	spouse of 22
Margaret Orr	child of 22

ROBINETTE
Mary Jane	spouse of 20

SCHNELL
    Mabel Marie   spouse of 52
SHOOK
    Flora May   spouse of 40
SMITH
    Emma J   spouse of 39
    Kathleen   spouse of 61
    Sarah   spouse of 2
STEEL
    Nancy   spouse of 4
SWAINGART
    Carson   child of 30
    Charles   spouse of 30
    Charles O   child of 30
    John Clair   child of 30
    Orr Arlo   child of 30
    Russell   child of 30
    Viola   child of 30
TATE
    Deborah   child of 56
    Diane   child of 56
    Donna   child of 56
    Elizabeth   child of 61
    Ethan   child of 61
    Helen June   55
    Jacob Marks   spouse of 49
    Jean   child of 49
    John Marks   56
    John Marks   child of 57
    Scott Vinson   61
    Stephanie Caroline   62
    Vinson Harold   57
WALTER
    Sarah   spouse of 34
WEISS
    Nicholas   spouse of 48

Robert Dr. Ph.D.   child of 48
William   child of 48
YATES
Adam Michael   child of 60
Joel Allen   child of 60
Larry   spouse of 60
Matthew Robert   child of 60

A link between Orrs in Apple Creek, Ohio and Mercer Co, Pennsylvania

I have been asked many times about possible links and have finally come across a connection between Ohio and Pennsylvania Orrs. It comes about through the marriages by male Orrs to Hofacre cousins.

Ross J Orr of Apple creek, OH, married Ethel May Hofacre 18 Jan 1919.

William Warren Orr, Mercer Co., PA married Martha Alice Hofacre in Perry Towenship, Mercer Co. PA.

The Misses Hofacre are cousins:

Ethel May`s ancestors are: Alonzo Lawrence (1869); John (1841); George (1794) and Michael (1767).

Martha Alice`s ancestors are: George Werner; George (1794); Johannes Michael (1769)

Michael and Johannes Michael Hofacre were brothers.

It may be a circuitous route to the connection, but they were all immigrants and had a common interest, especially in a community of farmers, to migrate to places where the land was available and, hopefully, cheap. They grasped opportunities when and wherever they could and would have been on at least nodding acquaintance, and probably members of the same church. There is some truth in the saying " the family that prays together, stays together".

A separate report of the William Orr & Mary Orrick/Elias Orr/ William Warren Orr line follows. This Register Report is a compilation and is given `as is` - a guide only to the relationships.

First Generation

1. William ORR. Born ca 1790 in Ireland. William died in Springfield Twp, PA. ca 1843, he was 53.

William married Mary ORRICK.

They had the following children:

2	i.	William (ca1801-)
3	ii.	John M (ca1804-)
4	iii.	Elias (ca1812-)
	iv.	James.
	v.	Robert.
	vi.	Jane.
	vii.	Elizabeth.

Second Generation

2. William ORR. Born ca 1801.

William married Elizabeth.

They had the following children:

i.	Rebecca J. Born ca 1828.
ii.	William. Born ca 1830.
iii.	Mary E. Born ca 1832.
iv.	Sarah Ann. Born ca 1835
v.	Elias. Born ca 1837.
vi.	Caroline. Born ca 1840.
vii.	John C. Born ca 1842.
viii.	Maria. Born ca 1845.
ix.	Amanda L. Born ca 1849.
x.	Joseph. Born ca 1856.

3. John M ORR. Born ca 1804.

John M first married Elizabeth M   JAMISON. Born ca 1806 in Mercer Co. PA. Elizabeth M died on 7 Oct 1854, she was 48.

They had the following children:

i.	Mary J. Born ca 1826.
ii.	William. Born ca 1827.
iii.	Isabella.
iv.	Hiram. Born ca 1832.
v.	John.
vi.	Elizabeth. Born ca 1837.
vii.	David P. Born ca 1839.
viii.	Margaret. Born ca 1842.
ix.	James. Born ca 1844.
x.	Joseph S. Born ca 1846.

John M second married Martha DENNISTON. Martha died on 7 Sep 1871.

4. Elias ORR. Born ca 1812 in Mercer Co., PA.

ca 1830 when Elias was 18, he married Margaret HOLIDAY, in Mercer Co., PA.

They had the following children:

	i.	Mary. Born ca 1841, who married Clint LACKEY.
	ii.	Robert. Born ca 1842. Occupation: Insurance business, Mercer, PA.
5	iii.	Beriah (1843-1903)
	iv.	Sarah. Born ca 1845.
	v.	James Robert. Born ca 1846. Occupation: Farmer, Springfield IL.

vi.   Jane. Born ca 1848.

6   vii.   Margaret (1853-1945)

viii.   Samuel. Born ca 1853. Occupation: Agriculturist (farmer).

ix.   John. Born ca 1857. Occupation: Farmer.

Third Generation

5. Beriah ORR. Born on 2 Jul 1843. Beriah died in Fairview, PA in 1903, he was 59.

Beriah first married Malinda HAZEN, daughter of William HAZEN & Dorothy. Born in Lawrence Co. PA. Malinda died in 1878 in Fredonia, PA.

They had the following children:

7   i.   William Warren (1868-1942)

ii.   James. Occupation: Sawmill business, Haronsburg.

iii.   Albert. Occupation: Telephone business, Mercer Co., PA.

iv.   Alice. She married William BEAN.

Beriah second married Martha DYKE, daughter of Henry DYKE.

They had one child:

i.   Charles.

Beriah third married Esther YOUNG, daughter of C. YOUNG. She had been previously married to a Mr PADEN.

They had the following children:

i.   Wayne. Occupation: Lumber inspector, Butler, PA.
ii.   Luella. Occupation: Hotel business with mother & sister. Fredonia, PA.
iii. Iola. Occupation: Hotel business with mother and sister, Fredonia, PA.

6. Margaret ORR. Born on 23 May 1853 in PA. Margaret died in Youngstown on 16 Apr 1945, she was 91.

Margaret married Josiah LUCE. Born ca 1848. Josiah died ca 1915, he was 67.

They had the following children:
i.   Maude. Born ca 1871.
ii.   Vera. Born ca 1878, died ca 1911, aged 33. Vera married Evan A JONES, in Sharpsville, PA.
iii. Grace. Born ca 1882.

Fourth Generation

7. William Warren ORR. Born on 25 Aug 1868 in Fairview Twp, Mercer Co., PA. William Warren died on 2 Nov 1942, he was 74.

William Warren married Martha Alice Hoffacker daughter of George Werner Hoffacker & Sophia Leipply. Born on 18 Nov 1871 in Perry Township, Mercer County, PA. Martha Alice died on 19 Feb 1943, she was 71. Through this marriage there is a connection to Ross J Orr of Apple Creek, who married a cousin, Ethel May Hofacre. See the separate Register Report for Orrs of Orrville.

They had the following children:
8   i.   Ralph George (1893-1968)
9   ii.   Granville B. (1897-1981)
10 iii. Olive Ida (1902-1957)

Orr of Ralston

From Geo. Robertsons *History of Renfrew Shire* (1818) p 330

The late William Orr, Esq; of Ralston, was the second son of Robert
Orr, manufacturer in Paisley. He went to Ireland in his youth,
where, along with his brother, John Orr, Esq of Dublin, he
introduced and brought to great perfection the art of printing linens.
There, by an assiduous attention to business, and an integrity in his
transactions, that procured him unbounded confidence, he acquired
a handsome fortune, with which he returned to his native place
about the end of the last century. In 1797, he acquired, from the Earl
of Glasgow, part of the lands of Ingliston, on which he built one of
the most elegant villas in the county. About two years after, when
the late Wlliam Macdowall, Esq of Castlesemple, was disposing of
the adjacent Barony of Ralston, about a mile and a half east from
Paisley, he purchased the greater part of it - and called the whole
property there by the name of Ralston.

He married Margaret, daughter of the late James Kibble, Esq; of
Whiteford, [24 April 1779 in Paisley] by whom he had three sons
and four daughters. He died in 1812, and was succeeded by his
eldest son, Robert Orr Esq; now of Ralston, who married Miss
Anne Duffie of Dublin. His daughter Margaret married Mr John
Duffey Junior, of Ballsbridge, in June 1804.

Part X

THE ORR COAT OF ARMS, CRESTS AND TARTAN

Heraldry is a science all its own and bound about with strict rules as to who may bear arms, and use heraldic devices and crests. A coat of arms can be obtained in only two ways - by applying for a grant to the appropriate Herald`s office or by proving descent from someone who was legally entitled to have arms. It is a very expensive thing to do.

Being of the same name as someone with arms does not confer any right to use it. The `family crest` which goes with a coat of arms is also personal property. To use or claim an arms to be your own is technically a civil wrong and punishable by the courts. In Scotland the Lord Lyon King of Arms, through his Court in Edinburgh, matriculates (approves) coats of arms and has wide powers under an Act of Parliament.

The designs shown here are representations of arms used by Orr in the past. Various versions are offered by commercial firms which differ mainly in the shape of the shield on which the design is mounted. Buying such creations does not confer a right to use it on letterheads etc.

The armorial description is

Gule. Three piles in point argent, on a chief or, a torteau between two crosslets fitchee of the field. Crest Cornucopia proper.

Meaning: On a red shield, three silver piles. On a gold upper third, a red circle between two red crosses - crosslets fitchee. Crest a naturally coloured cornucopia (a horn of plenty).

The Orr armorial. Photo by the author

The Ulster version above is that of James Orr of the Villa Antoinette, Cannes, France and Belfast. It has a trefoil added.. He was the second son of James Orr of Ballygowan and Holywood House, a Belfast banker. A brother was the Rev Alexander Orr, rector of Lambeg, His mother was Jane Stewart of the Stewarts of Ballintoy. His grandfather was Alexander Orr.

The armorial description given in Burkes *General Armory* is: Gule. Three piles in point argent, the centre pile charged with a trefoil slipped vert on a chief or, a torteau between two crosslets fitchee of the field. Crest Cornucopia proper charged with a trefoil slipped as in the arms. The motto is *Bonis Omnia Bona* - To the Good, All is Good.

Crests.

Other crests and mottoes given in *Fairbairn's Crests* include:

A cornucopia proper (meaning in its natural colours). *Virtutia fortuna comes.* Fortune the companion of virtue.

A cornucopia proper. Motto: *Bonis omnia bona.* To the good all is good.

Out of a heart, a dexter hand bearing a scimitar. Motto True to the end.

Also, similar but with a sword in the hand. Motto: True to the end.

A lion passant proper, resting dexter on a torteau. No motto.

(meaning a lion standing up facing left, with front right paw resting on a disc).

William Orr of Coleraine was a large linen manufacturer who used the design as a quality mark on his cloth.

WILLIAM ORR'S
Coleraines.

OLD LINEN SEAL OF THE ORRS
(in possession of Robert May).

Illustration from *Northern Leaders of '98 (No 1) William Orr*, by F J Bigger. Maunsel & Co, Dublin, (1906).

Tartans

There is much mystique accorded to the subject of tartans although they are a relatively late garment that has been considerably hyped by interested parties since Victorian times. The official base line for which tartan belongs to which clan was only approved by The Highland Society in 1816. Most Scotsmen merely wore a plaid and did not have the colourings or `sett` for the purpose of identification in battle. If anything the colour of their bonnet or cockade or ribbon in the bonnet served that purpose. For example the Covenanter armies in the 17th century wore blue bonnets and, or a blue ribbon across their chest. However, it is not my purpose to debate the issue only to provide information about the tartan that might be worn by an Orr.

As has been previously mentioned, the Orrs are an acknowledged sept of Clan Campbell and would be entitled to wear the standard tartan of the clan. There are four tartan setts in existence for Clan Campbell approved by MacCailein Moir: Campbell (sometimes called the darker version, or Argyll); Campbell of Cawdor; Campbell of Breadalbane; and Campbell of Loudon. Generally the Campbell or Argyll tartan is worn; the other Houses being applicable only when there is clear descent and with the permission of MacCailein Moir.

281
Appendices

1. 17th Century Burials, Greyfriars Church, Edinburgh

2. Orr in Lochwinnoch Parish, 1881 Census

3. Orr in Kilbarchan Parish, 1881 Census

4. Orr in Kilbirnie Parish, 1881 Census

5. Orr in Beith Parish, 1881 Census

6. Orr in Dumfries & Kirkcudbright, 1881 Census

7. Orr in Wigtownshire, 1881 Census

8. Orr Marriages in the *Ulster Pedigree*

9. Extract of Orr in the Super Index of Irish Wills

10. Orr in Ulster, Griffiths Valuation & Tithe Applotments

11. Flax Growers Index

12. Fugitives and Banished Persons 1798

13. Orr Who Served in the Royal Irish Constabulary, 1816-1921

14. Orr Related Papers in PRONI

15. Orr in Pallot`s Marriage Index of England, 1780-1837

16. Orr Miners Killed at their Work

Appendix 1

17th Century Burials, Greyfriars Church, Edinburgh

17th century Orr interments in the Greyfriars Kirk Yard, Edinburgh.

Chr. Name		Date interred	Spouse	Father	Note
Margaret	ORR	27 Aug 1661	Robert SALMOND		Spouse merchant at head of West Bow.
John	ORR	16 Mar 1666		Thomas ORR	Son of Thomas Orr, brewer.
Thomas	ORR	19 Aug 1666			Brewer.
	ORR	29 Apr 1667		Thomas ORR	Infant. Father a poultryman.
	ORR	24 Nov 1667		Thomas ORR	Father a tailor.
Thomas	ORR	16 Jul 1668	Elizabeth COWIE		Spouse buried.
Catherine	ORR	18 Jun 1669	Adam THOMSON		Spouse a brewer.
Janet	ORR	18 Dec 1669	Andrew JOHNSTONE		Spouse a brewer, at foot of West Bow.
Margaret	ORR	26 May 1673	MOSMAN ?		Buried in John Mosmans tomb.
	ORR	22 Jun 1673		Robert ORR	Infant.
Thomas	ORR	8 Jun 1673	Margaret FAIRLIE		Spouse buried.
	ORR	20 Aug 1674		Robert ORR	infant bastard ch of Robert Orr, writer.
Bessie	ORR	10 Oct			A poor burial

	ORR	1674 15 Dec 1675		William ORR	Gentleman. Infant.

	ORR	1674 15 Dec 1675		William ORR	Gentleman. Infant.
Robert	ORR	24 Dec 1675			Baker. His ch.d. infants bur 22 Jun 1673, 1 Sep 1676.
	ORR	8 Apr 1676		William ORR	Indweller. Infant.
	ORR	1 Sep 1676		Robert ORR	Infant
David	ORR	10 Dec 1684			Candlemaker
Margaret	ORR	13 Jun 1688			Poor burial, east end of kirk.
Robert	ORR	5 Jul 1689			Bur. Naismith tomb.
Elizabeth	ORR	10 Jan 1690	James SHAW		Spouse merchant, predeceased her. bur Cheislie tomb.
Agnes	ORR	12 Jul 1691	James BORLAND		Bur. Naismith tomb. Sp a writer. Burgess by right of wife and late Thomas ORR merchant burgess d 29 Jul 1674. Sister Jonet marr Andrew Johnstoun, also B by right.
Margaret	ORR	24 Dec 1693			Poor burial. Middle Road.
	ORR	6 Feb 1695		Thomas ORR	Father soldier. infant nr south door.

Laurence	ORR	5 Sep 1695			Buried Canegit.
Margaret	ORR	5 Nov 1696			Domestic servant.
Mary	ORR	28 Dec 1696	Laurence SCOT		Spouse merchant, predeceased her. Bur Heriot gate.
	ORR	18 Apr 1697		Thomas ORR	Father soldier. Infant.
	ORR	19 Jan 1699		Andrew ORR	Stillborn child.

Appendix 2

Orrs Residing in Lochwinnoch Parish, 1881 Census.

Name	Address		Occupation	Status	Age	Year born	Place born
Thomas	Belltrees Farm		Farm servant	M	42	1839	Lochwinnoch
Margaret	Belltrees Farm	Wife		M	34	1847	Kilbirnie
Thomas	Belltrees Farm	Son	School	U	15	1866	Lochwinnoch
Janet	Belltrees Farm	Dtr	School	U	14	1867	Lochwinnoch
Annie	Belltrees Farm	Dtr	School	U	8	1873	Lochwinnoch
Robert	Risk Farm		Farmer 60 ac.	U	42	1839	Lochwinnoch
John	Risk Farm	Bro.		U	24	1857	Lochwinnoch
Robert	Millbank Farm		Retd Farmer	U	72	1809	Lochwinnoch
John	Millbank Farm	Bro	Retd. Draper	W	61	1820	LOchwinnoch
James	Kaimhill		Dog Trainer	U	34	1847	Kilbirnie
Andrew	Kaimhill	Bro	Dog Trainer	U	20	1861	Kilbirnie
John	High Linthills		Farmer 98 ac	U	69	1812	Lochwinnoch
James	High Linthills	Bro	Farm Lbr.	U	59	1822	Lochwinnoch
Jane	Crooks Farm		Farmer 35 ac	W	49	1832	Lochwinnoch

Robert	Crooks Farm	Son	Farm Lbr	U	25	1856 Lochwinnoch
Helen	Crooks Farm	Dtr	Farm Lbr	U	22	1859 Lochwinnoch
James	Crooks Farm	Son	Farm Lbr	U	20	1861 Lochwinnoch
Robert	Heathfield		Gardener	M	37	1844 Lochwinnoch
Jane	Heathfield	Wife		M	31	1850 Fenwick
Robert	Heathfield	Son	School	U	8	1873 Lochwinnoch
John	Heathfield	Son	School	U	6	1875 Lochwinnoch
Agnes	Heathfield		Servant	U	14	1867 Kilbirnie
Christina S	East Kaim		Annuitant	W	42	1839 Lochranza,Bute
William O	East Kaim	Son	School	U	14	1867 Lochwinnoch
Mary	East Kaim	Mother		U	79	1802 Lochwinnoch
	Mother of Alexander Bartlemore, Farmer ae 50					
Robert	West Knockbartnoch		Farmer 90 ac	M	58	1823 Lochwinnoch
Elizabeth	West Knockbartnoch	Wife		M	48	1833 Houston
William	West Knockbartnoch	Son	Farm Lbr	U	19	1862 Lochwinnoch
John	West Knockbartnoch	Son	Farm Lbr	U	14	1867 Lochwinnoch
Maggie	West Knockbartnoch	Dtr	School	U	12	1869 Lochwinnoch
Mary	West Knockbartnoch	Dtr	School	U	10	1871 Lochwinnoch

Name	Place	Relation	Occupation	Status	Age	Year	Parish
Bessy	West Knockbartnoch	Dtr		U	4	1877	Lochwinnoch
Robert	Markethill		Hort. Lbr retd.	M	80	1801	Lochwinnoch
Janet		Wife		M	76	1805	Lochwinnoch
Robert		Son	Gardener	U	37	1844	Lochwinnoch

Janet Ferguson Gd dtr. U ae 17 yrs, servant. b Lochwinnoch

Name	Place	Relation	Occupation	Status	Age	Year	Parish
Anne	Calder Haugh House		Servant	U	37	1844	Lochwinnoch
Agnes	Calder St.		Nurse	U	69	1812	Lochwinnoch
James	Cross		Lic. Grocer	M	58	1823	Lochwinnoch
Margaret	Cross	Sis	Annuitant	U	48	1833	Lochwinnoch
Elizabeth	Church St.		Draper	U	50	1831	Lochwinnoch
Mary	Church St	Sis	Draper	U	45	1836	Lochwinnoch
Ann	Calder St		Housekeeper	W	74	1807	Lochwinnoch
Robert	Calder St	Son	Railway Lbr	U	34	1847	Lochwinnoch

Appendix 3

Orrs Residing in Kilbarchan Parish, 1881 Census.

Name	Address		Occupation	Status	Age	Year born	Place born
John	9 Steeple Square		Gardner	W	79	1802	Lochwinnoch
Sarah	4, Steeple St.		Hotel Keeper	W	63	1818	Johnstone
John	24 Steeple St		Weaving agent	M	39	1842	Kilbarchan
Jeanie	24 Steeple St	Wife		M	38	1843	Kilbarchan
John	24 Steeple St	Son		U	12	1869	Kilbarchan
Alexander G	24 Steeple St	Son		U	7	1874	Kilbarchan
William	36 Steeple St.		Thatcher	M	76	1805	Kilbarchan
Agnes	36 Steeple St.	Wife	Wool winder	M	50	1831	Kilmarnock
Agnes	36 Steeple St.	Dtr	Paper Mill worker.	U	15	1866	Glasgow
Janet	36 Steeple St.	Dtr	Flax Mill worker	U	12	1869	Johnstone
Thomas Smith Orr	36 Steeple St.	S/son	Gasfitter & plumber	U	19	1862	Glasgow
William	Glencart House		Thread Manufacturer	M	56	1825	Paisley
Isabella	Glencart House	Wife		M	53	1828	Neilston
James	Glencart	Visitor	Interest in	M	47	1834	Paisley

	House		money				
Eliza	Barnsbrock Farm		Dairy maid	U	26	1855	Lochwinnoch
William	Muirhead		Iron miner	M	29	1852	Ireland
Jane	Muirhead	Wife		M	27	1854	Ireland
Rebecca	Muirhead	Dtr		U	7	1874	Kilbarchan
Jane	Muirhead	Dtr		U	6	1875	Kilbarchan
William	Muirhead	Son		U	3	1878	Kilbarchan
Thomas	Muirhead	Son		U	1	1880	Kilbarchan
William	3, Blackstoun Row		Agr. lbr.	M	70	1811	Ireland
Martha	3, Blackstoun Row	Wife		M	60	1821	Ireland
James	3, Blackstoun Row	Son	Iron stone miner	M	24	1857	Ireland
Jane	3, Blackstoun Row	Dtr in law		M	23	1858	Paisley
James MITCHELL	3, Blackstoun Row	Gd son	Iron stone miner	U	17	1864	Barrhead
Martha MITCHELL	3, Blackstoun Row	Gd Dtr		U	10	1871	Linwood
John MITCHELL	3, Blackstoun Row	Gd son		U	5	1876	Linwood
William	3, Blackstoun	Gd son		U	1m	1881	Linwood

	Row						
John	15 Clippens Row	Boarder	Coal miner	U	21	1860	Johnstone
John	Crawfords Lands		Colporteur	W	64	1817	Lochwinnoch
Agnes	Crawfords Lands	Dtr		U	32	1849	Kilbarchan

Appendix 4

Orrs Residing in Kilbirnie, 1881 Census.

Name	Address		Occupation	Status	Age	Year born	Place born
Andrew	Townhead		Power loom twister	M	41	1840	Kilbirnie
Elizabeth	Townhead	Wife		M	38	1843	Port William, Wigtown
Robina	Townhead	Dt	Reeler	U	17	1864	Kilbirnie
Jane	Townhead	Dtr	Winder	U	14	1867	Kilbirnie
Elizabeth	Townhead	Dtr	School	U	8	1873	Dalry
William	Townhead	Son		U	4	1877	Kilbirnie
Elizabeth (Orr) Crawford	Lochridge West	Wife	Farm of 88 ac	M	40	1841	Kilbirnie
Margaret	Lochridge West	Mother	Annuitant	W	84	1797	Largs
Margaret	Redheugh House		Dom. servant	U	19	1862	Kilbirnie
James	Gateside Farm		Farmer 67 ac	M	54	1827	Kilbirnie
Mary	Gateside Farm	Wife		M	43	1838	Kilbirnie
Jane	Gateside Farm	Dtr	Fishing net worker	U	18	1863	Kilbirnie
Janet	Gateside Farm	Dtr	Fishing net worker	U	15	1866	Kilbirnie
Mary	Gateside Farm	Dtr	School	U	12	1869	Kilbirnie
Margaret	Gateside Farm	Dtr	School	U	10	1871	Kilbirnie

Annie	Gateside Farm	Dtr	School	U	8	1873	Kilbirnie
Hugh	Low Glengarth		Farmer 60 ac	M	50	1831	Kilbirnie
Agnes	Low Glengarth	Wife		M	47	1834	Kilbirnie
Agnes	Low Glengarth	Dtr		U	22	1859	Kilbirnie
Janet	Low Glengarth	Dtr		U	20	1861	Kilbirnie
James	Low Glengarth	Son		U	17	1864	Kilbirnie
Jane	Low Glengarth	Dtr		U	15	1866	Kilbirnie
William	Low Glengarth	Son	School	U	9	1872	Kilbirnie
Hugh	Low Glengarth	Son	School	U	5	1876	Kilbirnie
Robert	Low Glengarth	Son		U	2	1879	Kilbirnie
Rev John	The Manse		Minister	M	69	1812	Dreghorn
Jessie	The Manse	Wife		M	59	1822	Lesmahagow
Marion M	The Manse	Dtr		U	28	1853	Kilbirnie
Jessie B	The Manse	Dtr	School	U	15	1866	Kilbirnie
Margaret	Schoolwynd St.		Housekeeper	W	69	1812	Kilbirnie
William	Schoolwynd St.	Son	Masons Lbr	U	38	1843	Kilbirnie
Margaret	Schoolwynd St.	Dtr	Fishing net worker	U	25	1856	Kilbirnie
Agnes	Schoolwynd	Dtr	Fishing net	U	22	1859	Kilbirnie

	St.		worker				
Agnes	Cochran St		Fishing net gaurder	U	55	1826	Kilbirnie
Jane	Cochran St	Dtr	Fishing net worker	U	44	1837	Kilbirnie
Agnes	Cochran St	Dtr	Flax mill worker	U	15	1866	Kilbirnie
Agnes	Bridge St	Mother		W	74	1807	Lochwinnoch
Jane (Orr) Caldwell	Bridge St	Dtr		M	35	1846	Lochwinnoch
Mary	Bridge St		Dress maker	U	41	1840	Kilbirnie
John	Bridge St		Tenter,Wincey factory	M	66	1815	Kilbirnie
Jean	Bridge St	Wife		M	67	1814	Kilbirnie
John	Bridge St	Gd son	School	U	9	1872	Kilbirnie
John	Bridge St		Cabinet maker	M	32	1849	Kilbirnie
Maggie	Bridge St	Wife		M	32	1849	Cambusnethan
Martha J	Bridge St	Dtr	School	U	9	1872	Kilbirnie
Jane	Bridge St	Dtr	School	u	7	1874	Kilbirnie
Maggie	Bridge St	Dtr		U	5	1876	Kilbirnie
John	Bridge St	Son		U	3	1878	Kilbirnie
James	Main Street	Father		W	72	1809	Kilbirnie
Jeanie (Orr) Mackie	Main Street	Dtr	Flax thread mill worker	W	43	1838	Kilbirnie
William	Main St		Engine smith, flax factory	M	37	1844	Kilbirnie
Margaret (Lapraik)	Main Street	Wife		M	37	1844	Kilbirnie

Jeanie	Main Street	Dtr		U	2	1879	Kilbirnie
Jessie	Main Street	Dtr		U	1m	1881	Kilbirnie
Agnes LAPRAIK	Main Street	Step dtr	Fishing net weaver	U	17	1864	Dailly
Annie LAPRAIK	Main Street	Step dtr	School	U	12	1869	Dailly
Margaret	Bank St		Laundress		70	1811	Kilbirnie
William O Muir	Bank St	Gd son	Thread parter	U	14	1867	Kilbirnie
Margaret	Bank St		Newsagent	W	74	1807	Lochwinnoch
John Reid	Bank St	Gd son	Shoemaker	U	17	1864	Kilbirnie
John	Bank St		Flax store keeper	M	50	1831	Kilbirnie
Mary	Bank St	Wife		M	57	1824	Ireland
Annie	Bank St	Dtr	Fishing net weaver	U	31	1850	Glasgow
John	Bank St	Son	Linen thread dresser	U	23	1858	Kilbirnie
Robert	Bank St	Son	Pupil teacher	U	15	1866	Kilbirnie
Jessie	Bank St		News agent	W	65	1816	Monkton
Deborah	Bank St	Dtr	Reeler, Flax thread factory	U	29	1852	Kilbirnie
Robert	Newton St		Dairyman	U	73	1808	Kilbirnie
James	Bridgend St		Flax dresser	M	25	1856	Kilbirnie
Mary	Bridgend St	Wife		M	25	1856	Dalmellington
Catherine	Bridgend St	Dtr		U	4	1877	Kilbirnie
John	Bridgend St	Son		U	1	1880	Kilbirnie
James	Bridgend St		Iron miner	M	39	1842	Largs
Elizabeth	Bridgend St	Wife		M	38	1843	Kilbirnie
Hugh	Bridgend St	Son	Iron miner	U	18	1863	Kilbirnie

Annie	Bridgend St	Dtr	Flax spinner	U	16	1865	Kilbirnie
Jane	Bridgend St	Dtr	School	U	12	1869	Kilbirnie
Elizabeth	Bridgend St	Dtr	School	U	10	1871	Kilbirnie
John	Bridgend St	Son		U	5	1876	Kilbirnie
James	Bridgend St	Son		U	1	1880	Kilbirnie
William	Bridge St	Boarder	Gardener	W	70	1811	Kilbirnie
George	Bridge St		Thread finisher	M	27	1854	Kilbirnie
Marion	Bridge St	Wife		M	28	1853	Kilbirnie
Mary	Bridge St	Dtr	School	U	7	1874	Kilbirnie
Martha	Bridge St	Dtr		U	5	1876	Kilbirnie
John	Bridge St	Son		U	3	1878	Kilbirnie

Appendix 5

Orrs Residing in Beith Parish, 1881 Census

Name	Address		Occupation	Status	Age	Year born	Place born
Agnes	2&4 Whang St.		Grocer	W	62	1819	Dalry
Jessie Gibson	2&4 Whang St.	Dtr		U	39	1842	Beith
Agnes	2&4 Whang St.	Dtr		U	23	1858	Beith
Mary	2&4 Whang St.	Dtr		U	23	1858	Beith
Robert Longwill	Boghead		Merchant & Auctioneer	M	41	1840	Beith
Jane	Boghead	Wife		M	40	1841	Beith
Jane Smith	Boghead	Dtr	Pupil Teacher	U	15	1866	Beith
Agnes Longwill	Boghead	Dtr	School	U	13	1868	Beith
William	Boghead	Son	School	U	10	1871	Beith
Maggie Speir	Boghead	Dtr	School	U	7	1874	Beith
Ann	1 Cross	Wife		M	52	1829	Beith
George Bruce	1 Cross	Son	Joiner	U	18	1863	Beith
Robert Jr	1 Cross	Son	Stationer & Tobacc.	U	26	1855	Beith
Agnes Williams	1 Cross	Gd Dtr		U	2	1879	Beith
John	49 Buns		Chair	M	28	1853	Beith

Name	Address	Relation	Occupation	Status	Age	Year	Birthplace
	Wynd		maker				
Jane	49 Buns Wynd	Wife		M	27	1854	Beith
William	49 Buns Wynd	Son	School	U	7	1874	Beith
Jane	49 Buns Wynd	Dtr		U	3	1878	Beith
John	49 Buns Wynd	Son		U	1	1880	Beith
Elisabeth	Wardrop St			W	78	1803	Beith
Mary KENNEDY		Gd Dtr		U	9	1872	Beith
William	Crummock St.		Linen worker	M	23	1858	Beith
Jessie	Crummock St.	Wife		M	23	1858	Beith
George	Crummock St.	Son	School	U	5	1876	Beith
William	Crummock St.	Son		U	4	1877	Beith
William B	Crummock St.		Cotton Weaver	M	57	1824	Beith
Mary	Crummock St.	Wife		M	59	1822	Beith
Robert	Crummock St.		Flax mill mechanic	M	30	1851	Beith
Mary (McHARGE)	Crummock St.	Wife		M	26	1875	Kilwinning
William	Crummock St.	Son	School	U	7	1874	Beith

Name	Place	Relation	Occupation	M/U	Age	Born	Birthplace
Elisabeth	Crummock St.	Dtr	School	U	6	1875	Dalry
Mary	Crummock St.	Dtr		U	4	1877	Johnstone
Robert	Crummock St.	Son		U	2	1879	Lochwinnoch
Jane	Crummock St.	Dtr		U	4m	1881	Beith

Elisabeth McHARGE sis in law ae 15 Flax mill worker, b Kilwinning.

Name	Place	Relation	Occupation	M/U	Age	Born	Birthplace
Margaret	Gree			U	24	1857	Lochwinnoch
Martha	Gree	Sis		U	20	1860	Lochwinnoch
William	South Biggart		Farmer 96 ac	M	35	1846	Fenwick
Margaret	South Biggart	Wife		M	33	1848	Kilwinning
Robert	South Biggart	Son	School	U	9	1872	Govan
Marion S	South Biggart	Dtr	School	U	6	1875	Govan
William C	South Biggart	Son		U	4	1877	Beith
Agnes V	South Biggart	Dtr		U	1	1880	Beith
James K	Barrmill Village	Gd Son		U	10m	1880	Beith

Grandson of James Allan ae 48 b Kilbirnie & wife Ann ae 48 b Kilbirnie

Name	Place	Relation	Occupation	M/U	Age	Born	Birthplace
Robert	Barrmill Village		Overseer Thread Mfr.	M	54	1827	Beith
Agnes	Barrmill Village	Dtr	Housekpr.	U	14	1867	Beith

299

Appendix 6

Orrs Residing in Dumfries & Kirkcudbright, 1881 Census.

Name	Address	Occupn	Status	Age	Year born	Place born
Patrick	Downies Wynd, Annan, Dumfries	Labourer	U	30	1851	Glasgow
Matthew	Glentarras Distillery Langholm, Dumfries	Distiller	M	41	1840	Stirling
Mary	Glentarras Distillery Langholm, Dumfries	Wife	M	38	1843	Ireland
Emily D	Glentarras Distillery Langholm, Dumfries	Dtr	School	U	8	1873	Greenock
James	South Quintinespie, Balmaghie Kirkcudbright	Hotel keeper	M	25	1856	Borgue
Margaret	South Quintinespie, Balmaghie Kirkcudbright	Wife	M	26	1855	Irongray
Hugh	South Quintinespie, Balmaghie Kirkcudbright	Son	U	2	1879	Kelton
John	South Quintinespie, Balmaghie Kirkcudbright	Son	U	10m	1880	Kelton
Agnes	19 High St, Urr Kirkcudbright	Dom. servant	U	15	1866	Colvend

William	19 High St, Urr Kirkcudbright		Shoemak	U	18	1863	Colvend
John	Back St, Girthon Kirkcudbright		Retd Gardene	W	72	1809	Gatehouse of Fleet
Jane (Burnie)	High Rd. Kirkmabreck, Kirkcudbright	Dtr	Farmer`s widow	W	48	1833	Kirkmabreck

Dtr of Samuel & Janet Burnie of Kirkmabreck retd farmer ae 89 and wife Janet.

Hugh	Noggy, Rerrick, Kirkcudbright		Roadmar	M	53	1828	Ireland
Mary	Noggy, Rerrick, Kirkcudbright	Wife		M	45	1836	Anwoth
James M	Auldon Bank, Troqueer, Kirkcudbright		Draper`s son	U	5	1876	Maxwelltown
Thomas Alexande URR	Auldon Bank, Troqueer, Kirkcudbright	Son		U	3	1878	Maxwelltown

Appendix 7

Orrs Residing in Wigtownshire, 1881 Census

Name		Address	Relation	Occupation	Status	Age	Year	Birthplace
Jane		House Kirkcolm, Wigtown.		Dairy maid	U	22	1859	Stoneykirk
Ann		35 High St, Kirkowen, Wigtown		Washerwoman	U	47	1834	Kirkcowan
John		Smallmuir, Kirkinner Wigtown		Farmer 153 ac	M	59	1822	Mochrum
Jane		Smallmuir, Kirkinner Wigtown	Wife		M	34	1847	Anwoth
Jane		Smallmuir, Kirkinner Wigtown	Dtr		U	28	1853	Kirkinner
Annie		Smallmuir, Kirkinner Wigtown	Dtr		U	18	1863	Kirkinner
John		Airlies Farm House Kirkinner, Wigtown		Ag. lbr	U	21	1860	Mochrum
Allan		Mochrum, Wigtown		Labourer	M	66	1815	Penninghame
Elizabeth		Mochrum, Wigtown	Wife		M	57	1824	Kirkcowan
Isabella		Mochrum, Wigtown	Dtr		U	24	1857	Kirkcowan
James		Mochrum, Wigtown	Son	Shepherd	U	16	1865	Mochrum
Agnes ANDERSON		Mochrum, Wigtown	Gd Dtr		U	5	1876	Mochrum
William ANDERSON		Mochrum, Wigtown	Gd Son		U	2	1879	Mochrum
Jane		Miltonise Farm, New Luce, Wigtown		Dom. Servant	U	21	1860	Glasgow
John		Low Airyolland Farm, New Luce, Wigtown		Farmer 240 ac	M	50	1831	Inch
Grace		Low Airyolland Farm, New Luce, Wigtown	Wife		M	38	1843	Ireland

Grace Allan	Low Airyolland Farm, New Luce, Wigtown	Dtr	School		U	14	1867	New Luce
Margaret	Low Airyolland Farm, New Luce, Wigtown	Dtr	School		U	12	1869	New Luce
Emma Douglas	Low Airyolland Farm, New Luce, Wigtown	Dtr	School		U	10	1871	New Luce
Thomas Stewart Allan	Low Airyolland Farm, New Luce, Wigtown	Son			U	3	1878	New Luce
Thomas	Low Airyolland Farm, New Luce, Wigtown	Father	Ret. Farmer		M	88	1793	Ireland
William	Cults Cottages, Sorbie, Wigtown		Ag. lbr		M	27	1854	Kirkinner
Mary	Cults Cottages, Sorbie, Wigtown	Wife			M	21	1860	Stranraer
Robert	Cults Cottages, Sorbie, Wigtown	Son			U	1	1880	Sorbie
Robert	Cults Cottages, Sorbie, Wigtown		Ag Lbr		M	51	1830	Mochrum
Grave Mc C	Cults Cottages, Sorbie, Wigtown	Wife			M	52	1829	Glasserton
James	Cults Cottages, Sorbie, Wigtown	Son	Ag Lbr		U	20	1861	Glasserton
Robert	Cults Cottages, Sorbie, Wigtown	Son	School		U	12	1869	Glasserton
Jane	Cults Cottages, Sorbie, Wigtown	Dtr			U	6	1875	Glasserton
David	Penkiln Cothouse, Sorbie, Wigtown	Visitor			U	12	1869	Kirkinner
Mary	Low Cugroat, Stoneykirk, Wigtown		Dom. servant		U	15	1866	Stoney Kirk.
James	Low Cugroat,		Ag. Lbr		M	59	1822	Co. Down

Rosanna	Low Cugroat, Stoneykirk, Wigtown	Wife		M	59	1822	Co. Down
James	Low Cugroat, Stoneykirk, Wigtown	Son	Ag. Lbr	U	24	1857	Stoney Kirk
John	Low Cugroat, Stoneykirk, Wigtown	Son	Carpenter	U	20	1861	Leswalt
James	2 Princes St, Stranraer, Wigtown		Ag Lbr	M	50	1831	Co. Down
Mary A	2 Princes St, Stranraer, Wigtown	Wife		M	38	1843	Co. Down
Jane	2 Princes St, Stranraer, Wigtown	Dtr		U	7	1874	Stranraer
Margaret	2 Princes St, Stranraer, Wigtown	Dtr		U	4	1877	Stranraer
Thomas	20 Harbour St, Stranraer, Wigtown	Lodge	Clerk	U	17	1864	Stoneykirk
Jessie	50 Sheuchan St, Leswalt, Wigtown	Wife	Coach trimmers wife.	M	27	1854	Stranraer
Maggie	50 Sheuchan St, Leswalt, Wigtown	Gd Dtr		u	5	1876	Stranraer
John	50 Sheuchan St, Leswalt, Wigtown	Gd Son		U	3	1878	Stranraer
Mary	Drummarton Farm House, Whithorn, Wigtown		Servant	U	16	1865	Glasserton
Peter	1, Chapel Outon Cot House, Whithorn, Wigtown		Ploughman	M	24	1857	Glasserton

Elizabeth	1, Chapel Outon Cot House, Whithorn, Wigtown	Wife		M	21	1860 Minnigaff
George	Bladnoch Village, Wigtown		Iron Moulder	W	58	1823 Catrine, Ayr
George	Bladnoch Village, Wigtown	Son	Coach painter	M	30	1851 Ayr
Elizabeth	Bladnoch Village, Wigtown	Dtr		U	25	1856 Bladnoch
Mary	West High St, Sunnbrae House, Wigtown		Dom. Servant	U	19	1862 Kirkinner

Appendix 8

Surnames of People Who Married an Orr and Have an Entry in
The Ulster Pedigree

A Abernethy, Agnew, Alexander, Allen, Anderson, Andrew, Appleton, Armer, Armstrong, Arnold, Arthur, Auchinleak

B Bailey, Bailie, Ball, Barbour, Barnet, Barr, Barry, Basset, Bateman, Beard, Beaty, Beck, Bell, Bellamy, Bennet, Biggam, Bingham, Binsley, Black, Blackburn, Blair, Blakely, Blythe, Boden, Bole, Borrer, Bowman, Boyd, Boys, Bradly, Breeze, Brennan, Brice, Brown, Browne, Bryan, Bryson, Burgess, Burnett, Burns, Burt, Busby

C Cally, Cammack, Campbell, Carleton, Carlin, Carlisle, Carmichael, Carr, Carrenduff, Carse, Carson, Caruthers, Catherwood, Chain, Chalmers, Charters, Chatworthy, Christy, Clark, Clarke, Clegg, Cleland, Coats, Cochran, Cochrane, Conn, Conner, Connery, Cook, Cooper, Corbert, Corbet, Corry, Cosby, Cosgrove, Coulter, Cowan, Craig, Crawford, Creighton, Croft, Cross, Crossan, Crozier, Cultra, Cumberland, Cuming

D Dalzell, Davidson, Davison, Demster, Dickey, Dickson, Dobbin, Dodd, Doran, Dorman, Dougherty, Douglas, Downe, Drake, Duff, Dugan, Duglass, Dunbar, Dunlop, Dunn, Dunwoody, Dyer

E Eagleson, Eccles, Ellison, Erskine, Espy

F Falkender, Ferguson, Finlay, Finley, Fisher, Fleming, Folingsby, Forbes, Forcher, Ford, Foreman, Forester, Forsythe, Foster, Frame, Frazer, Freshfield, Frew

G Gabbey, Galway, Gamble, Garret, George, Gerrit, Gibson, Gill, Girvan, Gordon, Goudy, Gourley, Gowan, Graham, Grainger, Grant, Gray, Greer, Gregg, Gunning

H Hamilton, Hanna, Hannah, Hardy, Harper, Harris, Harrison, Harvey, Hays, Henderson, Henry, Herron, Hewit, Hill, Hitt, Hogg, Holyman, Hood, Houston, Howell, Hubbard, Huddleson, Hughs, Hunter, Hurd, Hurst, Hutchison, Hutton, Hyndman, Hynds

I Irvine

J Jackson, Jameson, Jamison, Jelly, Jennings, Joab, Johnson, Jordan

K Kearns, Kelly, Kennedy, Kernochan, Kernochen, Kerr, Killen, Kilpatrick, Kinear, King, Kinning, Kirk, Kitcher, Knight

L Lamont, Lapping, Lavery, Law, Lawrence, Laxmore, Ledgerwood, Legg, Leister, Letham, Levinson, Lewers, Lewis, Lindsay, Lindsey, Lingan, Linn, Littigo, Little, Lowry, Lyons

M Magee, Mageean, Malcom, Malcomson, Marshall, Martin, Matthews, Maxwell, Mayne, McAlpin, McAmon, McCartney, McBride, McBurney, McCalla, McCally, McCance, McCann, McCartney, McCaw, McCay, McClean, McCleary, McClelland, McClement, McClements, McClune, McClure, McComb, McConnell, McCoobry, McCormick, McCoughtry, McCoun, McCourt, McCracken, McCready, McCreary, McCrum, McCulloch, McCullough, McCullum, McCully, McCune, McCutchen, McDowell, McEwen, McFadden, McFee, McFerland, McGarraugh, McGarry, McGeehan, McGibbon, McGibbony, McGill, McGivern, McGoveny, McGowan, McGowran, McGrigor, McHarg, McIlvain, McIlveen, McKeag, McKean, McKee, McKelvey, McKelvy, McKibbin, McKinstry, McKittrick, McMahon, McMaster, McMillan, McMunn, McMurray, McQuoid, McRoberts, McVea, McWhinney, McWhirr, McWhirter, McWilliam, Melville, Miars, Miles, Miller, Milliken, Millin, Milling, Minnis, Mitchel, Montgomery, Moore, Moorehead,

Morris, Morrison, Morrow, Mullen, Mulligan, Mulree, Munse, Murdoch, Murdock, Murphy, Murray, Mussel, Mussen

N Neill, Neilson, Nesbit, Nevill, Nevin, Newberry, Norrit, Norwood

O Oakman, Orr, Owens

P Paisley, Park, Parker, Parry, Patten, Patterson, Patton, Paty, Peppard, Perry, Petticrew, Piper, Pollin, Pollock, Porter, Potts, Powell, Price

Q Quin

R Rainey, Ramage, Rankin, Rea, Read, Reid, Ricgardson Richey, Riddle, Ridgway, Roan, Robb, Robinson, Robison, Roddy, Roderman, Rodger, Ross, Rowntree, Russell

S Saul, Saunders, Scott, Shannon, Sharp, Shaw, Shearer, Shepherd, Shields, Simington, Simpson, Simson, Sinclair, Singer, Skelly, Sloan, Small, Smiley, Smith, Smyth, Snowden, Spiers, Steel, Steen, Steenson, Stevenson, Stewart, Stockdale, Stout, Strain, Summerside, Swan

T Taggart, Tate, Taylor, Templeton, Thompson, Tibbs, Todd, Torney, Trelford, Trimble

V Vance, Veacock, Vincent

W Waddle, Walker, Wallace, Walsh, Ward, Warren, Warwick, Watson, Watt, West, Whiggam, White, Wightman, Wilgare, Williamson, Wilson, Winter, Wolfenden, Wood, Woods, Wright, Wylie

Y Yates, Young

Marriagies of Orr in the female line with:

Appleton of Conlig	Johnson of Rathfriland
Barr of Bangor	Kennedy of Comber
Barr of Lisleen	Kennedy of Tullygirvan
Black of Gortrib	Kilpatrick
Blakely of Madyroe	Lewis
Boden of Craigantlet	Lowry of Ballymacashan
Burgess of Madyroe	Shaw
Burns of Cahard	Shaw of Clontinacally
Campbell	Steel of Maghrescouse
Clark of Clontinacally	MacWilliam of Ednaslate
Crawford of Carrickmadyroe	Malcolm of Bootan
Davidson of Clontinacally	Martin of Ballycloughan
Davidson Malcolm of Moat	Martin of Killynure
Dickson of Tulygirvan	Martin of Gilnahirk
Dinwoody of Carrickmadyroe	M' Burney
Dunbar of Slatady	M'Calla of Lisdoonan
Dunwoody of Madyroe	M'Clure of Clontinacally
Erskine of Woodburn	M'Connell of Ballyhenry
Frame of Munlough	M'Cormick of Ballybeen
Garret of Bal lyknockan	MCcoughtry of Ballyknockan
Garrit of Ballyknockan	M'Creary
Gregg	M`Creary of Bangor
Hamilton of Ballykeel	M'Cullock of Ballyhanwood
Hanna of Clontinacally	M`Culloch of Moneyrea
Hanna of Conlig	M`Fadden of Clontinacally
Harris of Ballymelady	M`Gee of Todstown
Harrison of Holywood	M'Gowan of Crossnacreevy
Henderson of Ballyhaskin	M' Kean
Hil of Gilnahirk	M'Kee of Lisleen
Huddlestone of Moneyrea	M`Kibbin of Haw
Hunter of Clontiriacally	M'Kibbin of Knocknasham
Hunter of Ravara	M'Kinning of Lisnasharock
Irvine of Crossnacreevy	M`Kittrick of Lisleen
Jamieson of Killaghey	M'Lean of Ballykeel

Jennings

M'Quoid of Braniel

M'Quoid of Donaghadee

Matthews

Miller of Conlig

Moore of Drummon

Morrow of Belfast

Murdock of Comber

Murdock of Gortgrib

Neilson of Ravara

Orr of Ballybeen

Orr of Ballygowan

Orr of Ballykeel

Orr of Ballyknoclcan

Orr of Bangor

Orr of Castlereagh

Orr of Clontinacally

Orr of Florida

Orr of Lisleen

Orr of Munlough

M"Munn of Lisleen

Patterson of Lisbane

Patterson of Moneyrea

Patterson of Tonachmore

Pettigrew of Ballyknockan

Piper of Comber

Porter of Ballyristle

Porter of Beechhill

Reid of Ballygowan

Riddle of Comber

Stevenson of Ballyrush

Stewart of Clontinacally

Stewart of Malone

Strain of Newtownards

Thomson of Newtownards

Todd of Ballykeel

Yates

Watson of Carryduff

White

Wright of Craigantlet

Male Orr Marriages with cousins (Orr) who resided at:

Ballyalloly

Ballybeen

Ballyblack

Ballycloughan

Ballygowan

Ballyhay

Ballykeel

Balyknockan

Ballymacarrett

Ballymisca

Ballyrea

Ballywilliam

Bangor

Bootin

The main concentrations

were around

Ballygowan

Ballykeel

Clontinacally

Braniel
Castleaverie
Castlereagh
Clontinacally
Cnotlig
Craigantlet
Dundonald
Gilnahirk
Gortg ib
Granshaw
Greyabbey
Killaghey
Killinether
Lisdoonan
Lisleen
Magherascouse
Moneyrea
Munlough
Newtownards
Saintfield
Tullyhubbert

Male Orr marriages with:

Abernethy	M'Creary
Agnew	M'Cullough
Barr	M''Garock
Boyd	M Kee
Bryson	M`Kibbin
Busby	M'Kinstry
Cally	M'Munn
Campbell	M'Quoid
Carr	M'Roberts
Carson	M'Whirter
Chalmers	Maxwell
Cleland	Miller

Corbett
Coulter
Cregg
Creighton
Cumminig
Dunlop
Ferguson
Frame
Gamble
G rey
Hamilton
Hanna
Harris
Irvine
Lamont
Lindsay
Malcolm
Malcomson
M`Birney
M`Caw
M`Cowan
M`Cleary
M'Connell

Milling
Minnis
Moorehead
Neilson
Patterson
Patty
Pollok
Porter
Rea
Reid
Rogers
Shannon
Smith
Smyth
Stevenson
Stewart
Taylor
Todd
Wallace
Walker
Wilson
Winter

Appendix 9

Extract of Orr from the Super Index of Irish Wills

The Super index ia a a compilation of available Irish will indexes, 1270-1860 compiled by Gloria Bangerter; edited and alphabetized by surname by Jeanne Jensen & Joyce Parsons. Also on microfilm at Salt Lake City: Filmed by the Genealogical Society of Utah, 2001 on 35 mm microfilm reels.

Vols. 1-3. -   Vault British Film [1145963 Items 11-13]
Vols. 4-8. -   Vault British Film [1145964]
Vols. 9-11. - Vault British Film [1145965 Items 1-3]

NOTE: The information in the table below serves as a Census substitute and only indicates that a person of that name died on or around the date shown. Be warned that the location and parish details have variable spelling and occasionally are townland names that appear in different Counties eg Carr, Corr and Curr are in Co. Tyrone.

There are Parish Maps and schedules of townlands at the Ulster Historical Foundation/Ulster Genealogical and Historical Guild site at www.ancestryireland.com.

Please do not raise your hopes that there is a document with all the family details on it. Most of these entries were probably `one liners` leaving all (and very little at that) to wife and eldest son. In many cases it was simply registering a death to protect the lease or tenancy of a son (tenancies were often given for two or three life times). Regrettably, virtually all the original Deeds and Wills of the Irish Prerogative and Consistorial Courts perished in the fire at the Royal Courts in 1922. There were some extracts made before then, such as Betham`s Index (FHL British Film 100113 Items 1-2), and the determined will hunter should look at the LDS Library Catalog under Probate for what may be available. Otherwise it is a trip to

Dublin and or Belfast, or hire a professional researcher to clutch at your straw.

Surname	Aka	Chr Name	Year	Type	Parish/County	Diocese

Abbrv. W = will proved. AB = Administration Bond.

Surname	Aka	Chr Name	Year	Type	Parish/County	Diocese
ORR		Agnes	1820	W	Drumbo	Down
		Alexander	1773	W		Prerogative
		Alexander	1811	W	Belfast	Prerogative
		Alexander	1739	W	Belfast	Prerogative
		Alexander	1766	W	Belfast	Connor
		Alexander	1842	W	Belfast	Connor
		Alexander	1766	W	Ballymoney	Connor
		Alexander	1825	W	Broad Island	Connor
		Alexander	1826	AB	Ballykeel	Connor
		Alexander	1837	W	Comber	Down
		Alexander	1813	W	Clontinacally	Down
		Alexander	1821	AB	Tullyhubbert	Down
		Alexander	1854	W		Derry
		Alexander	1801	AB	Rahan	Raphoe
		Andrew	1806	W	Loughanisland	Down
		Andrew	1840	W	Ballymartin	Down
		Anne	1841	W	Kilclieff	Down
		Anne	1843	W	New Street	Dublin
		Arthur	1753	AB	Collesker	Armagh
		Arthur	1800	W	Callesker	Armagh
		Arthur	1760	W	Cooney, Fermanagh	Clogher
		Arthur	1809	W	Comber	Down

	Charles	1805	W	Lisnafeffry, Down	Prerogative
	Charles	1831	W	Killagan	Connor
	Charles	1788	AB	Lisnafifey	Dromore
	Charles	1788	W	Lisnafifey	Dromore
	Daniel	1822	W		Armagh
	Daniel	1730	W	Ballymoney	Connor
	Daniel	1766	W	Menlagh	Down
	Daniel	1807	W	Holywood	Down
	David	1851	W	Belfast	Connor
	David	1841	W	Munlough	Down
	David	1856	W	Ballymiscaw	Down
	David	1807	W	Saintfield	Down
	David	1805	W	Comber	Down
	David	1716	W	Ballykeel	Down
	Deborah	1726	O		Dublin
	Edward	1855	W	Templecorran	Connor
	Elizabeth	1775	C	Curr, Tyrone	Armagh
	Elizabeth	1713	W	Killinether	Down
McGaresh	Elizabeth	1749	W	Bellyallely	Down
	Elizabeth	1816	W	Killinchy	Down
	Elizabeth	1805	W	Newtownards	Down
	Francis	1797	W	Kilstroll/Ardstraw	Derry
	Gawin	1771	AB		Raphoe
	George	1831	AB	Ballyon Lib. of Derry	Derry
	George	1760	W	Ballynascreen	Derry
	Hugh	1807	W	Newtownards	Down

Hugh	1851	W	Grand Canal Harbour	Dublin
Hugh	1770	W	Gobnescale Templemore	Derry
Jackson	1851	W		Down
James	1808	W	Gorton, Derry	Prerogative
James	1842	AB	Annarea	Armagh
James	1842	W	Annarea	Armagh
James	1806	W	Loughgall	Armagh
James	1823	W	Loughgeele	Connor
James	1819	W	Crumlin	Connor
James	1808	W	Ross	Connor
James	1800	W	Broadisland	Connor
James	1797	W	Cravery Parish,Antrim	Connor
James	1853	W	Ballybeen	Down
James	1820	W	Comber	Down
James	1828	W	Comber	Down
James	1832	W	Munlough	Down
James	1838	W	Ballykeel	Down
James	1842	W	Munlough	Down
James	1846	W	Kirkcubbin	Down
James	1734	C	Castle Avery	Down
James	1728	W	Munlagh/ Munlough	Down
James	1852	W	Lismastrain	Down
James	1817	W	Comber	Down
James	1812	W	Kirkcubbin	Down
James	1803	W	Killinchy	Down

	James	1802	W	Granshough	Down
	James	1798	W	Comber	Down
	James	1788	W	Ballykeel	Down
	James	1784	W	Lisleen	Down
	James	1742	AB	Cumber	Down
	James	1737	AB	Newtown	Down
	James	1758	AB	Ballybeen	Down
	James	1813	AB	Kirkcubbin	Down
	James	1750	W	Ballygoun	Down
	James	1761	W	Ballylesson	Down
	James	1773	W	Lisnasallagh	Down
	James	1776	W	Moyesset, Derry	Derry
	James	1709	AB	Letterkenny	Raphoe
	Jane	1740	W	Ralloo	Connor
Walker	Jane	1740	W		Down
	Jane	1791	W		Down
Brison	Jane	1826	W	Saint Andrews	Down
	Jane	1801	AB		Derry
	Janet	1755	W	Bellygown/ Ballygowan	Down
	John	1771	W	Killyncather, Down	Down
	John	1780	W	Ballybritain, Derry	Prerogative
	John	1807	W	Magherafelt, Derry	Prerogative
	John	1699	W	Letterkenny	Prerogative
	John	1801	AB	Ballyeglish	Armagh

John	1831	AB	Armagh	Armagh
John	1815	W	Mullantine	Armagh
John	1831	W	Armagh	Armagh
John	1832	W	Ballymagerney	Armagh
John	1801	W	Ballynick	Armagh
John	1787	AB	Tattenclave	Clogher
John	1856	W	Ballintoy	Connor
John	1853	W	Derryaghy	Connor
John	1729	W	Belfast	Connor
John	1742	W	Coleraine	Connor
John	1770	W	Coleraine	Connor
John	1777	W	Connor	Connor
John	1787	W	Portrush	Connor
John	1795	W	Cavehill	Connor
John	1802	W	Greencastle	Connor
John	1822	W	Raloo	Connor
John	1851	W	Derryaghy	Connor
John	1802	W	Saintfield	Down
John	1802	W	Cunningburn	Down
John	1803	W	Comber	Down
John	1805	W	Donaghadee	Down
John	1809	W	Ballyaloly	Down
John	1810	W	Comber	Down
John	1812	W	Drumbo	Down
John	1823	W	Drumbo	Down
John	1832	W	Moneyrea	Down
John	1837	W	Ballywilliam	Down
John	1839	W	Ballykeel	Down

John	1840	W	Clontinacally	Down
John	1842	W	Granshaw	Down
John	1847	W	Ballyaugherty	Down
John	1742	W	Ballyrolly	Down
John	1722	W	Clintincally	Down
John	1801	W	Saintfield	Down
John	1789	AB	Portaferry	Down
John	1803	AB	Cumber	Down
John	1806	AB	Knockbreda	Down
John	1758	W	Ballytriel	Down
John	1765	W	Clantenacally	Down
John	1773	W	Ballykeel	Down
John	1797	W	Comber	Down
John	1800	W	Lisleen	Down
John	1852	AB	Kernon Tullylish	Dromore
John	1852	W	Kernon Tullylish	Dromore
John	1742	A	Dublin	Dublin
John	1777	AB	Glenherdeal	Derry
John	1804	AB	Gortniskeig	Derry
John	1826	AB	Ballagan Desertoghill	Derry
John	1804	AB	Gortin	Derry
John	1844	W	Eden/Tamlag htocrilly	Derry
John	1786	W	Glencordial/C appagh	Derry
John	1779	W	Strabane	Derry

	John	1826	W	Ballyagin/De sertoghill	Derry
	John	1751	W	Killybracj/ Cappagh	Derry
	John	1767	W	New Ross	Ferns
	John	1773	W	Ballymartin, Down	New Mourne
	John	1806	W	Ballymartin	New Mourne
	John	1818	W	Turlagshill	New Mourne
	John	1728	AB		Raphoe
	John	1773	AB	Raphoe	Raphoe
	Joseph	1807	W	Ballymagerne y	Armagh
	Joseph	1839	W	Carrickpolan d, Ferm	Clogher
	Joseph	1825	W	Connor	Connor
	Joseph	1848	AB	Lisnamallard Cappagh	Derry
Coultert	Margaret	1721	W	Balleykill	Down
	Mary Ann	1746	W	Glenavy	Connor
	Mary	1851	W	Inishannon	Cork & Ross
	Mary	1847	W	Kircubbin	Down
	Mary Ann	1800	W	Comber	Down
Leathem	Mary	1821	W	Cumber	Down
	Mary	1803	W	Newtownards	Down
Risk	Mary	1810	W		Dromore
	Matthew	1800	AB	Killybrack Cappagh	Derry

Matthew	1807	W	Saul	Down
Matthew	1800	W	Killybrack/Cappagh	Derry
Matthew	1815	AB	Moness	Raphoe
Nancy	1853	W	Kirkinriola	Connor
Nathaniel	1831	W	Kilbride	Connor
Patrick	1783	AB	Dunmisk Parish	Armagh
Patrick	1734	W	Dunaghy	Connor
Patrick	1824	W	Drumhirk	Down
Peter	1744	W	Dunluce	Connor
Peter	1762	AB	Kirkcubbin	Down
Porter	1855	AB	Kirkcubbin	Down
Rebecca	1811	W	Harborne	Prerogative
Rebecca	1762	AB	Late of Curr	Armagh
Richard	1563	O	Clontarf	Dublin
Robert	1765	AB	Carragh Loughgall	Armagh
Robert	1846	AB	Annarea	Armagh
Robert	1846	W	Annarea	Armagh
Robert	1765	W	Corragh	Armagh
Robert	1839	W	Sionee, Tyrone	Clogher
Robert	1772	W	Drumin	Clogher
Robert	1773	AB	Drumin	Clogher
Robert	1856	W	Derryaghy	Connor
Robert	1768	W	Lambeg	Connor
Robert	1836	W	Belfast	Connor
Robert	1740	AB	Cumber	Down
Robert	1813	AB	Kirkcubbin	Down
Robert	1836	AB	Ballyhalbert	Down

Robert	1821	W		Down
Robert	1812	W	Kircubbin	Down
Robert	1780	W	Portgribb	Down
Robert	1808	W	Torbuoy, Log.	Ardagh
Robert	1794	W	Killybrack Cappagh	Derry
Robert	1706	W	Miniranoll (Moneyrannel)	Derry
Robert	1760	W	Bellior Clondermott	Derry
Robert	1798	W	Lisdoogan, Sligo	Kil/Achn
Samuel	1831	AB	Aney	Armagh
Samuel	1815	W	Drumnassoo	Armagh
Samuel	1831	W	Gorteclar	Armagh
Samuel	1760	W	Curr	Armagh
Samuel	1824	W	Antrim	Connor
Samuel	1733	W	Killead	Connor
Samuel	1765	W		Connor
Samuel	1768	W	Ballynure	Connor
Samuel	1796	W	Kilbegs	Connor
Samuel	1814	W	Antrim	Connor
Samuel	1849	AB	Levalleyreagh	Dromore
Samuel	1849	W	Levalleyreagh	Dromore
Samuel	1750	W	Shannamugh /Ardstraw	Derry
Sarah	1843	W		Cork/Ross
Sarah	1828	W	Strabane	Derry
Thomas	1839	AB	Ballynick	Armagh

Thomas	1839	W	Ballynick	Armagh
Thomas	1813	W	Belfast	Connor
Thomas	1813	W	Ballygowan	Down
Thomas	1806	W	Saintfield	Down
Thomas	1847	W	Clontinacally	Down
Thomas	1819	W	Drumbo	Down
Thomas	ND	AB	Ballyculla	Down
William	1757	W	Ballybeen	Prerogative
William	1819	AB	Gortlenaghan	Armagh
William	1831	AB	Aney	Armagh
William	1775	AB	Curr	Armagh
William	1808	W	Gorey	Armagh
William	1816	W	Coragh	Armagh
William	1819	W		Armagh
William	1770	W	Ballygurk, Derry	Armagh
William	1761	W	Ballywillen	Connor
William	1775	W	Ballylinney	Connor
William	1682	W	Belfast	Connor
William	1782	W	Ballymoney	Connor
William	1783	W	Ballyeaston	Connor
William	1815	W	Antrim	Connor
William	1857	W	Ballymoney	Connor
William	1856	W	Ballymoney	Connor
William	1853	W	Antrim	Connor
William	1842	W	Inishannon, Cork	Cork & Ross
William	1800	W	Ballykeel	Down
William	1800	W	Tallyhobert	Down

	William	1803	W	Newtownards	Down
	William	1815	W	Saintfield	Down
	William	1818	W	Donaghadee	Down
	William	1820	W	Drumbo	Down
	William	1825	W	Bangor	Down
	William	1833	W	Raffery	Down
	William	1844	W	Roddins	Down
	William	1727	W	Lisbane	Down
	William	1714	W	Clontinacally	Down
	William	1773	W	Grey Abbey	Down
	William	1766	W	Conligg	Down
	William	1730	W	Ballybeen	Down
	William	1727	W	Comber	Down
	William	1797	AB	Saintfield	Down
	William	1855	AB	Roddins	Down
	William	1822	AB	Tullaloob	Dromore
	William	1785	W	Strabane	Derry
	William	1838	W	Omagh	Derry
	William	1790	W	Gorton, Derry	Derry
	William	1724	W	New Buildings	Derry
	William	1745	AB	Cooladerry	Raphoe
	William	1709	AB	Taughboyne	Raphoe
ORRE	Alexander	1699	AB	Raphoe	Raphoe
ORRE	James	1716	W		Down
ORRE	John	1792	W	Mulerton	New Mourne

Prior to 1857 wills were proved in the Consistorial Court of the Bishop or Ordinary of the diocese in which a person dwelt. But if there were effects valued at £5 in two or more dioceses the will had to be proved in the Prerogative Court of the Archbishop of Armagh, Primate of All Ireland. The latter was the supreme court in matters where there was ecclesiastical jurisdiction. The jurisdiction of the Church Courts was abolished and transferred to the Probate Court in 1857.

Separate to the Church Courts, since 25 March 1708 there has been a Registry of Deeds in Ireland. Transcripts of wills and other devises or deeds including mortgages, conveyances, marriage settlements, rents, rights of way, and partnerships. These are recorded in shortened version and bound into large books that may be inspected at the Registry. The original memorials are stored separately in a fire proof vault. The Registry of Deeds has a vast amount of material besides wills, that can be of assistance to the researcher.

Have a look at what PRONI has to say – go to their web site at http://proni.nics.gov.uk/records/deeds.htm

Appendix 10

Griffith Valuation & Tithe Survey, Index of Orr

Total Number of ORR Householders in COUNTY ANTRIM

Householders Recorded; Civil Parish;(Barony *) Poor Law Union;
Year of Valuation; Present In Parish; Year of Survey

* The name of the barony is included only where the civil parish is
located in more than one barony.

10 Connor Antrim & Ballymena 1862 Yes 1835
8 Templecorran Larne 1861 Yes 1833
7 Tickmacrevan Larne 1861 No 1832
7 Derryaghy (Upper Massereene) Lisburn 1862 Yes 1827
6 Blaris Lisburn 1862 Yes 1834
5 Loughguile (Upper Dunluce) Ballymoney 1861 Yes 1832
5 Finvoy Ballymoney 1861 No 1834
5 Ballymoney (Upper Dunluce) Ballymoney 1861 Yes 1825
4 Antrim (Antrim Upper) Antrim 1862 Yes 1833
3 Kirkinriola Ballymena 1862 Yes 1833
3 Shilvodan Grange Antrim 1862 Yes 1833
3 Grange Of Dundermot Ballymena 1862 Yes 1834
3 Island Magee Larne 1861 Yes 1834
3 Grange Of Ballyscullion Ballymena 1862 No
2 Rasharkin Ballymena & Ballymoney 1861 No 1834
2 Raloo Larne 1861 Yes 1830
2 Skerry Ballymena 1862 Yes 1833
2 Kilbride Antrim 1862 Yes 1833
2 Craigs (Lower Toome) Ballymena 1862 Yes 1825
2 Antrim (Part Of Toome Upper) Antrim 1862 No 1833
2 Ballyclug Ballymena 1862 No 1825
2 Ballintoy Ballycastle 1861 No 1824
1 Templepatrick (Lower Belfast) Antrim & Belfast 1862 No 1833
1 Magheragall Lisburn 1862 No 1827

1 Larne Larne 1861 No 1834
1 Newtown Crommelin Ballymena 1862 No 1833
1 Racavan Ballymena 1862 No
1 Shankill (Upper Belfast) Belfast & Lisburn 1861 Yes 1834
1 Killagan (Upper Dunluce) Ballymoney 1861 No 1832
1 Kilwaughter Larne 1861 Yes 1834
1 Inver Larne 1861 No 1833
1 Carncastle Larne 1861 No 1834
1 Carnmoney Belfast 1861 No 1826
1 Billy (Lower Dunluce) Ballymoney & Coleraine 1861 No 1826
1 Derryaghy (Upper Belfast) Lisburn 1862 Yes 1827
1 Carrickfergus Larne 1861 No 1827
1 Dunaghy Ballymena 1862 Yes 1825
1 Glynn Larne 1861 No 1833
1 Dunluce Ballymoney & Coleraine 1861 No 1828
1 Drummaul Antrim And Ballymena 1862 Yes 1834
1 Ahoghill (Lower Antrim) Ballymena 1862 No 1825
0 Ballyrashane Ballymoney & Coleraine 1861 Yes 1832
0 Ballyscullion Ballymena 1862 Yes 1828
0 Killead Antrim 1862 Yes 1827
107 Total Householders Recorded

Householders in COUNTY ARMAGH

Householders Recorded; Civil Parish (Barony *); Poor Law Union;
Year Of Valuation; Present In Parish; Year Of Survey

16 Loughgall (Oneilland West) Armagh 1864 Yes 1830
7 Kilmore (Oneilland West) Armagh 1864 No 1833
4 Grange (Oneilland West) Armagh 1864 Yes 1832
4 Keady (Armagh) Armagh 1864 No 1825
4 Kildarton (Oneilland West) Armagh 1864 No
3 Magheralin Lurgan 1864 Yes 1834
3 Shankill Lurgan 1864 Yes 1833
3 Mullaghbrack (Fews Lower) Armagh 1864 Yes 1834
3 Drumcree Lurgan 1864 No 1827

3 Derrynoose (Armagh) Armagh 1864 No 1825

3 Kilclooney (Fews Lower) Armagh 1864 No

2 Tartaraghan Armagh, Lurgan 1864 Yes 1833

2 Lisnadill (Fews Lower) Armagh 1864 No

2 Lisnadill (Armagh) Armagh 1864 No

2 Mullaghbrack (Oneilland West) Banbridge 1864 Yes 1834

2 Seagoe Lurgan 1864 No 1830

2 Armagh (Armagh) Armagh 1864 No 1833

1 Tynan (Tiranny) Armagh 1864 Yes 1827

1 Loughgilly (Orior Lower) Newry & Banbridge 1864 No 1834

1 Loughgall (Armagh) Armagh 1864 Yes 1830

1 Grange (Armagh) Armagh 1864 No 1832

1 Kilclooney (Orior Lower) Armagh 1864 No

70 Total Householders Recorded

Householders in COUNTY CAVAN

Householders Recorded; Civil Parish: (Barony *); Poor Law Union;
Year of Valuation; Present In Parish; Year of Survey

2 Shercock Bailieborough 1857 No 1825

2 Kilbride Cavan & Oldcastle 1856 Yes 1825

1 Bailieborough (Clankee) Bailieborough 1856 Yes 1826

1 Killinkere (Castlerahan) Bailieborough & Oldcastle 1857 No
1833

0 Drumlane Bawnboy & Cavan 1857 Yes 1829

6 Total Householders Recorded

Householders in COUNTY DONEGAL

Householders Recorded; Civil Parish;(Barony *) Poor Law Union;
Year of Valuation; Present In Parish; Year of Survey

6 Moville Upper Inishowen 1857 Yes 1828

5 Taughboyne Derry & Strabane 1857 Yes 1826

4 Raphoe Strabane, Stranorlar & Letterkenny 1857 No 1841

328

3 Burt Londonderry 1858 No 1837
3 Donaghmore Strabane & Stranorlar 1857 Yes 1828
2 Culdaff Inishowen 1857 Yes 1829
2 Muffderry & Inishowen 1858 No 1837
2 Killea Derry 1857 Yes 1830
2 Kilmacrenan Dunfanaghy, Letterkenny & Millford 1857 No 1825
1 All Saints Letterkenny & Derry 1857 No
1 Aghanunshin Letterkenny 1857 No 1834
1 Clonleigh Strabane 1857 Yes 1826
1 Clonca Inishowen 1857 Yes 1828
1 Clondavaddog Millford & Letterkenny 1858 No 1834
1 Inver Donegal 1857 No 1825
1 Tullyfern Millford 1858 No 1830
1 Tullaghobegly Dunfanaghy 1857 No 1830
1 Urney Strabane 1857 Yes 1825
0 Fahan Lower Inishowen 1857 Yes 1829
0 Kilteevoge Stranorlar 1857 Yes 1834
38 Total Householders Recorded

Householders in COUNTY DOWN

Householders Recorded; Civil Parish; (Barony *) Poor Law Union;
Year of Valuation; Present In Parish; Year of Survey

21 Kilkeel Kilkeel 1864 Yes 1823
12 Newtownards (Ards Lower) Newtownards 1863 No 1833
9 Donaghadee Newtownards 1863 Yes 1834
5 Newtownards (Castlereagh Lower) Newtownards 1863 No 1833
5 Ballyphillip Downpatrick 1863 Yes 1827
5 Bangor (Lower Ards) Newtownards 1863 No 1833
5 Grey Abbey Newtownards 1863 No 1833
4 Saul Downpatrick 1863 Yes 1833
4 Tullylish Banbridge & Lurgan 1864 Yes 1833
4 Killinchy (Castlereagh Upper) Newtownards & Downpatrick
1863 Yes 1833
3 Magheralin Upper Half, Lurgan 1864 Yes 1834

3 Shankill Upper Half, Lurgan 1864 Yes 1833

3 Donaghmore Newry 1864 Yes 1829

3 Killinchy (Dufferin) Downpatrick & Newtownards 1863 Yes 1833

3 Downdownpatrick 1864 No 1833

3 Ballyhalbert (St Andrews) Newtownards 1863 Yes 1834

3 Killinchy (Castlereagh Lower) Newtownards 1863 Yes 1833

2 Saintfield Downpatrick & Lisburn 1863 Yes 1834

2 Seapatrick (Iveagh Upper) Banbridge 1864 Yes 1828

2 Magherahamlet Downpatrick & Lisburn 1864 No 1827

2 Drumbo Lisburn 1863 Yes 1829

2 Donaghcloney Upper Half, Lurgan 1864 No 1834

2 Comber (Castlereagh Upper), Lisburn & Newtownards 1864 Yes 1834

1 Seapatrick (Iveagh Lower), Banbridge 1864 Yes 1828

1 Tullynakill Newtownards 1863 No 1833

1 Loughinisland Downpatrick 1863 No 1828

1 Magheradrool, Downpatrick & Lisburn 1863 Yes 1834

1 Knockbreda (Castlereagh Lower), Belfast 1864 Yes 1833

1 Kilmood Newtownards 1863 Yes 1829

1 Knockbreda (Castlereagh Upper) Belfast & Lisburn 1864 Yes 1833

1 Kilmore (Kinelarty) Downpatrick 1863 No 1836

1 Killyleagh (Dufferin) Downpatrick 1864 No 1827

1 Dromara (Iveagh Lower), Banbridge & Lisburn 1864 No 1826

1 Dundonald Belfast & Newtownards1863 Yes 1834

1 Maghera Kilkeel 1863 Yes 1831

1 Ardkeen, Downpatrick & Newtownards 1863 No 1834

1 Ballyculter Downpatrick 1863 No 1834

1 Inishargy Newtownards 1863 No 1833

0 Dromore Banbridge & Lisburn 1864 Yes 1834

0 Dromore Banbridge & Lisburn 1864 Yes 1834

0 Kilclief Downpatrick 1864 Yes 1830

122 Total Householders Recorded

Householders in COUNTY FERMANAGH

Householders Recorded; Civil Parish (Barony *); Poor Law Union; Year of Valuation; Present In Parish; Year of Survey

2 Aghalurcher, Lisnaskea 1862 Yes 1833
1 Aghavea Lisnaskea 1862 Yes 1832
1 Derryvullan (Tirkennedy), Enniskillen 1862 Yes 1835
4 Total Householders Recorded

Householders in COUNTY LONDONDERRY

Householders Recorded; Civil Parish (Barony *); Poor Law Union; Year of Valuation; Present In Parish; Year of Survey

11 Artrea Magherafelt 1859 No 1829
7 Clondermot (Tirkeeran)
Londonderry 1858 Yes 1834
6 Faughanvale, Londonderry & Newtownlimavady 1858 Yes 1835
6 Cumber Lower Londonderry 1858 No 1827
5 Tamlaght Finlagan, Newtownlimavady 1858 No 1826
5 Templemore (N W Liberties), Londonderry 1858 No
4 Templemore (North Ward), Londonderry 1858 No
3 Templemore (East Ward), Londonderry 1858 No
3 Aghadowey, Coleraine & Ballymoney 1859 Yes 1833
3 Bovevagh Newtownlimavady 1859 No 1827
3 Coleraine Coleraine 1859 No 1827
3 Templemore (South Ward), Londonderry 1858 No
2 Desertoghill, Coleraine & Ballymoney 1859 Yes 1832
2 Tamlaght O'crilly (Loughlinsholin), Coleraine & Magherfelt 1859 Yes 1833
2 Ballynascreen Magherafelt 1859 Yes 1825
2 Ballyaghran Coleraine 1859 Yes 1829
1 Kilcronaghan Magherafelt 1859 Yes 1828

1 Errigal Coleraine 1859 No 1825
1 Tamlaght O'crilly (Coleraine), Ballymoney 1859 Yes 1833
1 Tamlaghtard Agilligan), Newtownlimavady 1858 No 1826
1 Aghanloo Newtownlimavady 1858 No 1829
1 Balteagh Newtownlimavady 1858 Yes 1829
1 Clondermot (East Ward), Londonderry 1858 No
1 Cumber Upper Londonderry & Newtownlimavady 1858 No
1 Lissan Magherafelt 1859 No 1827
1 Maghera Magherafelt 1859 Yes 1828
0 Dungiven Newtownlimavady 1859 Yes 1833
0 Magherafelt Magherafelt 1859 Yes 1828
0 Derryloran Magherafelt 1859 Yes 1826
0 Ballyscullion Magherafelt 1859 Yes 1828
0 Ballyrashane Coleraine 1859 Yes 1832
0 Banagher (Keenaght), Newtownlimavady 1858 Yes 1826
0 Desertmartin Magherafelt 1859 Yes 1827
0 Killowen Coleraine 1859 Yes 1830
0 Macosquin Coleraine 1859 Yes 1830
0 Termoneeny Magherafelt 1859 Yes 1828
77 Total Householders Recorded

Householders in COUNTY MONAGHAN

Householders Recorded; Civil Parish (Barony *); Poor Law Union;
Year of

Valuation; Present In Parish; Year Of Survey

14 Clontibret Castle Blayney & Monaghan 1860 Yes 1830
1 Drumsnat Monaghan 1860 Yes 1827
15 Total Householders Recorded

Householders in COUNTY TYRONE

Householders Recorded; Civil Parish (Barony *); Poor Law Union;
Year of Valuation; Present In Parish; Year of Survey

11 Artrea Cookstown 1860 No 1833

11 Ardstraw (Omagh West), Castlederg 1860 No 1833

10 Ardstraw (Lower Strabane), Castlederg, Gortin, Omagh & Strabane 1860 Yes 1833

6 Donaghcavey (Clogher), Clogher & Omagh 1860 Yes 1827

6 Drumragh Omagh 1860 Yes 1830

6 Clogherny Omagh 1860 Yes 1826

5 Clonfeacle Dungannon 1860 Yes 1833

3 Donaghmore Dungannon 1860 Yes 1815

2 Killeeshil Dungannon & Clogher 1860 Yes 1829

2 Ballyclog Cookstown 1860 Yes 1826

2 Aghalurcher Clogher 1862 Yes 1833

2 Ardboe Cookstown 1860 Yes 1826

2 Leckpatrick Strabane 1860 No 1827

1 Termonamongan Castlederg 1860 No 1826

1 Donaghcavey (East Omagh), Omagh 1860 Yes 1827

1 Donaghedy Strabane & Gortin 1860 No

1 Errigal Keerogue, Clogher & Dungannon 1860 No 1833

1 Bodoney Lowergortin 1859 Yes 1830

1 Camus Strabane 1858 Yes 1827

1 Cappagh (Omagh East) Omagh 1860 No 1826

1 Carnteel Clogher & Dungannon 1860 No 1827

1 Bodoney Uppergortin 1859 No

1 Lissan Cookstown 1860 No 1827

1 Pomeroy Cookstown & Dungannon 1860 No 1829

0 Termonmaguirk (East Omagh), Omagh 1860 Yes 1825

0 Derryloran Cookstown 1860 Yes 1826

0 Dromore Omagh & Lowtherstown 1860 Yes 1834

0 Dromore Omagh & Lowtherstown 1860 Yes 1834

0 Longfield West Castlederg 1860 Yes 1826

0 Kilskeery, Enniskillen & Lowtherstown 1860 Yes 1826

79 Total Householders Recorded

Appendix 11

Irish Flax Growers List, 1796

The 1796 Flax Growers Bounty List is held in the Linenhall Library, Belfast which gives the names of farmers in all parishes who were awarded spinning wheels and looms for growing areas of flax. Lists are available for all the counties of Ireland except for Dublin and Wicklow, and are arranged in parishes within the county. Unfortunately the townlands are not given. It is especially useful for Co Donegal as there are some 7000 names (from a total of about 55,000 on the list). Some women feature in entries especially in the province of Munster.

The list is in the Latter Day Saints library. British film area 12, fiche # 6341104.

ID County Surname Given Name

263 Antrim Orr Robert
818 Antrim Orr Thomas
974 Antrim Orr James

1457 Armagh Orr Joseph
2453 Armagh Orr Robert
3817 Armagh Orr William
4169 Armagh Orr James
8333 Donegal Orr William
8334 Donegal Orr James
9985 Donegal Orr William
10155 Donegal Orr Agnis
11643 Donegal Orr Andrew
12194 Donegal Orr Alexander
2489 Donegal Orr Arthur
12768 Donegal Orr Robert

13534 Donegal Orr Andrew
13807 Donegal Orr Robert
13852 Donegal Orr Robert
13873 Donegal Orr David
14210 Donegal Orr Matt
14507 Donegal Orr Mathew
14536 Donegal Orr James
14558 Donegal Orr Robert
14612 Donegal Orr David
14652 Donegal Orr Mathew
14654 Donegal Orr Jane
15014 Donegal Orr Widow

16646 Down Orr Samuel
16684 Down Orr Charles
16720 Down Orr Thomas
16780 Down Orr John
17016 Down Orr John
17017 Down Orr Gowan
17032 Down Orr James
17066 Down Orr John
17960 Down Orr Charles
18236 Down Orr William
18578 Down Orr Matthew
18581 Down Orr John
18637 Down Orr Samuel

18987 Fermanagh Orr John

23457 Londonderry Orr John
24320 Londonderry Orr William
24779 Londonderry Orr John, jun
24798 Londonderry Orr John, sen
25114 Londonderry Orr Elizabeth
25134 Londonderry Orr William
25867 Londonderry Orr Richard

26072 Londonderry Orr Hugh
26196 Londonderry Orr Samuel
26255 Londonderry Orr Joseph
26324 Londonderry Orr Isaac
26448 Londonderry Orr James
26452 Londonderry Orr George

31940 Longford Orr Robert

47773 Sligo Orr Robert
48530 Tyrone Orr Walter
48589 Tyrone Orr Joseph
49060 Tyrone Orr James
49504 Tyrone Orr James
49915 Tyrone Orr William
49916 Tyrone Orr Robert
49937 Tyrone Orr John
49956 Tyrone Orr Patrick
50099 Tyrone Orr George
50126 Tyrone Orr William
50582 Tyrone Orr William
50598 Tyrone Orr David
50635 Tyrone Orr George
50646 Tyrone Orr William
50647 Tyrone Orr David
50740 Tyrone Orr Samuel
50762 Tyrone Orr Alexander
50868 Tyrone Orr Allen
50927 Tyrone Orr Hnery
52720 Tyrone Orr William
52787 Tyrone Orr Patrick
52944 Tyrone Orr James
53644 Tyrone Orr Samuel
54335 Tyrone Orr William

4

Appendix 12
Fugitives and Banished Persons after the 1798 Rebellion.

Fugitives

After the Rebellion was at an end, apart from deserters and desperados excluded from the amnesty proclaimed by Lord Cornwallis, every individual of any note connected with the Revolutionary movements, had either been pardoned or expatriated. The more timid evaded the vengeance of the government by voluntary exile and of the more prominent leaders, the following brief abstract of the names included in the Fugitive and Banishment Acts, will generally tell their fate.

Under the Fugitive Act were included:

Adair, Henry	Lewins, Edw. John
Bashford, Thomas Gunning	Lowry, Alexander
Burke, William .	M'Can, Authony
Burke, James	M'Cormick, Rich
Bryson, Andrew	M'Guire, John
Campbell, William	M'Mahon, Arthur
Cooke, Patrick	Matthew
Cormick, John	Morris, Harvey
Cullen, William	Mouritz, Joseph, or Joshua
Delany, Michael	Neale, James
Derry, Valentine	Nervin, John
Dixon, Thomas	O'Finn, Edward
Duckett, John	O'Brien, John
Duignan, Miles	Orr, Joseph
Egan, Cornelius	Orr, Robert
Fitzpatrick, Mich	Plunkett, James
Holt, Joseph	Reynolds, Michael
Houston, Thomas	Scully, John
Hull, James	Short, Miles
Jackson, John	Short, Owen

Jackson,
Kenna, Matthew James
Kelly, James
Keogh, Bryan
Lawless, William

Swift, Deane
Teeling, Bart
Townsend, James
Turner, Samuel *

* Shot afterwards in a duel, in the Isle of Man.

The Banishment Act contained the names of::

Andoe, Thomas
Astley, Alexander
Aylmer, William
Banks, Henry
Bannen, Peter
Barrett, John
Boyle, Edward
Brady, Thomas
Bushe, James M.
Byrne, Richard
Byrne, Patrick
Byrne, Patrick
Byrne, Garret
Carthy, Dennis
Castles, John
Chambers, John
Comyn, John
Cormick, Joseph
Corcoran, Peter
Cuff, Farrell
Cumming, George
Cuthbert, Joseph
Daly, Richard
Davis, Joseph
Dillon, Richard
Devine, Patrick

Lacy John
Lube, George
Lynch, John
Lynch, Patrick
M'Cabe, Wm. Putnam
M' Dermott, Bryan
Macneven, William James
Macan, Patrick
Martin, Christian
Madden, Patrick
Meagher, Francis
MWiken, Israel
Mowney, Patrick
Mulhall, Michael
Neilson, Robert
Neilson, Samuel
O'Connor, Arthur
O'Reilly, Richard
Quigley, Michael
Redfern, Robert
Reily, John
Reynolds, Thomas
Rose, James
Russell, Thomas
Sweetman, John
Smyth, James

338

Dorney, John
Dowling, Matthew
Doyle, Michael
Dry, Thomas
Emmett, Thos. Addisn.
Evans, Hamden
Farrell, Andrew
Farrell, Denis
Fitzgerald, Edward
Flood, Michael
Geraghty, James
Goodman, Robert
Goodman, Rowland
Greene, John
Griffin, Lawrence
Haffey, James
Hanlon, Patrick
Harrison, John,
Houston, William
Ivers, Peter
Jackson, Henry
Kavanagh, Morgan
Keane, Ed.
Keenan, John
Kelly, Lawrence
Kennedy, John
Kennedy, Jn. Gorman
Kinkead, John
Kinselagh, John

Sampson, William
Speers, Henry
Swing, John
Tierman, James
Toland, Daniel
Ware, Hugh
Young, John

Appendix 13

Orr Who Served in the Royal Irish Constabulary, 1816–1921

The Royal Irish Constabulary was disbanded in 1922 and replaced by the Garda Siochana in Ireland and the Royal Ulster Constabulary in Northern Ireland. These records are on microfilm from the LDS.

Name	Chr. name	Age	Born	Married	Enlisted
ORR	William	18	Kilkenny	Y	1867
	James	18	Limerick		1875
	Samuel	21	Longford	Y	1870
	Joshua	19	Londonderry	Y	1881
	David	19	Londonderry		1876 d1882
	James	18	Londonderry		1881 d1884
	Robert	18	Meath		1862
	William	18	Queens		1867
	John	22		Y	1868
	John	19	Wicklow		1873 d1894
	Daniel	28	Antrim	Y	1837
	David	19	Londonderry		1847
	James	26	Wicklow	Y	1826
	James	20	Londonderry	Y	1852
	James	19	Wicklow		1848 d1866
	John	20	Cork	Y	1830
	Joseph	19	Tipperary		1852
	William	28	Armagh		1832
	David	20			1849

	John	23	Armagh		1853
	Robert	20	Tipperary	Y	1855
	John	19	Londonderry		1856
	John	20			1857
	Thomas	26	Londonderry	Y	1857
ORR	Thomas	19	Kilkenny		1858
	John James	19			1859
	James	21	Antrim	Y	1850
	William James	19	Londonderry went to Australia		1860
	Jacob	20	Armagh		1872 d1876

341

Appendix 14

Orr Related Documents in PRONI.

Orr & Rountree solicitors papers	D/1716
Orr and Garvin document	T/1877
Orr and Robb document	D/583
Orr David document	T/655
Orr document	T/1222
Orr document	T/2027
Orr document	T/3301
Orr documents	T/569
Orr family document	T/1824
Orr family documents	T/2034
Orr Joseph & Sons Ltd, Milltown Mills (Benburb) papers	D/2130
Orr M T (depositor) papers	D/2934
Orr papers	D/1717
Orr papers	D/1786
Orr papers	D/2908
Orr R solicitors papers	D/1707

Appendix 15.

Orr in Pallot's Marriage Index for England: 1780-1837

Orr, Ann
Spouse: Bodden, Wm Marriage Date: 1830 `
Parish: Clerkenwell

Orr, Ann
Spouse: Dawson, John Marriage Date: 1796
Parish: Exeter

Orr, Ann
Spouse: Dawson, John Marriage Date: 1796
Parish: Exeter

Orr, Ann
Spouse: Nelham, Thos Chas. Marriage Date: 1806
Parish: Shadwell, St. Paul

Orr, Charlotte
Spouse: Davis, Wm Marriage Date: 1791
Parish: St. Anne, Soho

Orr, Charles
Spouse: Whitaker, Eliz Marriage Date: 1824
Parish: Doncaster

Orr, Christopher
Spouse: Clifton, Mary Marriage Date: 1807
Parish: Heysham

Orr, David
Spouse: Parrington, Agnes Marriage Date: 1807
Parish: Heysham

Orr, Elizabeth
Spouse: Bird, Thos Marriage Date: 1823
Parish: Chelsea, St. Lukes

Orr, Elizabeth
Spouse: Wood, Thos Marriage Date: 1825
Parish: Stratford Le Bow

Orr, Francis.
Spouse: Newey, Mary Marriage Date: 1816
Parish: Westminster

Orr, George.
Spouse: Fullerton, Elizth Marriage Date: 1835
Parish: Alverstoke

Orr, Hannah.
Spouse: Schroder, Charles Marriage Date: 1809
Parish: Holy Trinity Minories

Orr, Hannah.
Spouse: Schroder, Chas Marriage Date: 1809
Parish: Holy Trinity Minories

Orr, Hugh.
Spouse: Stewart, Rebecca Amelia Marriage Date: 1830
Parish: Charlton

Orr, Henry.
Spouse: Rogers, Margt Marriage Date: 1796
Parish: Shadwell, St. Paul

Orr, Isabella.
Spouse: Williams, Richd Marriage Date: 1817
Parish: Shoreditch

Orr, Janet.
Spouse: Hatch, John Marriage Date: 1829
Parish: Westminster

Orr, James.
Spouse: Rogers, Mary Ann Marriage Date: 1797
Parish: Southwark

Orr, John.
Spouse: Slade, Sophia Marriage Date: 1803
Parish: St. Boltolph Without Aldgate

Orr, John.
Spouse: Slade, Sophia Marriage Date: 1803
Parish: St. Boltolph Without Aldgate

Orr, Johnston.
Spouse: Foocks, Sarah Marriage Date: 1832
Parish: St. Giles In The Fields

Orr, Mary Ann.
Spouse: Bryant, James Marriage Date: 1812
Parish: St. Magnus The Martyr

Orr, Peter.
Spouse: Williams, Sarah Marriage Date: 1836
Parish: St. Michael Cornhill

Orr, Robert.
Spouse: Harridman, Mary Marriage Date: 1810
Parish: St. Boltolph Without Aldgate

Orr, Samuel.
Spouse: Hornby, Ellen Marriage Date: 1799
Parish: Heysham

Orr, Sarah.
Spouse: Goldwin, Wm Marriage Date: 1817
Parish: St. Dionis Backchurch

Orr, Susanna.
Spouse: Sherwood, Richard William Marriage Date: 1797
Parish: St. Pancras

Orr, William.
Spouse: Darling, Ann Marriage Date: 1815
Parish: Stepney

Orr, William.
Spouse: Graves, Emily Marriage Date: 1826
Parish: St. Swithin

Orr, William.
Spouse: Graves, Emily Marriage Date: 1826
Parish: St. Swithin

Orr, William.
Spouse: Longden, Mary Marriage Date: 1802
Parish: Westminster

Orr, William.
Spouse: Morgan, Susannah Marriage Date: 1797
Parish: St. George In The East

Appendix 16
Some Orr Miners Killed at Their Work.

The information available about accidents and deaths in the mines has varied enormously in earlier times. In some cases accidents were reported to the authorities and formal enquiries may have followed. Anybody who has lived in a mining community will admit to a frisson of fear when the sirens sound and the vehicles of the Mines Rescue Team scream past, they know a friend and colleague may be in serious trouble. A very good museum is The Scottish Mining Museum, LadyVictoria Colliery, Newtongrange, Midlothian. The Durham Mining Museum web site is also well worth a visit - http://www.dmm.org.uk/mindex.htm

Charles E Orr was killed while working at in the Hartford Pit, Cramlington, about 10 miles north of Newcastle on Tyne ca 1928.

D. D. Roach Orr, died following an accident at Murton Colliery, about six miles south of Sunderland46 He was a hewer, that is a man who actually dug the coal and filled the tubs that took the coal topsides. He was severely injured in the arm, chest, and internally when jumping off a set of empty wagons on which he had been riding, His coat caught, and he was dragged and run over. He died the following day, 20 Feb 1897, aged 46 years.

David Orr was a hewer at Greenside Colliery about 7 miles west of Newcastle on Tyne. He suffered a broken thigh caused by a fall of stone on 10 December 1910 and died from his injuries on 09 Jan 1911 He was 23 years old.

Henry Orr was killed in an accident on 28 Apr 1913 at Silksworth Colliery, about 2 miles south west of Sunderland.

Hugh Joseph Orr, died ca 1930 at the New Hartley mine about 9 miles north east of Newcastle on Tyne.

Joseph Orr, aged 35, worked at Hebburn Colliery about 4 miles north east of Newcastle on Tyne. He was killed in an explosion caused by a naked light igniting firedamp on 6 May 1852. The explosion occurred on what was called the Monkton Flat. There were over 200 hundred men in the pit at the time but not all in close proximity to the explosion. But 20 men and 2 boys were in the Flat and 14 of them perished. Joseph left a wife and 3 children

Matthew Orr, died 29 Sep 1887 aged 22. He was a hewer and was killed in a fall of stone at Whitehaven Colliery, 1 mile from Whitehaven itself.

Matthew Orr. He was a landing lad at the Clara Vale colliery about 7 miles west of Newcastle on Tyne. He was not a healthy lad at best of times being consumptive (pulmonary tuberculosis) and suffering from a tumour on his neck. It seems that his condition worsened following work on 9 Jan 1906 although he continued to go in to work for a further week. He saw a doctor who examined the tumour and referred him to the Newcastle Infirmary where it was removed. On return home his condition worsened and he died on 28 May 1906. The doctor at the inquest said phthisis was the immediate cause of death, but it was perhaps called into activity prematurely by some injury and the subsequent operation, and that any extra exertion would have caused pain. The jury found that he died from phthisis accelerated by an injury received whilst employed as a landing lad.

Robert Orr died in 1931 at Newbiggin Colliery about 16 miles north east of Newcastle on Tyne.
William Orr died in 1933 also at Newbiggin Colliery. He and Robert Orr may have been related.

William Orr, aged 56, was a hewer at Silksworth Colliery about 2 miles south west of Sunderland. He was killed whilst trespassing on the Ryhope Private Railway 07 Jan 1905. The accident was not classified as a colliery accident.

Index

ORR James of
Ballycarry 162,
James of Ballygowan
78, 277,
James of Cannes 277,
James of Cranfield 169,
James of Creavery 169,
James of Fiddyglass 52,
James of Holywood 63,
James of
Johnsonville 122,
James of Letterkenny
107, 109, 161,
James of
Lochwinnoch 84, 85,
James of Raphoe 51,
James of Rich Hill 109,
James Campbell 123,
James Lawrence 117,
160, James M 28,
Jane 68, 88, 163, 186,
271, 273,
Janet 88, Janet of
Lorabank 94, 188,
Jannet MA 186, 187,
John 66, 82, 85, 87,
88, 89, 90, 91, 92, 93,
94, 99, 125, 162, 167,
271, 272, 273,
John of Ayr 164,
John of Ballinderry
52, 107,
John of Belfast 110,
John of Castlefin 52;

ORR John of Corstorphine
report *integral index*
link to McCullough,
Australia 188;
John of Donoughmore
52, John of Dublin 275,
John of Dunluce 52,
John of Girvan 123,
John of Hills 83,
John of Jamacia 79,
John of
Jamphraystock 83,
John of Killinchy 111,
John of Legnathraw 52,
John of Letterkenny
52, 107, 109, 161,
John of Lochwinnoch
84, 86, Jr 85,
John of Moy 3, 4, 81,
John of Ontario 181,
John of Quente Bay 182,
John of Raphoe 107,
John of Tasmania 122,
John of The Folly 169,
John Boyd, Lord 164,
John Bryson
58, 156, 157, 158,
John Clement of NZ 151,
John Forbes 122,
Rev John Henry 163,
John M 271, 272,
John Richard 123,
John William
of NZ 124,

10049235R10211

Made in the USA
San Bernardino, CA
27 November 2018